# Information-Systems Development

# Information-Systems Development

Systems thinking in the field of information-systems

Paul J. Lewis

The Management School
Lancaster University

PITMAN
PUBLISHING

PITMAN PUBLISHING
128 Long Acre, London WC2E 9AN

A Division of Longman Group Limited

First Published in Great Britain 1994

© P.J. Lewis 1994

A CIP catalogue record for this book can be obtained from the British Library.

ISBN 0 273 03107 4

Printed in England by Clays Ltd, St Ives plc

*The Publishers' policy is to use paper manufactured from sustainable forests.*

# Contents

# Part I Systems ideas

## Chapter 3    Fundamental concepts

## Chapter 4    Systems ideas in the field of IS

# Part II Decisions, support and data

## Chapter 5    Decision-making

## Chapter 6    Supporting the organisation

# Chapter 7    Problems with data analysis

# Part III Using soft systems thinking

## Chapter 8      Soft systems methodology

## Chapter 9      Interpretative data analysis

## Chapter 10    The Millside Medical Practice: an illustrative use of systems thinking

*"New occasions teach new duties:*
*time makes ancient good uncouth*
*They must upward still, and onward,*
*who would keep abreast of Truth"*

James Lowell

# 1 Mapping out the territory

## 1.1 THE NEED TO UNDERSTAND INFORMATION-SYSTEMS

The subject of this book is the use of information within human organisations, and in particular how an organisation's need for information may be supported by computers and other forms of information technology. Its contents should therefore be of interest to managers and administrators as well as to students and computing professionals who wish to better employ their technical skills in the commercial world.

The need to understand how information can be used and managed has never been more important, for computer-based information-systems have entered our lives at an astounding pace; the change from a situation where they were to be found in only the largest public and private organisations to the present situation, where they pervade all our professional and social lives, has occurred at a rate that surprises even those who have been responsible for it. Unfortunately, our understanding of how to develop and manage information-systems has not developed at the same pace as our ability to create them.

The dramatic increase in the availability, and the capability, of information technology has faced managers with a host of new questions. Which of all the possible information-systems that might be created, should be created? How may information-systems be used to gain or protect competitive advantage? How can we ensure that the new information-systems contribute to rather than endanger the long term viability of the organisation?

The resulting uncertainty has over the years provided rich rewards for numerous consultants and management gurus, each offering their own particular universal panacea in the shape of some new technique and methodology. Sadly, each such offering seems to give but temporary respite, and the same questions soon recur. Managers are increasingly realising that the issues of information-systems are management issues, and that it is only they themselves who may resolve them, in ways that are appropriate to their organisation and its particular needs. This is, however, not easily done; many of the confusions and issues in the field of information-systems arise from there being no shared concepts or any agreed language through which the subject may be discussed.

This is where we hope this book may make some contribution, for it offers to managers and organisations a set of ideas and a framework for addressing the subject of information-systems. We suggest that it is systems thinking that can provide the concepts and language for information-systems work and that many of the issues to be dealt with are precisely those which the newer forms of systems thinking have been developed to address.

One of the most important themes that we shall develop is that the correct place to start thinking about information-systems is not with the information-systems themselves, but with the organisational activity that they are meant to serve. This is a most basic principle, but one that has not been followed in the past. Understanding information-systems has in the past been too often equated with understanding the enabling technology, with the result that too much attention has been given to technical issues and too little to the needs of the organisation and the impacts upon those within it. As a result analysis has been driven by what is technically *possible* rather than by what is organisationally *desirable*. The consequences of this include a number of costly failed investments in information-systems, the disenfranchisement of management and an accepted use of development methods that are insensitive to the social and political contexts within which the information-systems are to be used.

Such problems cannot be solved by piecemeal changes to practice such as trying to involve potential users more in the development process (more participative development) or by passing on to managers and users the responsibility for creating new information-systems (the information centre approach). If the same underlying concepts and language are used to think about why and how development takes place, then the outcomes of such refinements will not be significantly different from what went before.

We believe that it is necessary to re-examine some of the basic assumptions of work in information-systems, of the notions that underlie our present understanding of the nature of information, of why information-systems are needed and the process by which they are developed. In this book we do this through a particular set of ideas, those of systems thinking, and from a particular perspective, that information-systems cannot be discussed in isolation from the social contexts in which they exist and which imbue data with meaning.

When one understands information-systems to be socially constructed artefacts, which merely *happen to be implemented* through a novel technology, that of the computer, the subject of information-systems and their use appears in a different light. Rather than problems of data-processing or information technology one must instead address complex issues of organisational management, and begin to think, not of developing computer systems, but of *managing* information.

## 1.2 THE EMERGING FIELD OF INFORMATION SYSTEMS

Some re-examination of the basic ideas used in information-systems work is now due, for one of the lessons of history is that the greatest effects of a technological innovation can arise not from the technology itself but from the changes that are subsequently engendered in how we view the world. This is most literally true of the telescope, which was developed so that merchants could gain commercial advantage through knowing earlier the identity of incoming cargo ships. Its existence, of course, allowed a more detailed study of planetary motions and led eventually to the heliocentric view of the universe. The shift in thinking which accompanied the realisation that the Earth and Man did not exist at the centre of all things affected every area of religion, politics, art and science thereafter.

It is not too fanciful to suggest that, from a future perspective, the greatest effects of the computer might be seen as concerning, not such things as how we shop or bank, but how we think about and understand information-systems and human organisations.

It will however be many years before any such patterns become discernible, for the organised study of information-systems is yet in its early stages. This is hardly surprising, for computers have existed for less than fifty years and studying their use in organisations has been done for a much shorter time. If there is a new discipline of information-systems, then it is for the moment a most undisciplined one, plagued with confusions and disagreements; even a suitable name has not been firmly decided, although the most common label, that which we use in this book, is 'Information Systems' or more simply 'IS'.

The comparative youth of IS as a field of study means that its boundaries remain much debated and the means by which it may be studied are still emerging; the degree to which the academic journals and conferences of IS contain discussions of research paradigms and appropriate methods far exceeds that found in more established disciplines such as the natural sciences, where such things have long since been agreed.

The emerging field of IS has, though, already made some important contributions to practice. One of these is the change to viewing information-systems as not merely collections of data processing procedures and machinery but as complex combinations of both machines and people. With this has come the realisation that they cannot be 'engineered' in quite the same way as physical artefacts such as buildings, bridges or space rockets: because a new computer-based information-system may have widespread organisational, economic, cultural and political implications its creation cannot be treated as a purely technical exercise.

It is a mistake to believe that this means only that the developers of information-systems need more training and more knowledge. This conclusion is, however, often drawn and developers are certainly now expected to have a greater range of expertise than in the past. It is no longer felt to be enough for the designer of a computer-based information-system to be technically proficient; they must now have knowledge of finance and economics to appreciate the business consequences of the information-system, the management sciences to satisfy the needs for management and control, the behavioural sciences to manage the intervention and achieve successful change. All this whilst still being competent enough in the computer sciences to properly understand the possibilities and limitations of the technology.

The result of such an eclectic 'tool kit of techniques' response is that any honest appraisal of present IS practice and education reveals a loss of intellectual coherence.

The field of IS has become a disorganised aggregate of ideas and theories from many different disciplines, some of which have incommensurable philosophical bases. The goal-oriented models of human behaviour often used in the area of decision support systems, for example, conflict sharply with the models of human behaviour employed elsewhere.

## 1.3   A CYCLE OF LEARNING

Here, then, we have the roots of the confusions surrounding the subject of information-systems. We have computer-based information-systems becoming increasingly vital for organisational survival, managers needing to manage the impacts of new technologies, a young field of study still struggling to establish and define itself, and relevant ideas being separately borrowed from many different disciplines.

To attempt to make sense of and take control of this area must seem to the busy manager a daunting prospect. But there is a way for such managers to approach the subject without fear. This is because, to be of any real use, knowledge must be organised so as to create a means of enquiry and used within a cycle of learning,

We use later in this book a basic model for rational enquiry that includes a framework of basic concepts and ideas together with a suitable methodology for applying those to a particular application area. The essence of this model is that we should learn from every attempt to apply our basic concepts to the real-world, by reflecting upon the experience and where necessary making modifications to both concepts and methodology (Figure 1.1).

In this book we hope to provide the reader with the basis for operating their own version of such a learning cycle in one particular application area. That application area is of course the use of computer-based information-systems in organisations, their role and how they may be created. Some of the ideas and  techniques that we shall look at are well-known and will be familiar to anybody who has experience of working with information-systems. But others, such as the organising principles of the framework of concepts, the idea of four types of support, specific techniques and the soft systems methodology through which we suggest those techniques be used, belong to systems thinking.

We cannot guarantee that what is offered in this book will make simple the subject of information-systems or resolve all of anybody's problems. We do believe, though, that it will provide the basis for individuals and organisations to learn their own way towards solutions and resolutions. The nations of the Third World know only too well that literacy is a key factor for economic and social development; in the same way, for organisations and individuals to be part of and thrive in a post-industrial information society then they must be 'information literate'. Information literacy requires above all else a coherent set of concepts through which to understand information-systems and a flexible methodology through which those concepts may then be applied to any actual

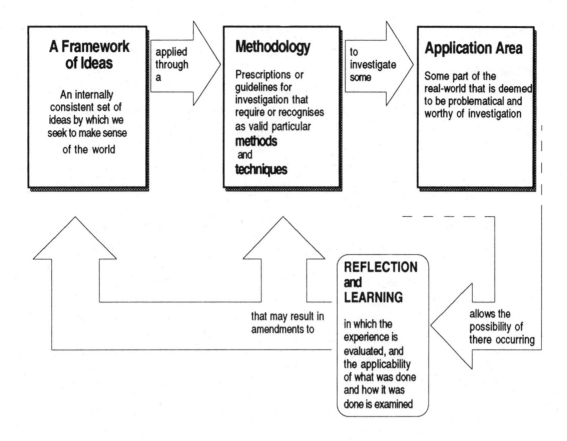

**Figure 1.1**     *Operating a cycle of learning*

situation. We believe, and hope to convince the reader, that both of these can be provided by systems thinking.

## 1.4   THE STRUCTURE OF THIS BOOK

Our text is divided into three parts.

### IN PART I:

We introduce the basic concepts of systems thinking and see how these may be used as the basis for understanding information-systems and their use within organisations.

#### In Chapter 2:

We see that the complexity of the modern world led to a search for new means of enquiry that could be used to intervene in the real-world and to tackle problematical situations; the most successful of these has been the systems approach. We examine the development of systems thinking and look at the most important variants of the systems approach. Systems thinking has continued to develop and be refined, leading to new systems approaches, better suited to the subtle complexities of the problems found in human organisations. Some of the differences between this newer, soft systems thinking and that which went before are described.

**In Chapter 3:**

We describe the basic concepts of systems thinking. When used properly these can be powerful analytical tools, allowing us to untangle complexity and place structure upon a confusing variety of issues, difficulties and suggested solutions. Some of these, such as the most basic notion of 'a system', have become so familiar to us over the last thirty years that they are now part of our everyday language. But in many cases this has meant that their precise meaning, and therefore their true value, has been lost. In this chapter we therefore explain some of the fundamental concepts of systems thinking and attempt to re-establish what exactly is meant by such terms as 'system', 'sub-system', or 'inputs and outputs'.

**In Chapter 4:**

Before applying these basic ideas to the subject of information-systems, we first examine the extent to which systems thinking is already therein employed. After all, many methodologies for information-systems development justify themselves with the claim that they are 'systems approaches'. We suggest that it is actually only a limited and limiting range of systems ideas that have been adopted by the field of IS, and even these are often used in isolation rather than in any coherent way.

We see that the influence of systems thinking upon the IS thinking field was strongest perhaps thirty years ago, when methods and ideas such as that of development life-cycles were borrowed from systems analysis and systems engineering. It is the systems ideas of that past era that are still echoed in present IS practice.

This historical inheritance has constrained much thinking about information-systems, suggesting that the development of information-systems is analogous to the construction of designed physical artefacts such as buildings and bridges. This has led to a tradition of information-systems development that focuses upon technical problem-solving and gives insufficient consideration to the special characteristics of organisations. These special characteristics derive from the fact that organisations do not exist independently of the human beings who form them, and that organisations, and the information-systems that serve them, are above all else social systems.

## IN PART II:

We begin to see how systems ideas can provide the foundations for understanding information-systems, and in its more recent forms can recognise the special nature of human organisations.

**In Chapter 5:**

We begin by looking at decision-making. One of the most basic tenets of conventional thinking about information-systems is that they exist to serve decision-making.

Decision-making is therefore taken to be a central concern of, and justification for, all forms of information-systems development.

If information-systems are seen as serving decision-making then the view which one adopts about how decisions are made becomes of crucial importance, but in the study of information-systems too little attention is given to what exactly is meant by decision-making. In Chapter 5 we investigate decision-making, introduce the idea of appreciation and show how this may provide us with an enriched model of decision-making. This model reveals decision-making to be a convenient shorthand expression for a complex process, in which organisations adapt and change in response to their environments. It also provides the means for distinguishing between 'data' and 'information' by means of the cognitive frameworks through which the world is perceived.

**In Chapter 6:**

We build upon this richer interpretation of decision-making by considering the different ways in which information-systems may support decision-making. This provides a basic taxonomy of information-systems, allowing us to make some sense of the plethora of descriptive labels (decision-support, executive information systems etc) that abound. We then examine some characteristics of data and look at the type of data required in different decision-making situations.

**In Chapter 7:**

Gaining an understanding of the data in a problem situation is a long established part of systems development and few would doubt its utility or importance. Data analysis is though not without problems, and in this chapter we look at some of these. The time is ripe for this, for data analysis is now being used in a rather different way than it was previously, and at an earlier stage in the development process. Work here requires recognition of the social and political construction of meaning that occurs within any human situation and the cultural context within which business and information-systems planning take place.

We suggest that the current theory and techniques of data analysis are effective tools for the purposes for which they were originally conceived, but are not well suited to use in the early stages of development; rooted in an objectivist paradigm, they do not allow for the possibility of multiple, equally valid views of reality. They rely on there being a high level of agreement as to the nature of the present situation, what is 'the problem' and what any new information-system should do. This makes them particularly unsuitable for use at the earliest stages of analysis, where it is just such things which are undecided, and which form the major subject for investigation and debate.

At the end of this chapter we return to the idea of appreciation. This not only provides a model of human sense-making that explains much of the present practice of data analysis but also opens up the possibility of an alternative form of data analysis, one more suited to the requirements of early investigations of a problem situation.

## IN PART III:

We turn to the particular subject of information-systems development, and how systems thinking may help us to create information-systems that genuinely benefit the organisation that they are meant to serve. This is a very large subject and some of the topics within it, the planning of information-systems to gain competitive advantage or applying ideas of systemic control towards the evaluation of IS investments, are worthy of whole books to themselves. Rather than merely scrape the surface of such topics we use the remainder of this book to discuss the uses of soft systems thinking.

### In Chapter 8:

We look in detail at the soft systems methodology (SSM), the most developed example of the newer systems thinking. We see how it tackles the difficulties of intervening in complex human problem situations, and how it may be used as the basis for information-systems work.

The assumptions underlying SSM are rather different to those to be found in conventional information-system development methodologies. SSM declines to view organisations as goal-seeking mechanisms, or to use analysis of present procedures and practices as the basis for designing new information-systems. Instead both organisations and information-systems are seen as complex social constructs, so that due consideration must be given to the varied ways in which the participants perceive their situation.

This means that if SSM is to be used for information-systems work then attention must first be given to the human activity that the information-system is intended to serve and support. Thinking about information-systems must begin with reaching agreement as to the essential purposes of the organisation and activities that are required. Only then can one begin to think about what data might be necessary to the enacting, or supporting the enacting, of those activities, and finally how that data should be collected, stored or communicated through new technologies. The focus is therefore upon the organisation rather than the information-system, and the planning of new information-systems is based upon what is demanded by the organisation's purposes.

One may use soft systems ideas on a large scale, to understand the planning, development and use of information-systems. In doing so there is a shift away from regarding information-systems as a 'technical fix' to individual problems. Instead, information is seen as essential for the process of organisation itself, and one focuses upon the need for a continuous matching of the information needs of the organisation with the information supplied by its information-systems.

Systems ideas may, though, also be of use, on the smaller scale, in the development of individual information-systems. It is here that an interpretative form of data analysis may be most needed, and so it is to examining the possibility for this that we now return.

**In Chapter 9:**

SSM does not presently allow for any consideration of data issues, and conventional forms of data model are not suitable for use with SSM because they embody philosophical presuppositions that are different to, and match badly with, the phenomenology of SSM. This is clearly an obstacle to using SSM in information-systems work or any problem situation that involves the storage of data or the provision of information. We suggest that this deficiency might be remedied by using an interpretivist form of data analysis alongside an SSM analysis.

We see how, when we define a human activity system in SSM, we may identify a number of 'cognitive categories' that are meaningful in relation to that system. From these, and the associations between them, we may create a System Data Model. This can be valuable in that it defines a shared vocabulary, with which one may better discuss the system and alternative possibilities for the organisation. But it can also act as a guide to data storage requirements and so contribute to information-systems design.

**In Chapter 10:**

We present an illustrative use of some of the ideas that we have discussed. The case study which is used here is somewhat different in kind to that usually found in texts concerned with information-systems development. Rather than describe the problems of a well-structured commercial trading organisation we consider the situation surrounding a medical practice; here the difficulties are not only technical (how to store data and make it available to people within the organisation) but very obviously also social, political and moral.

One of the great strengths of soft systems thinking is that it can be tailored to the particular needs of each situation in which it is used. No description of its use can, therefore, ever be typical or act as a complete guide for future applications. In looking at the Millside Medical Practice we hope, though, to illustrate some characteristics of the use of soft systems thinking and show how it might be used in situations where more technically oriented approaches would falter or over-simplify.

## 1.5 STYLE OF THIS BOOK

We have tried to make all the material in this book as accessible as possible for the general reader without simplifying to the extent that the already knowledgeable reader is dissatisfied. Despite this we recognise that the book is in places not a particularly 'easy read', for we have tried to do justice to the variety of ideas that exist about each of the topics that we discuss. It behoves us therefore to explain certain conventions used in this book.

First, our commitment to systems thinking presents us with a particular difficulty of language, namely that we do need to use the word 'system' in a rather formal way that is different to the way in which it is used in casual, everyday speech. For this reason we have adopted the convention of hyphenating the phrase 'information-system' whenever we wish to use it as a label for some real-world collection of machines and software or procedures. We hope that the reader will accept this as necessary precision rather than pedantry.

Secondly, we have given full references to other authors whose work may be illuminating or provide a fuller discussion of certain topics. If the inclusion of such references in the text is daunting to the general reader then we crave their indulgence. Such references are essential for academic users of the book and useful to those who wish to pursue particular topics in greater detail.

Finally, we recognise that some of the material in this book is likely to raise in the readers' minds more questions than it answers. Somewhat in amends, therefore, we end some chapters with answers to a few of the most commonly asked questions relating to the material therein.

## 1.6  CONCLUDING REMARKS

We would not suggest that understanding the subject of information-systems in the way that we suggest in this book will, by itself, provide solutions to all the issues that confront us today. But we do believe that the ideas found within the following chapters can provide a framework through which we may discuss those issues clearly and perhaps learn our way forward.

It is our contention that the management and use of information-systems must not be seen as the responsibility of technical experts but as an organisational issue, and the responsibility of those who will use, benefit or suffer from their existence. Those managers who are able to employ computerised information-systems to most advantage are not those who have the greatest technical knowledge of computers, but those who have a clear understanding of both the information that their business requires and *why* that information is required.

In future, even if systems thinking influences the IS field in the way that we hope it may, some things will probably continue as before. Data processing departments will probably continue to carry out development projects and users will probably still complain that they cannot get the information-systems that they really need. Those organisations that learn from systems thinking will, though, seek to actively manage their information provision, to effectively plan and control their use of data. We believe that such will thrive and prosper, whilst those who ignore the need to manage information will disappear as surely as would any organisation that did not adequately manage its financial affairs. Such is the reason that we commend the use of systems thinking to the reader.

## 1.7 ACKNOWLEDGEMENTS

It would be hard to over-emphasise my debt to colleagues Peter Checkland, Brian Wilson, David Brown, Mark Winter and Sue Holwell. Many of the ideas in this book have arisen from work we have undertaken together and the challenging discussions that we have had over the years. Credit is due too to all those students of the Management School of Lancaster University who have attempted to use systems ideas in often difficult real-world situations; their successes and failures have been the basis for much of our own learning.

# Part I

## *Systems ideas*

# 2 Systems thinking

## 2.1 INTRODUCTION

One of the distinguishing characteristics of human beings is the desire for improvement; we are all capable of looking at the world in which we live, visualising a different world where things are organised differently and 'better', and then striving to change the world in order to bring about the desired improvements. Whether the desired changes are relatively limited in scale, such as better business procedures, or globally large, such as the abolition of nuclear weapons, there must exist some process of inquiry, included within which is a set of internally consistent mental constructs which leads the observer to perceive the world in a particular way, to recognise some 'problem' or 'opportunity', and guides them towards some end.

The best known such method of inquiry is probably the scientific method which began to be codified in 16th century Europe; its methodology of formulating hypotheses and testing them via controlled and repeatable experiments is a familiar one and one which has become the epitome of rational investigation. Our understanding of the scientific process has been modified by the work of Popper (1959, 1963, 1972) and Kuhn (1962) and we now understand its end result to be convincing and tested explanations of the world rather than the discovery of absolute truths about it; nevertheless, the development of the scientific method of inquiry has rightly been described as the great triumph of Western civilisation, underlying as it does all the scientific and technological advances which surround us in our everyday life. Indeed, ours has been described as a

> "... scientific civilisation ... a civilisation in which science is only a Latin word for knowledge." Bronowski (1973) p. 437.

As powerful as the scientific method of enquiry has proved to be it has limitations when used outside the well-controlled conditions of the laboratory. Whilst the scientific method of inquiry has been spectacularly successful as a means of understanding the physical world it has become clear over the last one hundred years that it is not a suitable method of inquiry for every branch of knowledge because of the complexity and social nature of many problem situations.

This is illustrated well by the destruction of North European and Canadian forests by 'acid rain', something which is widely felt to be undesirable and therefore a 'problem'. The present situation may be perfectly understood in terms of chemistry (the nature of the chemical reactions involved), physics (the movements of chemical pollutants through the atmosphere) and biology (the effects of pollutants upon plant life), and yet the situation remains problematical and unchanged many years after its existence was first established. It is not easy to determine what should be done in response to this problematical situation because there is not a single problem to be investigated but a number of inter-related problems.

In addition to the complexity of the scientific problems of understanding the unpredictable effects of releasing a complex mix of chemicals into varying, uncontrolled atmospheric conditions there exist political problems (obtaining international recognition of the damage caused and acceptance of responsibility), economic problems (the costs of abandoning cheap but polluting means of power production) and social problems (the unemployment caused by abandoning polluting industries, the unacceptability of alternatives such as nuclear power). These cannot be dealt with in isolation from one another because a 'solution' to any of them may exacerbate others.

Such complex webs of interrelated problems are sometimes described as 'messes'(Ackoff, 1974) and 'messiness' is typical of the problems which most concern us in the modern world. It was the need to deal with such problems which led to the emergence of a different method of enquiry, that of systems thinking.

## 2.2 THE EMERGENCE OF SYSTEMS THINKING

Some elementary systems thinking may be found in the work of the Gestalt psychologists such as Wertheimer, Koffka and Kohler, who emphasised the study of perception, learning and thinking in whole units, not by analysis into parts; the papers in Ellis (1938) provide an interesting insight into this earliest systems thinking. It is though from the work of the organismic biologists, and in particular the contribution of Bertalanffy (1950, 1951, 1968) in converting the ideas of organismic biology into a set of general concepts, that modern systems thinking developed.

The problem identified by the organismic biologists and explored by the first systems thinkers was that the scientific method deals with complexity by reductionism, by breaking a large, complex domain of investigation down into smaller, less complex sub-domains and investigating each of these in turn. When this logic is applied to 'real-world' problem solving the underlying assumption is that a large and complex problem is nothing more than the sum of a number of smaller less complex problems; and that solving all of those smaller component problems will equate to a solution for the larger problem. It is assumed that identifying the individual elements of a situation, studying them in isolation, and searching for both causes and effects will uncover the nature of the problem and lead to the identification of solutions.

However, studying the problem elements in isolation may cause important interactions to be overlooked, for the effects of the interactions *between* the elements may be just as important as the effects of the individual elements themselves. The early systems thinkers felt that reductionism did not allow for the possibility that complex entities might have properties which did not belong to any of their constituent parts; if such *emergent properties* occurred only when the individual parts were brought together in a particular, organised way then they could not be examined by reductionist approaches. Scientific analysis, which sought to understand that entity only in terms of the component parts, would overlook an essential part of the area of study.

The possibility of emergent properties, a possibility already recognised in Aristotle's dictum that "The whole is more than the sum of the parts", implied that if such complex entities were to be fully understood then new methods of enquiry would have to be developed, methods which would allow a study of those things *as a whole* rather than a study of the parts in isolation. The distinctive new idea which systems theorists proposed was that of using the concept of 'a system' as the basis for making sense of some part of the real-world. The system concept, it was argued, could provide the basis for a *holistic* approach to analysis which was not solely concerned with the nature of the individual problem components but also with their organisation and the relationships between them.

That such a holistic method of inquiry might be applicable in many different fields was indicated by the backgrounds of the founders of the Society for General Systems Research (Bertalanffy, Rapaport, Boulding, and Gerard) being in such diverse fields as biology, mathematics, economics and physiology. The meta-level nature of systems thinking has subsequently been demonstrated by the emergence of systemic approaches in a wide range of disciplines, from anthropology through to zoology, and to the establishment of at least one entirely new discipline, that of ecology.

The field in which systems ideas have had most impact however has been that of organisational and management science. Here the potential for systems ideas in the study of the problems which arise from the increased size and complexity of modern industrialised society was recognised at a very early stage and systems thinking has developed to become the predominant form of enquiry and of immense practical importance. Churchman *et al* (1957) provide an explanation for this through their argument that as organisations grow and become more complex so individual parts of the organisations become more specialised in their function, leading to a need for greater co-ordination and control by management. It was serendipitous that as, during the post-war period, organisations grew in size and complexity and increasingly encountered such needs the newly emerged discipline of systems thinking was able to offer a way of managing the process of management, providing both a language for discussing complex problems and an approach to resolving them. Systems ideas now provide the intellectual structure for most studies of organisations and their management, the works of Emery & Trist (1960), Katz & Kahn (1966), Maurer (1971) providing, just some amongst many, examples of their use.

## 2.3 HARD SYSTEMS APPROACHES

Even within the single application area of management and organisational science there are many different approaches to using the same basic concepts of systems thinking. The three variants which have had most influence upon IS thinking however are systems engineering, systems analysis and operational research, amongst which Checkland (1978) finds sufficient similarities to identify as one, predominant form of the systems approach, that of 'hard' systems thinking.

This phrase 'hard systems thinking' is often misunderstood and because the distinction between 'hard' and 'soft' strands of systems thinking is one which we shall use repeatedly we must be careful about what it means. It does not mean that this form of systems thinking is particularly difficult (though it may be) nor that it is concerned with 'hard' (or quantifiable) systems. It does mean that systems ideas are employed as the mechanism for selecting between alternative ways of achieving a defined and unquestioned goal. The 'hardness' is, essentially, characteristic of the method of inquiry, not of that which is being investigated.

Systems analysis, systems engineering and operational research all emphasise the use of systems concepts as a means of investigating and taking rational action in complex situations. There is though little agreement about precisely where the boundaries of each approach lie. Systems analysis is, for example, sometimes seen as being the precursor to systems engineering. Machol (1965), for example, describes systems analysis as

> " ... *the study of a system which does not yet exist (at least in the modification under study) in an attempt to elucidate its effectiveness or performance, its cost in dollars or other factors, and the effect of parameter variations on these quantities.*"

whilst associating systems engineering with the design process, its outputs being

> "... *a set of specifications suitable for use in constructing a real system out of hardware.*"
>
> *Machol (1965) pp. 1-4.*

Machol's further distinction that the operational researcher is more often concerned with the optimisation of existing systems whilst the systems engineer is more likely to be concerned with the creation of new systems is now untenable, for the concerns of operational research have expanded considerably since the time that Machol was writing. The OR practitioner is now just as likely to be concerned with the creation of expert systems or strategic planning as with more traditional queuing problems.

Black (1968), whilst still regarding systems analysis as the earlier stage which identifies the result wanted, defines systems engineering more widely to include the co-ordination of the work of groups doing sub-tasks and achieving the realisation of the designed system. Wymore (1976) takes a still wider view, regarding systems engineering as the overall task with component activities of both systems analysis and systems design, where systems analysis refers to the process of developing and manipulating a model of a large-scale, complex, man/machine system that is already in existence, whilst system design means to develop a model from which a new design will be created.

However one wishes to delineate the boundaries between the three approaches the similarities in their aims and the activities by which they achieve those aims are very great. Let us look briefly at each to see what those similarities are and the influence each has had upon thinking related to information-systems.

### 2.3.1 Systems engineering

Systems engineering emerged during the 1940s and 1950s as systematic means of organising large-scale, complex endeavours and the stages of a typical systems engineering project are shown in Figure 2.1. Its roots lay in the desire to create complex physical artefacts, and the greatest successes of systems engineering have been in the creation of such artefacts, whether these are vehicles for the exploration of space, complex communications networks or large-scale integrated manufacturing plants.

The reason why systems ideas are appropriate in such areas is not difficult to understand if we consider a problem typical of those tackled by systems engineers. Production of a saleable end product in the petrochemicals industry may require many intermediate processes, each process transforming an input chemical mix into the desired chemical output plus a number of 'waste' by-products. The 'waste' products of each of these production processes are however often not waste at all, since they may themselves be, or be converted by further processing into, another saleable product. Petrochemical production plants therefore consist of many linked processes, where thousands of pieces of equipment are linked together and where both the products and waste products of one chemical process are fed into other chemical processes. Any change in the operations of one process therefore has implications for the operations of the many others which depend, either directly or indirectly, upon its products or by-products. In such situations it is essential that one does not aim to manage each production process individually but takes a larger view and manages the plant as a 'whole'. If the managers of the chemicals plant were to maximise the efficiency of a single production unit without considering the consequent effects on other production processes they might find that this led to a drop in overall efficiency and financial returns. This possibility is recognised within systems thinking as the principle of sub-optimisation (Hitch, 1953), which states that optimising the performance of a sub-system independently will not in general move the performance of the system as a whole towards its optimum, and may actually worsen the performance of the overall system.

Systems engineering, in common with other 'hard' systems approaches, is concerned with finding a solution to a given problem. For a structural engineer the problem may be to design a way of crossing a river with a bridge which is strong enough for some predicted use but cheap and easy to build. The engineer's work begins when *the need* for the river to be crossed has been *already identified*. Systems engineering too is concerned with the creation of a system to satisfy a defined need; the systems engineer knows (or at least proceeds upon the basis that they know) *what* must be done; their skill, craft and techniques are directed towards deciding *how* to do it. Because there may be many possible, alternative ways in which to do it much attention must be given to the process by which to select the 'best' (variously interpreted as the most elegant, the most effective, most efficient or cheapest) way.

The influence of systems engineering upon IS thinking has been very great, in the ubiquitous idea of a generic 'systems development life cycle', in the organising of development through projects and in the view that both software and information-systems must be *engineered*. The roots of the latter may lie in history, for the justification for much early electronic data processing was that the computer would be able to carry out the *same*

**SYSTEMS STUDIES (OR PROGRAM PLANNING)**
A preparation phase in which decisions are made as to how resources will be allocated to individual projects, negotiations take place with potential clients and background information is assembled.

**EXPLORATORY PLANNING ( OR PROJECT PLANNING I )**
In which interest becomes focussed on a specific project, problem or area of need. Six inter-related functions in this phase, corresponding roughly to general problem solving, are :

**Problem definition**: Isolating and quantifying those factors which define the system and its environment. Gathering and analysing data to describe the situation, requirements, possible inputs and outputs, and economic considerations

**Selecting objectives**: The logical end of problem definition is the choice of objectives which will guide search for alternatives and provide the criteria for selecting the optimum system.

**Systems synthesis**: Compiling or inventing alternative systems which can satisfy the objectives. Each alternative is worked out in sufficient detail to permit evaluation and permit a decision as to its merits, relative to other alternatives.

**Systems analysis**: Deducing the consequences of the alternatives with regard to system performance, cost etc.

**Selecting the best system:** Evaluating the analyses and selecting a subset of the alternative systems which merit further study.

**Communicating results**: Reporting that either a specific development will solve the problem, that exploratory development is required in order to draw firm conclusions or that no further work is justified

**DEVELOPMENT PLANNING (PROJECT PLANNING II)**
Once it is decided that a development project will take place then more detailed analysis takes place, operationally this means repeating the previous steps of the previous phase in greater detail on a reduced set of choices.

**STUDIES DURING DEVELOPMENT (ACTION PHASE I)**
The system is developed according to plans produced by previous phases. Project specific techniques may be required to ensure adequate flows of information amongst the many parties involved in construction of the system.
Plans are drawn up for testing of the system and for training of future users.

**CURRENT ENGINEERING (ACTION PHASE II)**
This is an on-going phase that begins with the start of operational use of the system. Performance of the operational system is monitored, unforeseen design faults or unexpected weaknesses are corrected. The system may be modified in response to changes in the environment.

**Figure 2.1**     *The phases of systems engineering projects (after Hall (1962))*

operations more cost-effectively, so that the principal concern of the early developers was to speed the throughput of the information-system.

This was precisely the same sort of task as that undertaken by industrial engineers seeking to improve the flow of production in the process industries. Both the overall imagery, of developer as machine-builder, and the specific tools and techniques used, those of systems engineering, were therefore seen as transferable to the task of designing information-systems.

But the strength of those ideas has far outlasted their historical origins. Feigenbaum (1968), for example, conceptualises organisations as integrated man-machine-information structures and proposes that :

> *"The application of the first several generations of factory automation and of office computerization has demonstrated the necessity for systems engineering work in the specification and use of such equipments. We are learning to make the design of these equipments a function of what the system calls for. The force-fit use of technically-optimized but not systems engineered pieces of hardware simply does not meet the requirements for effective systems operations." p. B-729*

And similar sentiments endure within Boehm's (1976) call for 'software engineering' or the

> *" ... practical application of scientific knowledge in the design and construction of computer programs and the associated documentation required to develop, operate, and maintain them." p. 1226.*

Sadly, the multi-disciplinary nature of the IS field is such that the extent to which current practice has been oriented by systems engineering ideas is liable to be forgotten. Thus Macro (1990) suggests that 'software engineering' arose from structured programming, guidelines on good practice and the idea of 'life cycles' for development, though none of these pre-date the late 1960s. In Aktas (1987) the shared ancestry of computer systems development and large-scale engineering, which leads to shared images of a life cycle, is forgotten to the extent that the author sees the similarities between the two only as proof that they are essentially the same:

> *"Examining the life cycles for information systems that have been proposed by different authors at various times during the last 20 years, one notes their similarity. But the most crucial point is that information systems life cycles are very close to those followed by engineering systems; that is, planning, analysis, design, implementation, and maintenance are also the major phases for developing information systems. This is not a coincidence; once more it should be stressed that an information system development process is an engineering process and as such has to follow the same steps and obey the same general principles ..." p. 14.*

## 2.3.2 Systems analysis

Systems analysis here refers not to the rather more limited set of activities carried out by computer systems analysts but to the systematic form of enquiry which arose during the 1950s, becoming well known through the work of the RAND Corporation in California. The methodology of systems analysis is shown in Figure 2.2.

**1. *Formulation* ( the Conceptual Phase )**

1.1  Clarify, formulate and limit the *problem*
1.2  Classify and select the *objectives* one hopes to attain with
the system - and update when necessary
1. 3  Select *criteria* for measuring achievement of objectives - and
update continuously
1.4  State *hypotheses* (or possible solutions) in the light of statement
of problem.

**2. *Search* (the Research Phase)**

2.1  Establish *facts* and collect *data* on which analysis will be based
- attach *probabilities* to those facts subject to uncertainty.
2.2  Assess the *cost* of data collection
2.3  Generate *alternative* ways for achieving objectives

**3. *Evaluation* ( the Analytical Phase )**

3.1  Carry out *model building* (conceptual or mathematical) to predict
consequences of various alternatives - state *approximations* and
assumptions on which such modelling is based.
3.2  Carry out *computation* to explore consequences of model.
3.3  Assess *alternatives* by weighing cost against effectiveness.
3.4  Examine results of 3.3 from the point of view of *sensitivity* to
changes in *parameters* and changes in *assumptions*.

**4. *Interpretation* ( the Judgmental Phase)**

4.1  Take account of *non-quantifiable* and *incommensurable* factors.
4.2  Take account of *'real' uncertainty* as opposed to statistical
uncertainty.
4.3  Present conclusions, distinguishing between what the analysis
has shown and pooled judgement.

**5.    *Verification* (the Scientific Phase )**

If possible, test the conclusion by conducting *experiments*.

Iterate if conclusions not satisfactory

**Figure 2.2**      *Steps in the RAND Systems Analysis (after Jenkins (1983))*

According to de Neufville & Stafford (1971) :

*"Systems analysis is a co-ordinated set of procedures which addresses the
fundamental issue of design and management: that of specifying how men, money,
and materials should be combined to achieve a larger purpose ...*

*... A good systems analysis - at whatever level it is done - is one that carefully identifies
the important issues and alternatives and relates the several costs and benefits of
each project in a way that is meaningful to the persons responsible for approving a
program." pp. 2-3*

Thus systems analysis is primarily concerned with making rational choices between alternatives within complex situations. It is particularly associated with the creation of detailed cost-effectiveness comparisons.

Opportunity for RAND style systems analysis to make a particular contribution to IS thinking was particularly provided by increasing job specialisation, and the differentiation between analysis or problem-solving activities and those of design and construction. In the 1960s such specialisation was necessary not only because of the increasing complexity of the development process, as more complex information-systems were demanded, but also because of a wider perception of the developer's role. This was no longer restricted to simply producing information-systems on request but now involved actively investigating the reasons for such requests and whether or not a new system was organisationally desirable. Both the re-orientation regarding the objectives of development and the distinction between the activities of analysis and design are apparent in the comments of Gregory & Van Horn (1963):

*"The objective of systems analysis, then, is to learn enough about a system - equipment, personnel, operating conditions, and demands on it - to establish the foundation for designing and implementing a better system, if it is feasible to do so. A data-information system is better, if it increases the net over-all output of the organization after considering the costs of systems design as part of the total costs." p. 121*

*"It might seem that both analysis and design work could be done by analysts because they have the best insight into problems and are best armed to solve them. Although this may be so, analysis and design have an important difference. One involves fact-finding, whereas the other depends on creativity, imagination, and an awareness of what might be done." p. 136*

Early prescriptions on the development of information-systems such as ADS (Lynch, 1969), IBM's SOP (IBM, 1974) and the ARDI methodology (Hartman *et al*, 1968) all display some ancestry from RAND style systems analysis. The third phase of an SOP study, for example, is concerned with design and within it the processing requirements for each organisational activity are divided into a number of processing runs. Experimentation might then be used to decide between possible alternative means of achieving the required processing and to discover whether performance might be improved. Alternative hardware configurations and processing algorithms might all be tried, timed, evaluated and costed. Cost and benefit comparisons could then be made to choose the best processing methods, as well as to decide whether development should take place. We need only compare this to the phase 3 of Figure 2.2 to see the influence which systems analysis had upon early information-systems practice.

The desire for 'rational', 'scientific' choice in the design of information-systems is also clearly expressed in Sackman's (1967) proposition that information-systems development should be conducted through the application of scientific principles:

*"It is then proposed that the development of man-machine digital systems be conducted as an applied scientific enterprise, regulated in accordance with an evolving*

*set of hypotheses that relate system design to system performance and are*
*experimentally tested in anticipation of and in response to changing conditions." p. 172*

The influence of RAND style systems analysis in IS thinking has continued over the years, even though it is rarely acknowledged and many IS practitioners are unaware of the historical roots of the ideas that they use. It may be clearly seen in Youssef's (1975) discussion of the development of management information-systems. This displays both the characteristic RAND style of problem-solving methodology and the ontological use of the system concept of hard systems thinking, with computer systems analysis taken to be :

*"....the set of steps required to examine an existing system or sub-system in order to*
*identify the problems causing inefficiency or inadequacy. It should be noted that the*
*concept of systems analysis has a broad application; it can apply to the engineering*
*staff studying hardware structure and efficiency, or it can apply to the analysis of a*
*computer-based information-system in which the flow of information is the focal point.....*
*....Before a new system can be designed, the existing system must be analyzed in order*
*to evaluate its merits and limitations. Therefore, the discussion of systems analysis*
*procedures assumes the existence of some type of an information-system. Systems*
*analysis involves six major steps: (1) define the problem, (2) state the objectives, (3) list the*
*limiting factors, (4) gather pertinent data, (5) develop potential alternatives, and (6)*
*reach a conclusion." p. 26*

Whilst the emphasis upon rational choice between alternatives may be less marked in modern development methodologies some of their ancestry remains discernible. The Structured Systems Analysis and Design Method or SSADM (Downs *et al*, 1992), for example, includes steps such as 'Define business system options' and 'Select business system option' which employ a selection, on the basis of costs and benefits and impacts, of one from amongst a number of alternative solutions to an identified business problem. The thinking and problem-solving approach of RAND style systems analysis thus continues to influence a new generation of information-systems professionals.

### 2.3.3 Operational research

The origins of operational research lie in war time studies, such as those described by Waddington (1973), into such questions as what size of convoy would suffer least sinking losses, at what height should anti-submarine aircraft fly in order to have the best likelihood of locating their targets and how should fighter aircraft be distributed in order to best intercept incoming raiders. With the end of the war the scope for applying the same form of systematic quantitative analysis to the problems of organisations was quickly recognised.

The same emphasis upon a rational choice between alternative responses to a given problem which we have already seen in systems engineering and systems analysis is also evident in the methodology of classical operational research (Figure 2.3). The specific aim is to apply the methods of science to problems of management, and a particularly strong emphasis is given to employing quantitative models of the situation in order to predict and compare the outcomes of different decision alternatives.

**QUALITATIVE ANALYSIS**

An initial diagnostic phase in which an initial identification of the problem elements is made; critical factors identified should include
• the principal decisions which are required
• the controllable or decision variables
• the uncontrollable variables
• restrictions or constraints on the variables
• the objectives for defining a good solution
• the measures of effectiveness which may be used to choose between alternatives
• the  tradeoffs which are likely to be required.

**QUANTITATIVE ANALYSIS**

**FORMULATING THE PROBLEM**

Establishing the limits for the analysis and deciding which of the possibly multifold impacts shall be considered within the analysis

**MODEL BUILDING**

Constructing a mathematical representation of the situation by:

Identifying  the static and dynamic structural elements

Devising mathematical formulae to represent the interrelationships among the problem elements

Selection of time horizon within which the model will be used.

Gathering the required  historical, technological or judgmental data`

**PERFORMING THE ANALYSES**

Performing calculations: Using the model  to find the most favourable set of values for the decision variables and information about the costs of deviating from these values. This will frequently involve finding values for the decision variables that optimize one of the objectives and give acceptable levels of performance for others.

Sensitivity testing: Assessing the sensitivity of the solutions to the model specification, to the accuracy of the data used in the analysis

**IMPLEMENTING THE FINDINGS AND UPDATING THE MODEL**

**Figure 2.3**      *Stages of Operational Research (after Wagner (1969))*

One of the great insights of the early OR practitioners was to recognise that many problems, apparently completely different, share a common underlying structure. For example, designing the service levels of a lift, organising the layout of petrol pumps at a service station or deciding the number of check-out tills at a supermarket may seem to have little in common; yet in each case one entity is required to service the needs of queues of other, customer entities. All three cases may be seen as queuing problems, a class of problem with which OR practitioners are well familiar and for which a solution may be arrived at by a number of well proven techniques.

The success of this strategy of finding recurring problem types has led to two difficulties for the OR profession. The first is the accusation that OR too readily interprets a complex problem situation as being the kind of problem which it already knows how to tackle, and ignores those subtleties of the actual situation which do not fit into such a problem formulation. The second is that as the methods for solving standard problem types have become well publicised and software packages incorporating OR algorithms have become available, allowing those without specialised knowledge to apply them, so the demand for the original skills of the OR professional has declined. Perhaps because of both of these reasons the OR profession has in recent years been quite exceptionally self-reflective concerning their role and methods. Among the results have been a widening of the application areas and techniques of OR, as in the application of OR thinking to the problems of non-profit-making groups through 'community operational research', and the acceptance of 'softer' techniques, such as the cognitive mapping of Eden (1989), as valid within OR.

This change is important because until recently operational research has had little direct influence upon information-systems thinking or practice. Because of the similarities of approach with systems engineering and systems analysis there have been no incompatibilities between OR and the field of IS, but there has been only limited cross-fertilisation of ideas. OR has tended to be regarded as a sister discipline to information-systems development, and this was often reflected in organisational structures, with practitioners of the two fields located in separate departments and groups. With the broadening of views regarding what constitutes OR, with increased interest in decision support and knowledge-based systems, and a shift towards methods that are not exclusively mathematical, the situation is changing. In the future we may expect OR thinking to play a far more active role in guiding information-systems practice, particularly in respect to providing decision support.

## 2.4 CHARACTERISTICS AND CRITICISMS

It is the 'hard' systems approaches which are best known and generally described as being 'the systems approach'; perhaps as a consequence they are also the form of systems thinking which has been most criticised. Some criticisms, as those made by such as Berlinski (1976), may be disregarded here in that they are mostly directed at General Systems Theory, the somewhat esoteric, mathematical form of systems thinking which has had little real-world impact. Other criticisms, directed at poor practical execution of the methodologies, may be avoidable by better training and professional practice. Quade & Boucher (1968) for example give warning of a number of potential pitfalls; these include that technically oriented analysts may focus their energies upon the mechanics of modelling rather than upon the problem situation and that recognised limits to the confidence which can be attached to a model may be ignored and firm conclusions and recommendations unjustifiably produced.

More difficult to dismiss though are criticisms that the basic philosophy and methodology of the 'hard' systems approaches makes them unsuitable to applications in social situations, for there exists much corroborating case evidence of failure in such situations. In order to understand why this might be so we must examine some of the basic characteristics shared by the hard systems approaches.

### 2.4.1 Single level of analysis

Whenever a person or group of persons (for convenience we shall use the term 'analyst' to cover both possibilities) enquires critically of a situation with the intent of causing change then an intervention process occurs. Immediately the nature of the situation is changed and the behaviour of those in the situation may be altered, whether for good or bad. The intervention may, in itself, be regarded as evidence of a willingness for change and lead to positive, 'Hawthorne' effects; or it may be interpreted as interference and lead to a lack of co-operation; or the arrival of the analyst may be regarded as threatening, arousing concerns over future job security. This means that in any intervention the analyst is always working (whether or not consciously) at two levels of analysis (Figure 2.4).

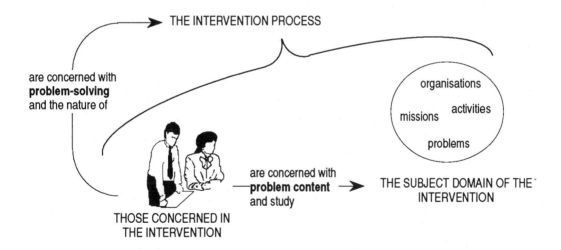

**Figure 2.4**     *Two levels of analysis within interventions*

The first and the most evident of these is the level of problem content. Here the inquiry is concerned with that part of the world which is seen as problematical and has caused the analyst to be there in the first place. At this level the analyst seeks to answer questions such as what organisation structure will serve the organisation best?, what plant layout will be most cost effective?, should a centralised or distributed design be used for a computerised information-system? The answers to such questions will form the content of any report that the analysts produce and attempting to answer such questions is what is normally recognised as 'doing the study'.

But at the same time as the analyst is addressing questions of problem content they must also address questions regarding the intervention itself. This second level of analysis concerns the nature of the intervention itself, how to interact with those in the situation, how to organise the intervention and the role of the analysts within the intervention. For example, is the analysts' role to 'solve' the client's problem or to help the client solve the problem? Is their role to directly cause or recommend some change or is it to act as a catalyst within the situation without influencing the results? Who should be taken as 'the client' for whom the analysts are working? What consideration shall be given to the views of those who are not 'the client' ?

Within the 'hard' systems methodologies it is only the first of these levels of analysis which is given much attention. The methodologies of systems engineering, systems analysis or (classical) operational research discuss how to deal with the problem content, prescribing the activities which should be done in order for the analyst to solve the problem; they do not consider the nature of the intervention itself to be problematical.

### 2.4.2  Problem-solving focus

Systems engineering, systems analysis and operational research all accept as given that the role of the analyst will be to solve particular problems on behalf of an identified client, that problem-solving is concerned with the making of rational choices amongst alternatives and that such choices may be made by focusing upon 'objectives, alternatives and ranking'. Miles (1973) describes the 'objectives, alternatives, ranking' approach to problem solving as being the father of the systems approach thus :

*"John Dewey stated the essence of problem solving some sixty years ago when he asked:*

*1. What is the problem?*

*2. What are the alternatives?*

*3. Which alternative is best?*

*... Dewey's formulation has today, largely through the influence of the communications and aerospace industries, evolved into the celebrated 'systems approach'. " p. 9*

and Findeisen & Quade (1985) echo this in the assertion that:

*"Most problems {Ackoff (1957) argues all problems, but see Checkland (1981, p. 155)} ultimately reduce to evaluating the efficiency of alternative means for a designated set of objectives. Analysis to assist someone to discover his best course of action may thus be considered as an inquiry into three basic questions:*

*1. What are his objectives?*

*2. What are his alternatives for attaining those objectives?*

*3. How should the alternatives be ranked?" p. 122*

Unfortunately social problems present a number of difficulties for the application of the 'objectives, alternatives and ranking' approach. In social situations the problem is rarely one of what course of action will be most cost effective in attaining objectives; it is often one of what *are* the objectives. And social situations are characterised by a wide range of values and beliefs which affect perceptions of the situation and what will constitute 'desirable' change, so identifying the criteria by which to compare alternatives is fraught with difficulty.

### 2.4.3  Adoption of power-holder views

One consequence of not explicitly questioning the nature of the intervention process is a tendency to support the status quo and views of existing power-holders. The methodologies of the 'hard' systems approaches allow that the initial stage of analysis is one of formulating the nature of the problem, where the domain of the analysis is determined and the problem is defined; within this stage the analyst would consider whether the client's initial definition of the problem is not merely a symptom of some other underlying problem. A later stage is to define suitable criteria by which alternatives may be evaluated. In both stages values play an important role, determining the choice of problem to be solved and the evaluation criteria which are to be used to choose between alternative solutions.

However, the views sought to resolve these questions and the sources of data gathered are almost certain to be those of the people with power in the situation; the managers, the administrators, those who are paying for the study. It is rare indeed to find a description of a 'hard' systems study which is participative and in which the views of all stakeholders are considered when deciding exactly what 'the problem' is. This may be just about excusable when the problem situation is clearly the property of some group; if Acme Industries runs a non-union shop and allows its staff no say in the management of its business then perhaps the analyst investigating some problem situation within Acme Industries can, with only minor ethical misgivings, accept that the management's view is the only one that in this situation needs to be considered. Such an approach is however severely limiting in that the results are unlikely to be of use or acceptable to anyone who does not share those beliefs and values.

In social situations where there are often a large number of different interest groups whose views must be accommodated but there may be little consensus of values, where power may be shared or where there are ethical requirements for participation, then the ready acceptance of power-holders' views as the basis for analysis is not practical. For example, in matters of national health care, then there are clearly difficulties with the tendency of 'hard' systems approaches' to not clearly distinguish between the customers and the beneficiaries of the system, the client who is paying for the study or the owner of the system. The political clamour which resulted from changes to the British National Health Service in the 1990s indicated only too clearly that it can by no means be assumed that medical professionals, governmental paymasters and patients requiring treatment have quite the same set of values or that they will find the same evaluation criteria acceptable.

### 2.4.4  Emphasis upon objectivity

The readiness to adopt the client's perspective upon the situation and their vision of what constitutes a problem partly arises from the 'hard' systems approaches' emphasis on providing not only a *rational* but also an *objective* analysis. The emphasis upon objectivity leads to a tendency to ignore those elements of a problem situation which cannot be easily quantified or modelled and to emphasise quantifiable, rather than qualitative, aspects and data. In practice though the hard systems approaches can never be genuinely objective or politically neutral. For example, the choice of criteria which can be used to evaluate the effectiveness of various alternatives must always mean acceptance of *some* group's value judgements about what is important.

Their inherent but un-admitted subjectivity also becomes clear with respect to the requirement to obtain clear objectives as the starting point of analysis. First, many different objectives can be identified for a complex entity such as a business organisation and attempts to explain their behaviour in terms of the pursuit of a single objective do not stand up to close examination. For example, the objective which is most commonly attributed to commercial organisations is that of making profits, yet we find that successful organisations restrict themselves to particular areas of business, even though the potential for increasing profitability by participating in other areas exists; large oil companies do not generally enter grocery retailing even though they would probably be very powerful and effective competitors in this area.

Secondly, human organisations do not themselves have objectives. Objectives are attributed to them by the observer and, clearly, different observers may attribute different objectives. The shareholders of a business may regard it as an income generating mechanism whilst the employees may regard it as a source of employment, an arena in which to fulfil themselves through practice of their skills or for some other form of social interaction. The 'hard' systems approaches have tended to perceive this as a problem of multiple objectives, continuing to assume that it is *the organisation* that has many objectives and ignoring the problem of objectives being subjective attributions. Such multiple objectives are dealt with by the idea of 'trade-offs', as in the suggestion that:

> "*In general, all systems have conflicting objectives, so that some form of compromise is essential. Therefore, a balance or* trade-off *must be sought between the conflicting objectives if the best overall result is to be obtained. ...*
>
> *... Reaching the best compromise between conflicting objectives poses many important questions which usually require detailed investigation at the beginning of a systems study.*" Jenkins (1969), p. 7.

Thus the analyst might for example have to balance the objective of increased profitability (an objective of management) with another objective of maintaining employment (an objective of the work force). This however merely disguises the problem in another level of supposed rationality, for conveniently forgotten is that the choice of *what is* an acceptable trade-off is itself a subjective and political act, based upon some group's value judgements.

## 2.4.5 Quantification and modelling

Model building is the essence of the 'hard' systems approaches and systems engineering, systems analysis and operational research all employ the construction and manipulation of quantitative models as a substitute for experimentation with the real-life system. Quade (1971) for example writes that:

> "Systems analysis, operations research, and similar techniques have functioned well for industry and defense, areas that lack the benefit of a comprehensive theory for guiding action, by relying on the systematic utilization of a large body of only partly articulated and largely intuitive judgement by experts in the fields involved. The standard research technique for such utilization is that of constructing an appropriate model of the situation." p. 24

Wagner (1969) too describes model building as the essence of the operational research approach and the counterpart to laboratory experimentation in the physical sciences, concluding that the model is a vehicle for arriving at a well-structured view of reality.

There are very good reasons for this emphasis upon model building, for even if a real-life system existed it would usually be far too complicated, costly or dangerous to test all possible changes under all the possible operating conditions and circumstances which might occur. Nevertheless, in some situations it is impossible to quantify all aspects of the situation or attempts at quantification may be so unacceptable to those involved in the situation that the results will never be considered worthwhile. A prime example of this occurs in problem situations involving the safety of human beings. Suppose the problem situation concerns whether or not new pedestrian road crossings should be installed. The effects of these on traffic flow could be simulated readily enough to give an estimate of the delays they would cause and some costs might be calculated based on lost working time etc. Against these however would have to be balanced the costs of the human injuries and lives lost if the new crossings were not installed. But how does one decide the value of a human life? Are all human lives equally valuable or is the life of a brilliant young student worth more than that of a retired elderly person? Perhaps the student's life is more valuable since they have the potential to make a great contribution to society. Perhaps the elderly person' life is more valuable since they have already contributed to society through taxation. No matter what value is put on a life then this will be far less than the value ascribed to it by its close relatives. Even if we try to be 'rational' about these questions, perhaps assuming that the law of averages will apportion the number of young students and elderly people killed for us, then our approach is not one which will be welcomed, and it is unlikely that our coldly rational analysis will be accepted as the basis for deciding whether or not those road crossings will be built. One may respond with the argument that whilst it is clear that we cannot yet quantify such things as human lives well, in practice the calculation is done implicitly anyway, when decisions are made, so why not at least try make it explicitly, however badly we may do it. Such an argument however is difficult to sustain in real life, contentious and political situations.

## 2.4.6 Applicability within social situations

The obvious success of 'hard' systems approaches led in the 1960s to their being applied in many different fields and to many types of problem. Attempts were made to apply the systems approach to problem situations in which social and political factors predominated. Designing a social system, it was claimed, was in essence no different from designing a more effective telephone network.

Wymore (1976), for example, expresses the view that the existence of human beings as participants (or as he views it, components or inputs) in social systems need not be a problem:

*"That there is no really satisfactory and totally encompassing theory of human behaviour, leads many to despair of ever being able effectively to design human beings into systems. On the other hand, such a total encompassing theory of behaviour is not necessary to build useful models of human beings, "useful" in the design and analysis of systems. After all, in many system design situations we do not have to deal with the total range of behaviour of the human being but we must be able to predict his behaviour as a component in a system or as an input to a system. Extant insights from the behavioural sciences are sufficient to enable the development of system-theoretic models of human behaviour in a restricted environment.*

*There is a great deal of extant scientific knowledge concerning social and behavioural phenomena that could be turned into technology for the design and analysis of social systems. We have more knowledge about these things than we have yet seen fit to apply, in an engineering sense. We are able to achieve very detailed models of human behaviour, models detailed enough to satisfy our most stringent requirements in the design and analysis of systems. Furthermore, behavioural sciences are developing at a rapid rate." Wymore (1976) p. 7*

There is here a somewhat naive belief that, in principle, human behaviour can be understood, and predicted, in the same way as physical phenomena. Experience, though, has suggested that this belief is not workable, for attempts to apply 'hard' systems thinking to socially based problems have met with little success. Even within comparatively well-structured situations it has been found that the conclusions reached as a result of a logical analysis have proved socially or politically unacceptable to the organisations involved. When attempts were made to use hard systems thinking in situations where there was not consensus over what the present situation was or what exactly 'the problem' consisted of, then the most disappointing results of all arose. Hoos (1972) provides a detailed and scathing critique of the attempted application of 'hard' systems thinking to social problems, locating the source of the failure of such attempts in the emphasis upon quantitative modelling and an ignoring of the unmodellable factors which are, in fact, most important.

*"Supposed to overcome the piece-meal fragmentation of other, more specialized approaches, the systems approach has provided a language that talks of total embrace of social processes and dynamics but delivers methods that reduces wholes to their arbitrary and often least important common denominators. Supposed to solve social problems, it has merely served to redefine them in a way amenable to the technical*

*treatment. ...*

*......In most social problems, even those attributable in large part to technology, aspects amenable to technical treatment are likely to be less important than those which are culture-bound, value-laden, and honeycombed with a political power network." pp. 241-242*

Dror (1971) concluded that although the management sciences (within which he specifically includes systems engineering, systems analysis and operational research) provided approaches useful for improving some types of decision-making they were unable to contribute much to policy making due to a number of weaknesses; these he identified as

- A neglect of the institutional contexts of the problems and the policy-making and policy-implementation processes.
- An inability to handle political needs.
- An inability to deal with irrational phenomena such as ideologies, charisma or self-sacrifice.
- An inability to deal with basic value issues.
- An ability to compare and choose between existing or easily identified alternatives but an inability to invent new alternatives.
- An inability to deal with situations where predictability in respect to the alternatives is absent.
- A reliance on quantification which leads to an inability to deal with complex social issues.
- Neglect of metapolicy (the level of policies on how to make policies) and an inability to improve the policy-making system.

## 2.5 TOWARDS NEW FORMS OF THE SYSTEMS APPROACH

So, the 'hard' systems approaches proved to be a powerful tool in the creation of physical systems such as buildings and engineering artefacts, in aiding decision-makers in cases where there was agreement over objectives and in studies where the task of the analyst was clearly defined to be to decide how to achieve some given objectives. But their early promise was not entirely fulfilled and by the 1970s it had become clear that there were special difficulties in applying the systems approach to the more complex and subtle problems of organisations. Where purposeful human beings were a major component of the problem, where there was a lack of consensus amongst those involved, where goals were fuzzy and poorly articulated then problems were ill-structured, 'wicked' and 'messy' and systems thinking seemed to be ineffectual.

One possible response was to modify the 'hard' systems approach. Quade (1971), for example, argued for a relaxation of the emphasis upon quantitative modelling through the adoption of a wider interpretation of the nature of a model as any device that provides a means to predict and compare the outcomes of alternative actions, regardless of its representative features or how efficient it is at optimisation. This, he argued, was required because traditional quantitative modelling was inappropriate in some situations.

*"Models in this tried but restricted sense are particularly difficult to create where political and social factors predominate. Some examples: how much of the city budget should be allocated to welfare and what portion of that spent on outpatient clinics, or whether local transportation needs are better served by a rapid transit system or by more and higher performance freeways, or if there is some legislative action that might end the increase in juvenile delinquency. Such questions involve more than the allocation of resources. Here, rather, the objectives or goals of the action to be taken must be determined first. It is not clear that "more efficient" has a meaning in these problems and the difficulties almost always lie more in deciding what ought to be done than in how to do it." Quade (1971) p. 25*

But it was by no means clear that any minor amendments such as merely using a different type of model was sufficient to allow the 'hard' systems approaches to be used successfully in social situations. More radical amendments might be necessary and alternative versions of the systems approach might be required.

### 2.5.1 Soft systems thinking

Since the 1970s new strands of systems thinking have emerged which are better able to cope with these less well defined problem situations. The most developed of these so far is the 'soft' systems methodology (SSM) which adopts a radically different approach to using systems ideas and whose history and use is described in detail in Checkland (1981), Wilson (1984) and Checkland & Scholes (1990).

The soft systems methodology was developed over a number of years through action research and practical experience in a large number and a wide range of consultancy projects. In early work it was found that the traditional systems approach was extremely powerful but not always sufficient or appropriate, this being particularly true with respect to socially located problem situations. This led to a gradual process of development, from the earliest forms of SSM which were merely amended forms of systems engineering, through both relatively minor refinements of technique and what may, with hindsight, be seen as major paradigm shifts in understanding to a fundamentally new version of the systems approach. Soft systems thinking now provides a means of inquiry for dealing with just those messy, ill-structured situations which have proved most problematical for the hard systems approaches.

Soft systems thinking differs from other systems approaches in a number of ways, amongst them being that it abandons the goal-seeking model of human behaviour and rejects the aim of engineering systems that will meet objectives. Before discussing soft systems concepts in detail and how they may be applied it is therefore useful to highlight these differences.

## 2.6 DISTINGUISHING CHARACTERISTICS OF SOFT SYSTEMS THINKING

### 2.6.1 Different use of the concept of a system

The hard systems approaches use the concept of 'a system' ontologically, that is to say, as a label for things in the real-world, and analysis proceeds on the basis that the world *is composed of* systems and sub-systems. Soft systems thinking however emphasises that the concept of 'system' is an epistemological device for *thinking about* some part of the world rather than an ontological description *of* part of the world. Whilst a very powerful tool for analysis, the notions of system and sub-system are only mental constructs through which we may *choose* to make sense of an external world. This difference is of great import for both systems theory and for the practical use of systems thinking, for it :

> " ... *transfers systemicity from the world to the process of inquiry into the world."*
> *Checkland (1983), p. 672.*

Reason demands that we act quite differently when our intervention is based upon beliefs such as "A university *is* a system to produce a better qualified work force for the future" and "A university *might be regarded* as a system to produce a better qualified work force". The former is, rightly or wrongly, definitive. If we accept it then it follows that all activities of the institution are to be focused upon producing individuals equipped with management skills. Any expenditure of time or money upon activities not directly concerned with the equipping of students with such skills must be seen as irrational or inefficient. The latter belief though is exploratory. We may, for the purposes of the investigation, examine what activities are implied by choosing to see the university in this way. But we do not rule out other possible concerns and it helps us to learn and understand about real-life universities rather than pass judgement upon them in any absolute sense.

### 2.6.2 Possibility of multiple perspectives

The change from using the system concept as a description *of* the world to a tool for thinking *about* the world allows soft systems thinking to explain why different interpretations of 'the problem' exist and cope well with what, in the language of hard systems thinking, would be described as multiple and conflicting objectives.

The de-coupling of the idea of a system from the real-world allows the possibility that some part of reality may be regarded simultaneously as many different systems, each perhaps having different purposes. It becomes possible to undertake phenomenological forms of enquiry and to utilise discussion and debate as a means of sharing insights and achieving learning rather than mere confrontation. Neither of these possibilities are, of course, available if one assumes that systems exist within the real-world in a form independent of their observer.

### 2.6.3 Inclusion of values and beliefs within analysis

An important aspect of soft systems thinking is then that it allows that a situation could be regarded differently by observers with different personal sets of values and beliefs. So a cocktail party may be regarded as an opportunity for social intercourse and relaxation or as an opportunity to make business contacts; a foreign war may be interpreted as a defence of democracy or as an exercise to protect foreign investments. The meaning of the situation is dependent upon the values, beliefs and past history of the observer.

Hard systems thinking has no mechanism for dealing with such differences in perceptions of the situation but soft systems thinking takes these, and their cause, to be an important component of the problem situation. It explicitly considers values and beliefs both through social and political analyses and through the 'weltanschauungen', or world-views, which makes any particular concept of a system meaningful. Such weltanschauungen may be not only large scale ideologies (capitalism, Marxism, or Christianity) but also small scale, personally held views of what is 'good' or 'bad', desirable or not, which provide a context within which behaviour can be seen to be consistent and actions meaningful.

This provides an explanation of the phenomena which hard systems thinking finds so difficult to account for, namely why the rational solutions which the analyst defines are often so difficult to implement. Now it can be seen that whilst the analyst's recommendations may be both feasible and rational in their own terms they may have little meaning for others. Unless the real-world participants are sympathetic to the views and values upon which the analysis has been based, then it is unlikely that they will agree with the analyst's notion of what 'the problem' is, or consider their recommendations desirable or even particularly relevant to their concerns.

### 2.6.4  No 'right' definition of a system

One of the assumptions of the hard systems thinking is that the 'real-world' is composed of systems, waiting to be identified and classified. If two individuals examine the same situation and do not reach the same conclusions about it then this must be due to faulty observation, and one set of conclusions can in principle be shown to be more correct (that is to say, closer to reality). Differences in motivation, norms and values (in short all those things which make an individual essentially human) are all possible sources of error, and obstacles to achieving this 'correct' objective knowledge of the situation.

But the nature of social situations is such that no 'right' definition may be achievable. For example, if I should define a bicycle as a two-wheeled personal transportation system operating through the application of human effort then you may test whether my observation is correct through simple data collection. Do, for example, all bicycles have two wheels? If however I say that a prison may be usefully seen as a limited access facility for the punishment of wrong-doers then you may collect all the data about prisons that you wish but still disagree with me about the nature of a prison. You might instead see it as a support facility for the rehabilitation of socially irresponsible individuals. Neither of these views of a prison can ever be *proved* as 'right' or 'wrong'. Both of these views, and many others, could be defended in terms of the data collected about real-world prisons, and all could be correct in terms of a particular set of beliefs and values held by an observer.

In soft systems thinking the shift to using the concept of 'a system' as an epistemological device together with the notion of weltanschauungen avoids such fruitless searches for the 'right' definition of a system or 'the solution' to a problematic situation.

### 2.6.5 The nature of organisations

Hard systems thinking regards human organisations as rationally arranged, goal-seeking mechanisms. The task of management is then necessarily taken to be to organise and allocate resources so as to maximise the likelihood of goal achievement and to control the operation of the goal-seeking strategies and tactics in a turbulent environment. Human organisations may, it is then assumed, be engineered using the same methods and techniques as are used in the engineering of physical artefacts.

Soft systems thinking, rather than seeing organisations as such 'goal-seeking machines' in which human beings merely happen to carry out some of the necessary tasks, considers organisations to be complex and ever-changing social entities whose nature is continually re-defined by those within it. As such, the organisation's view of itself and the world around it is created, defined and re-defined, by a continuous interaction of roles, norms and values.

This is in accord with much modern management thought. Pfeffer (1981), for example, points out that organisations can be understood not only in terms of enactment of a functional purpose but also as political arenas and as

*"... social systems populated by individuals who come to the system with norms, values, and expectations and with the necessity of developing understandings of the world around them so there can be enough predictability for them to take some action" p. 4.*

Pfeffer's conclusions are that understanding organisations requires two distinct levels of analysis. The first is concerned with the organisational actions and decisions that have observable, substantive outcomes such as inventory levels or the average time taken to satisfy an order. The second is concerned with understanding how such organisational activities are perceived, interpreted and legitimated. As we shall see, soft systems thinking addresses itself to both of these.

### 2.6.6 Nature of the intervention

As discussed previously, the hard systems approaches accept: that the role of the analyst (systems engineer, systems analyst or operational research practitioner) lies in engineering improvements to real-world systems: that the route to such improvements lies in discovering the most efficient, cost-effective means of meeting a defined objective: that such discoveries will be made through rational and primarily quantitative methods, especially through the creation and manipulation of models which mirror the real-world. As a consequence there needs to be little discussion concerning the nature of the intervention process.

Soft systems thinking, in contrast, takes human organisations to be complex and ever-changing social entities whose nature is changed merely by the fact that some kind of intervention is taking place. Because the arrival of the analyst changes the problem situation, the nature of the intervention is, in itself, something which must be carefully considered and managed. Furthermore, politics are not regarded as an aspect of the situation which interferes with rational analysis, not as confusing 'noise', but as a very important part of the situation. Negotiation and debate will therefore be necessary in order that the analyst and those in the situation may reach agreement or at least accommodation as to the nature of the present situation, what is problematical, what might constitute a solution and what role the analyst may play. This means that soft systems thinking requires that the analyst specifically address the second level of analysis which takes place in any intervention, that concerning the nature of the intervention process itself. Assumptions concerning who is 'the client', who 'owns' the problem, and what the role of the analyst is to be in this situation are subjects for examination and debate.

That soft systems thinking may also be used to conduct this second level of analysis highlights a further distinction between 'hard' and 'soft' systems thinking. Hard systems thinking makes use of the concepts of system, sub-system etc for understanding the real-world and builds systems models as a way of deciding between alternatives in an organised way. So we may say that it uses *systemic* ideas in a *systematic* way. Soft systems thinking, however, goes further than this. Not only are systems ideas employed in the study of problem content but also the whole process of inquiry may itself be regarded as 'a system for inquiry'. This makes soft systems thinking systemic in both its concepts and methodology, whereas hard systems thinking is merely systematic in the latter.

### 2.6.7 Human activity systems

Boguslaw (1973) argues that the essential difference between work with social systems and other types of system is not to be found in the proportion of components of the system which are human beings, nor in the variability or reliability of the system under examination, but rather in the attitude with which analysis is approached.

> "*The question ultimately is one of the definition of system objectives and, in a much deeper sense, a question of purpose, goals and values. It depends on what it is that you regard as being important.*
>
> *If you begin, or are predominantly preoccupied, with materials and how these can be assembled for some given system purpose, then no matter how high the ratio of human components used in your system, you will, in my view, continue to be a designer of nonsocial systems. If, on the other hand, you are predominantly concerned with people and view them sui generis- as things important in themselves- if you regard them as more or less self-generating, independent entities which represent the ultimate definers of all system goals - if you are ethnocentric about the race of mankind- then you are somewhat prepared to enter into the activity of social system design." pp. 181-182*

The hard systems approaches treat the human components of the problem situation as essentially no different to other components or resources. However, human beings have characteristics which set them apart from all other things in the world. Only human beings can attribute meaning to observations of the world, set objectives, take purposeful action to achieve those objectives and, crucially, later choose to change those objectives. It is the ability to select, re-select and possibly change yet again their own objectives which makes human beings *purposeful* rather than merely *purposive* in their actions. This distinction is used by Ackoff & Emery (1972), who emphasise this ability to change purposes or goals as a defining characteristic of purposeful individuals or systems that

> "*... can produce (1) the same functional type of outcome in different structural ways in the same structural environment and (2) can produce functionally different outcomes in*

*the same and different structural environments.*

*Thus a purposeful system is one that can change its goals in constant environmental conditions; it selects goals as well as the means by which to pursue them. It thus displays will." p. 31*

It is failure to recognise this distinction and that, using the phrase of Vickers (1983), 'human systems are different' that lies at the root of the shortcomings of attempts to apply hard systems approaches in social situations. In soft systems thinking though the special ability of human beings to display purposeful behaviour is attended to by the idea of a special class of systems, human activity systems. These are in Checkland's (1971) taxonomy of systems distinct from other classes of system such as designed physical systems (buildings, missile systems etc), and require their own methods for analysis.

One word of caution is required here. The concept of a 'human activity system' is an epistemological device of soft systems thinking. That is to say, the premise underlying its use is that it may be useful and lead to insights if we *choose to regard* some part of the real-world, a part in which human beings play a major role, as a human activity system. We should not fall into the error, regrettably common, of believing that any part of the world is by its very nature a human activity system. In discussing human activity systems Checkland & Scholes (1990) emphasise this by using the term 'holon' (instead of 'system') to describe the abstract idea of a whole with emergent properties.

*"Those who write about 'human activity systems' as if they exist in the world, rather than being holons which can be compared with the world, are failing to grasp the essence of soft systems thinking, namely that it provides a coherent intellectual framework ... as an epistemology which can be used to try to understand and intervene usefully in the rich and surprising flux of everyday situations." p. 24*

Though the use of the term 'holon' is not one which we shall use in this book, the confusing multiplicity of ways in which the term 'system' is employed is a problem, and something of which the reader must continually aware.

## 2.6.8 An approach to learning rather than problem-solving

Hard systems approaches, based upon the idea that systems exist in the real-world, take the task of the analyst to be one of engineering improvements in those real-world systems by discovering optimal, or at least satisficing, solutions to perceived problems. Soft systems thinking instead employs systems ideas as a means of enquiry and is based upon a paradigm of learning rather than optimisation. Checkland (1981) declares that:

*"... the methodology declines to accept the notion of 'the problem'. It works with the notion of a situation in which various actors may perceive various aspects to be problematical. It tries to provide help in getting from a position of finding out about the situation to a position of taking action in the situation. ...*

*... Its emphasis is thus not on any external reality but on people's perceptions of reality, on their mental processes rather than on the objects of those processes." p. 279*

A result of this shift is that organisational learning is as valid an end result for an intervention as any more tangible 'deliverables' or changes to the situation; consequently, although soft systems studies most commonly result in changes to the situation their end result may, in certain cases, be not a 'problem' now 'solved' but a change in perceptions about the situation. The study may end successfully with those who previously saw a situation as problematical no longer finding it so.

### 2.6.9  Underlying philosophy

Systems theory is usually regarded as essentially positivist in nature but the introduction of the concept of a human activity system marks a shift in the philosophical basis of 'soft' systems thinking towards phenomenology. Soft systems thinking argues that in studying the human organisations we require a fundamentally different approach from that which we might use to study the natural world (science) or designed physical systems (hard systems thinking) because of the special nature of human beings. Human beings have consciousness and free will; they do not simply react to the world in which they live but are able to interpret and place meanings upon their sensations of the world. In order to understand the actions of human beings it is therefore necessary to investigate those meanings and the values which give rise to them, and in any study of human organisations the meanings created by those involved and the perceptions which arise from them cannot be excluded from the analysis.

### 2.7  CONCLUDING REMARKS

It may seem that the subject of much of this chapter is far removed from the technical questions of how to create computerised information-systems. We hope though that the reader will appreciate that this is not so. For the way that we currently think about using and creating information-systems has been influenced by systems thinking, and all our development methodologies enact, at least to some extent, a systems approach. A proper understanding of those ideas is therefore essential for looking at the subject of information-systems and, as we shall see in later chapters, using those ideas differently through soft, rather than hard, systems thinking, has important consequences for the study of information-systems.

# 3 Fundamental concepts

## 3.1 INTRODUCTION

In Chapter 2 we saw that systems thinking developed in response to the need to deal with complex problem situations, and found some differences between the original 'hard' forms of systems thinking and the more recent and complementary soft systems thinking. Though we looked at three variants of hard systems thinking there are many others, notably the cybernetics of Beer (1966, 1967, 1972, 1979) and the system dynamics modelling of Forrester (1961, 1969), which lack of space prevented us from discussing. There are therefore many versions of 'the systems approach', but all consciously employ certain fundamental concepts. Those concepts are the subject of this chapter but two provisos must be made about what follows.

First, the view taken of each concept varies somewhat between adherents of different systems approaches; for example, we have already indicated that the concept of 'system' is employed differently in soft systems thinking than in hard systems approaches such as systems engineering. As there can be no neutral description of the concepts we must declare in advance that we shall introduce the concepts primarily from a soft systems standpoint, and that in places the descriptions we give may differ from those that might be given by adherents to other schools of thought.

Second, in a book such as this it is necessary to introduce the concepts individually but this is potentially misleading, for the concepts of systems thinking have no real meaning in isolation from each other. Take, for example, the ideas of 'system' and 'system boundary'. To accept that some part of the real-world might be thought of as a system implies the existence of some sort of boundary, an imaginary line of classification and discrimination which separates those things which are part of the system from those things which are not. It is impossible to use the concept 'system' without, at the same time, using the concept 'boundary of a system', and vice-versa.

The concepts described individually in the succeeding pages must therefore eventually be understood as a whole. To assist in this Figure 3.1 shows how some of the propositions of systems thinking relate to each other. The reader may care to refer back to this diagram at times during this chapter.

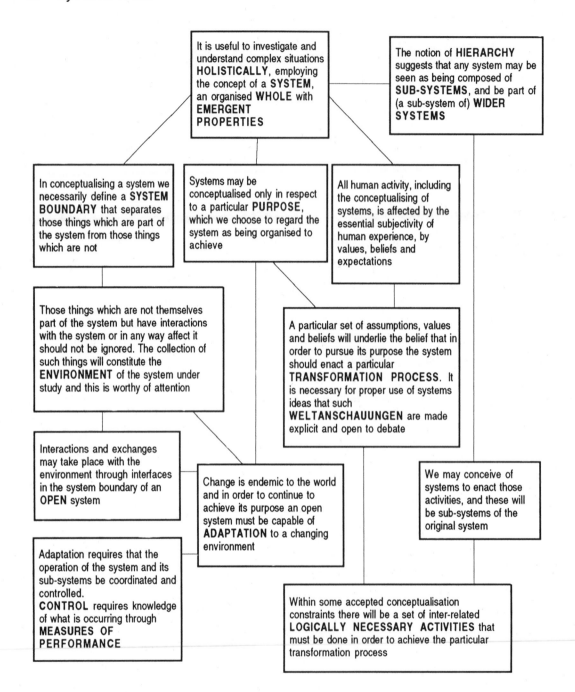

**Figure 3.1**     *Relationships between some of the propositions of systems thinking*

## 3.2  THE HOLISTIC CONCEPT OF A SYSTEM

The most basic concept of systems thinking must surely be the notion of 'system' itself. Phrases such as 'central heating system' are part of our everyday language, but if we look at some typical uses of the word 'system' in the field of information-systems (Figure 3.2) it is all too clear that this familiarity can be dangerous, leading to imprecision in meaning through the word being used for very different purposes.

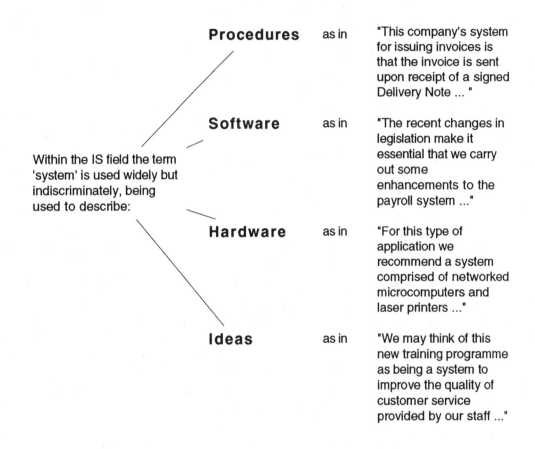

**Procedures**  as in  "This company's system for issuing invoices is that the invoice is sent upon receipt of a signed Delivery Note ... "

**Software**  as in  "The recent changes in legislation make it essential that we carry out some enhancements to the payroll system ..."

Within the IS field the term 'system' is used widely but indiscriminately, being used to describe:

**Hardware**  as in  "For this type of application we recommend a system comprised of networked microcomputers and laser printers ..."

**Ideas**  as in  "We may think of this new training programme as being a system to improve the quality of customer service provided by our staff ..."

**Figure 3.2**    *Different, conflicting uses of the term 'system' are made in the IS field*

Within systems thinking the word 'system' is used rather more precisely. The notion of 'a system' arises from the need to be able to investigate complex situations in a holistic way that takes account of the possibility of emergent properties. A basic definition of a system is then of a set of inter-related components *organised* together to form an entity that, as *a whole,* has *emergent properties* that belong to no single component or subset of the components of which it is formed.

All systems approaches make a distinction between **systems**, which have organisation and therefore purpose, and **aggregates,** which do not. Angyal (1941) distinguishes between these in that in a system it is significant that the parts are organised and arranged whereas in an aggregate it is significant that parts are added or removed. This difference is perhaps easiest to understand when we apply the concept of a system to parts of experienced reality. The nature of a physical aggregate such as a randomly organised pile of stones remains substantially unchanged if we re-arrange the pile; we do not now have anything different from that with which we started. If we add more stones to the pile we have something that is only quantitatively different, namely a larger, weightier pile. In contrast, the dry-stone walls commonly found in the North of England are carefully organised for the purpose of containing livestock. Such walls are not held together by mortar but by the careful arrangement of each component stone and the removal or movement of a single stone may change the nature of the whole; the wall may collapse and be unable to serve its purpose.

Figure 3.3 illustrates another example of what might be regarded as an aggregate and a system. The components of a bicycle have individual properties of shape, hardness, colour etc, but only when they are arranged together in a particular way does a new whole arise, the bicycle, which has amongst its *emergent properties* the potential for providing personal transport.

**AGGREGATE**
A collection of individual, isolated components unrelated other than by spatial relationships or similarities of kind

**SYSTEM**
Purposefully arranged together, the whole has emergent properties that belong to none of the component parts.

**Figure 3.3**    *An example of an aggregate and a system*

These two examples are easy to understand because they refer to real-world objects with which we are familiar. The notion of a 'system' is though more generally applicable and can be used to examine a wide range of phenomena, including those of which we can have no direct experience. It can be used in the analysis of physical objects (such as an automobile's ignition *system*), transient activities and procedures (a company's order processing *system*), the natural world (a biological eco-*system* or the solar *system*), or even ideas such as the agreed rules by which a society is regulated (the legal *system*).

### 3.2.1 Taxonomies of systems

The apparent universality of applicability of the concept of a system is seductive and has led to a number of attempts to create 'taxonomies of systems' capable of classifying all experienced reality. These are primarily of interest for the characteristics of systems which are used for classification. Boulding (1956, 1985), for example, has proposed taxonomies of systems based upon the degree of complexity of organisation displayed by a system (Figure 3.4), finding it possible to:

> *"... describe a list - indeed something of a hierarchy- of systems that we have good reason to believe correspond to something in the real world." Boulding (1985) p. 18.*

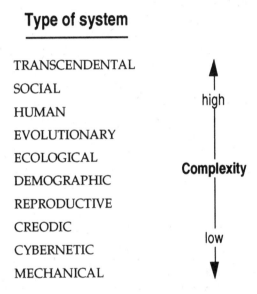

**Figure 3.4**     *A hierarchy of system types suggested by Boulding (1985 )*

The taxonomy of systems suggested by Jordan (1968) is founded upon three "bipolar types that are somewhat similar to dimensions". These are the rate of change (which may lie somewhere between structural and very low to functional and very high), the degree to which a purpose is exhibited by the system (represented by the extremes of the system being purposive to non-purposive) and the connectivity of the system (this being either mechanistic or organismic). By considering where any system lies upon the range of each of these, eight types of system are identified.

A notable feature of Jordan's hierarchy is that it makes *intentionality*, the having of a purpose or the quest for a goal, a required characteristic of a system. Checkland (1981) though identifies a logical weakness of Jordan's taxonomy to be that it ascribes purpose to the exemplar part of experienced reality; it assumes that a road *has* a purpose rather than that a purpose is *allocated to it* by the observer who has chosen to see it as being a system.

Checkland's own (1971) systems map of the universe (Figure 3.5) echoes previous taxonomies both in emphasising the applicability systems ideas to the full range of human experience and in suggesting that the universe is composed of various types of system. Its particular importance is in singling out the class of 'human activity systems' as the class of system with which the practical application of systems ideas is most concerned and as requiring its own special methods of analysis.

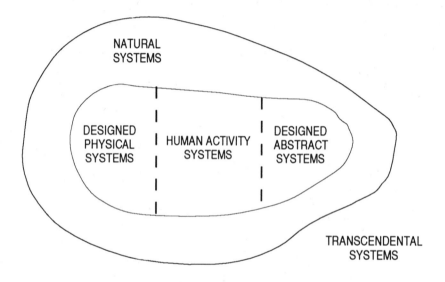

**Figure 3.5**    *Checkland's classes of system*

There have been few suggestions for taxonomies of systems made in recent years because of the changes that have occurred in the understanding of the concept of 'system'. The concept of system has become recognised to be an epistemological device, meaning that one may *choose* to regard some part of experienced reality as being a system, without believing that it by virtue of some inherent characteristics *is* a system. The power and range of applicability of the system concept then arise not because systemicity is somehow inherent in the world or that the hidden hand of some creator or nature is in any way revealed by its wide applicability: it just happens that 'system' is sufficiently powerful an epistemological device as to be applied to almost all human experience. This change in understanding has made the description of any single taxonomy of systems a somewhat meaningless activity, for there will always be alternatives and different possible system explanations of experienced reality.

## 3.3  PURPOSES AND TRANSFORMATION PROCESSES

The most general characteristics of any form of systems approach are then a commitment to holistic enquiry and the belief that it is useful to employ the *concept* of a system to *make sense* of complex and sometimes apparently chaotic experienced realities.

Part of our definition of a system was that it was organised However, it is clearly meaningless to describe something as 'organised' without being able to identify what that thing is organised to do. It is, for example, not unreasonable to believe that a collection of locomotives and rolling stock, track and signalling devices might constitute a 'railway system' but it is debatable what the purposes of such a system are. Is it organised to provide a communal service for the transportation of people and goods or should its purpose be to gain income and profits from the sale of transportation? Upon such questions rest all the debates concerning whether railway operations should be subsidised and whether branch lines that are non-economic but whose closure would damage local communities should be kept open. Without committing ourselves to one of these or some other purpose then we are not in any real sense employing the idea of a system. We can therefore only talk meaningfully of a system if we can clearly identify and communicate the purpose for which that system is organised. We may declare the purpose of a system within a system definition written in natural language, but such definitions are always ambiguous, so it makes sense to try to communicate the idea in other ways in addition.

One additional way is to highlight the intended transformations that would occur as a result of the system's existence. For example, we might define in English a system that is:

> "A nationally owned system that provides scheduled and reliable train services by the employment of locomotives, track and subsidiary equipment together with appropriately trained personnel in order to satisfy the travel needs of the population."

We could strengthen the chance of our conceptualisation of the system being correctly communicated to another person by stating that the transformation which the system is intended to perform, that we would expect any real-life manifestation of such a system to cause to occur, would be that shown below:

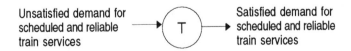

There is hidden here an assumption that causing such a transformation to occur will further the purpose of the system: in conceptualising the system we have, based on particular beliefs and values, accepted that providing scheduled and reliable train services will help to satisfy the population's travel needs. Only in the existence of such an assumption does the conceptualisation of the system make sense.

This means that if we choose to view some part of the real world as 'a system' we must declare as precisely as possible what system we are taking it to be, the associated transformation process of that system and, crucially, declare the fundamental assumptions (there may be several) or *weltanschauung* under which it is meaningful to believe that achieving the intended transformation will further the purposes of the system.

Precisely how the system and its purposes are defined will have immense consequences for any investigation that employs it. If we wish to think of a system relevant to the operations of a real-world prison then as Mowshowitz (1976) rightly points out:

> "Suppose one were to investigate the penal system from the systems point of view. A basic philosophical question concerning its objectives would have to be decided at the outset. Should the model embody a rehabilitative or retributive principle of justice?" p. 222.

If then one decides to view a prison as a system, the precise nature of that conceptualised system, including the essential purpose of the system, must be defined very precisely. Figure 3.6 shows two possible, equally valid, ways in which we might view a prison as a system, each enacting a different intended transformation. Quite clearly, if the intention is to investigate the workings of a real-world prison using such conceptualisations, each would lead to very different findings.

### 3.3.1 Intended and unintended transformations

We must remember that any system will have associated with it many different transformations, and not all of these will be intended. For example, a system to provide road transport facilities to service the needs of industry might have an intended transformation concerned with satisfying the requirement to move industrial loads rapidly by road. The operation of any real-world example of such a system would though have many effects and many possible transformation processes could be equally validly associated with the system: the unsatisfied desire of non-commercial drivers to travel between places quickly is transformed into a satisfied desire and the new roads rapidly become congested, concrete is transformed into roads, flyovers and bridges, and sites of natural beauty or scientific interest are destroyed. On a smaller scale any system concerned with manufacturing will cause the transformation of raw materials into finished products, but it will also transform raw materials into waste. Clearly the relative extent to which both transformations occur will be of great concern to the managers of that system.

To maintain a genuinely holistic stance the system thinker must give attention to not just the intended transformations of a conceptualised system (those which arise from its intentionality or help define its purpose) but also the full range of transformations that a system might cause to occur.

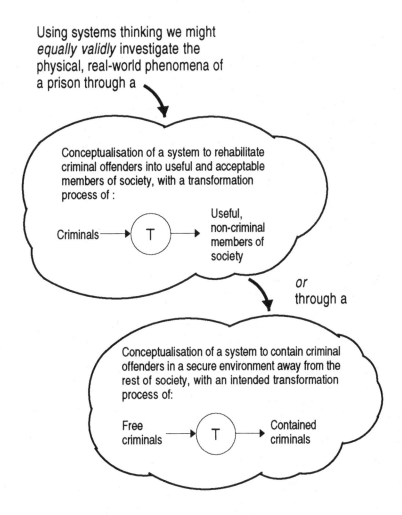

Using systems thinking we might *equally validly* investigate the physical, real-world phenomena of a prison through a

Conceptualisation of a system to rehabilitate criminal offenders into useful and acceptable members of society, with a transformation process of :

Criminals → T → Useful, non-criminal members of society

*or* through a

Conceptualisation of a system to contain criminal offenders in a secure environment away from the rest of society, with an intended transformation process of:

Free criminals → T → Contained criminals

**Figure 3.6**     *A prison seen as two different systems*

### 3.3.2  Purposes and goals

The intentionality of systems is an idea common to all systems approaches but is described in the literature in a variety of different ways. It is quite common for the idea of intentionality to be described by reference to 'goals' or 'objectives', as in McLeod's (1990) definition of system as:

*"An integration of elements designed to accomplish some objective" p. 890*

We would wish though to use the idea of a system to mean something more than a *designed* physical system. And words such as 'goal' and 'objective' are widely used in the management literature to describe things that may, at some foreseeable time in the future, be achieved. It is therefore preferable to use 'purpose' to describe the on-going intentionality of a system. In this way one might, for example, say that a manufacturing system has the objective of winning a major government contract but the purpose of always being one of the top ten profitable firms in the industry. At some point in the future the contract will be awarded, and the objective will have been achieved or not - but the company can never fully achieve its purpose; if the next years' accounts show that it remains one of the most profitable companies then it has continued to pursue its purpose well, but there is always next year's performance to strive for, and the purpose has not been finally achieved. Of course, to pursue the long term, continuing purpose it might be thought essential to achieve particular short term goals or objectives, such as winning the government contract.

This use of the terms is similar to that used in strategic planning where organisations are considered to have on-going 'missions' in the light of which particular 'strategies' and 'tactics' are chosen. In agreeing to a particular mission the executives are, in effect, choosing to view the organisation as being one particular system in preference to the myriad of others that they might see it as being.

## 3.4 HIERARCHICAL DECOMPOSITION: SYSTEM AND SUB-SYSTEM

The earliest systems thinkers recognised that what is taken to be 'the system' is always a somewhat arbitrary choice made by the analyst. Not only might the same part of experienced reality be regarded as different systems having very different purposes, but if the component parts of a system are examined in detail then those components might themselves be regarded as systems in their own right. Hierarchy has therefore been a central concept of systems thinking from its beginnings, and what is labelled as a 'sub-system' at one point in an enquiry may itself become 'the system' when enquiry becomes more focused and attention is given to what Klir & Valach (1965) describe as another level of resolution.

Of course, if every system may be seen as having sub-systems that may themselves be regarded as systems at a higher level of resolution then it follows that any system that we choose to investigate will be part of some wider system. So every system may be seen as being located within a hierarchy of systems, having sub-systems within it and itself being part of a wider system. This is important to remember because a wider system will inevitably place constraints upon and have expectations of the behaviour of the system under consideration, and that system will constrain the operation of its sub-systems.

The possibility of there being always a hierarchy of systems, *each having meaning only in respect to the purposes of the higher level system of which it is part,* allows the systems thinker to shift the focus of the analysis to increasing levels of detail, without falling into the traps of reductionism. For example, a motor car, which might be regarded as a system for providing convenient personal transportation, could be seen as composed of a number of sub-systems, such as those concerned with propulsion (the engine), electrical devices (ignition, indicators, lights) with transmission control (gearbox, steering and brakes) and human convenience (seats, luggage facilities etc). All or any of these might now be studied in greater detail without losing sight of the fact that each must contribute to the wider system's purpose of providing convenient personal transport.

### 3.4.1 A variety of possible system decompositions

To regard particular parts of a system as together forming sub-systems is, like the decision to regard part of reality as a system, a deliberate choice made by the analyst; this means that it is possible to decompose any system into a number of possible sets of sub-systems. This possibility is a particular strength when systems thinking is used as a means of organisational analysis, introducing variety in the depth as well as the breadth of the analysis. For example, a motor car can be regarded as many different systems, including a system for polluting the atmosphere. But without compromising our view of a motor car as a system for convenient personal transport, we might equally well regard it as composed of different sub-systems to those suggested above, perhaps having a mobility sub-system (engine, ignition, transmission and wheels), a mobility control system (steering, brakes and driver) and a cargo handling system (passenger seats, luggage space and roof rails).

The sub-systems that are most readily perceived in business organisations are those which reflect the functional partitionings that are formally defined within the organisational structures. In a trading organisation it is inevitable that we would find activities concerned with the sale or exchange of products, and those activities will usually be grouped together under the formal label of the Marketing Department. If one regards that organisation as a system it would then be very easy to identify sub-systems whose boundaries coincided with the formal organisation structures, including identifying a marketing sub-system that maps precisely onto the activities of the real-world Marketing Department. However, if the system concept is to be used to greatest advantage then it is important to not accept too readily existing organisational structures as the basis for analysis; looking at the organisation in a fresh way, as an alternative set of systems and sub-systems, will often yield valuable new insights into the causes of current problems.

For example, one might choose to regard a manufacturing organisation as a system that satisfies the market demand for a product by manufacture within the constraints of producing an agreed rate of financial return. Knowledge and experience of manufacturing firms tell us that, in practice, manufacturing is usually accompanied by a complicated set of activities concerned with purchasing raw materials, scheduling production, finding customers, arranging distribution, maintaining financial records, etc. The essence of using systems thinking as a means of investigating a real manufacturing organisation (as opposed to using just experience or common-sense) is to discover why those activities are required and how they might be best organised through methodical decomposition of the original system idea. Figure 3.7 shows one possible set of sub-systems for the conceptualised manufacturing system. This is very similar to what one might find enshrined in the real-world organisation's formal reporting structures and functional divisions.

But one might choose to consider the system to be composed of a different set of sub-systems, those shown in Figure 3.8. In this alternative set of sub-systems there is a different arrangement of responsibilities and some of the activities previously done by separate sub-systems have been subsumed into different groupings; the activities of the Personnel sub-system of Figure 3.7, for example, may now be a responsibility of the Resources sub-system together with activities concerned with purchasing raw materials that were previously included within the Production sub-system of Figure 3.7.

This alternative set of sub-systems does not merely represent 'old wine in new bottles', and it is not what would be labelled in computer systems analysis as a re-grouping of the same 'functional primitives' or basic activities. The 'customer satisfaction' sub-system is a re-thinking of the activities previously done by the Production and Marketing sub-systems; the new sub-system implies much closer links between the activities of producing products and knowing what the customer requires. Using this system as the basis for examining the real organisation would cause greater consideration to be given to such things as the quality of service provided to customers than would be the case using the previous systems model. Choosing either the decomposition of Figure 3.7 or 3.8 as the basis for analysing the workings and performance of the real-world manufacturing organisation will therefore have considerable implications for the results of the analysis.

## 3.5 SYSTEM BOUNDARIES AND SYSTEM ENVIRONMENTS

Whenever one chooses to view some part of the 'real-world' as a system then by defining that system one, at the same time, unavoidably delineates a system boundary for that system: a line is drawn between what should, and what should not, be considered part of that system.

This does not mean that we can henceforth ignore the existence of everything outside the system boundary, for there will be many things that while not themselves part of the system can affect the operation of the system. For example, if we choose to investigate a manufacturing organisation by means of any concept of a system then we need to recognise that the real-world organisation has intimate relationships with such things as its suppliers and fund providers such as banks. These would have to be considered as outside the conceptualised system since the system will have no direct control over their actions. However the actions of such environmental entities as banks may act as a major constraint upon the system. Changes in interest rates or restrictions on borrowing may require changes to the system's activities, and could even lead to a failure to survive. Systems thinking allows for such things to be taken account of by labelling the set of things which affect the system and exert influence on the operation of the system but which lie outside the systems boundary as the *environment* for that system (Figure 3.9).

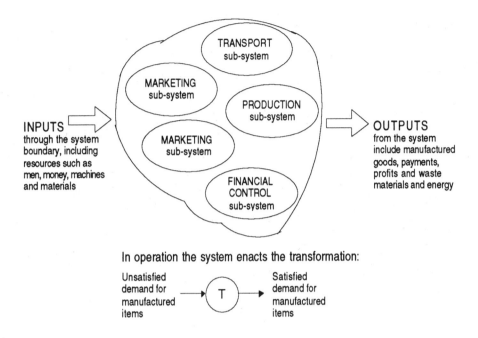

**Figure 3.7**     *Sub-systems of a manufacturing system*

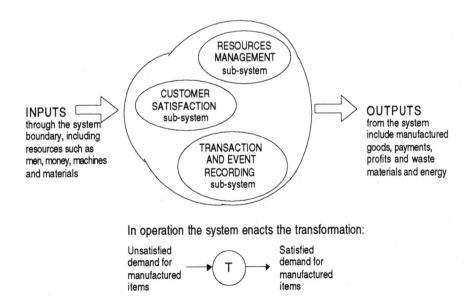

**Figure 3.8**     *Alternative set of sub-systems for a manufacturing system*

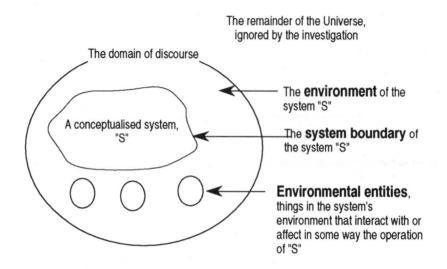

**Figure 3.9**     *Boundaries and environments*

A distinguishing feature of the environment is that the system has no control over events in the environment or the action of environmental entities although both will, in part, determine the system's performance.

Of course, there will be an infinite number of things over which a given system has no control but unless these interact with the system in some way then these will be considered to lie outside the domain of discourse and be unconsidered in the investigation.

Many of the things within a system's environment might themselves be validly seen as being systems in their own right. However, from the viewpoint of the one given system under study, these may be regarded as environmental entities like any others. For example, if we conceptualise a system relevant to the marketing department of an organisation then one environmental entity that we might identify for that system would be 'customer', reflecting that customers are something with which our system has direct interaction but which could not be considered as part of the system itself.

Another thing with which the system may have direct interaction might be the production department of the same company, perhaps informing that department of product sales so that future production may be changed in response. Although it might be quite reasonable to regard the production department as being a system in its own right, *from the viewpoint of the sales system* no distinction need be made between the customers and the production department as environmental entities.

### 3.5.1 Exchanges across the system boundary

The environment will greatly determine the performance of the system and it is therefore very important to identify the nature of the relationships between entities in the environment and the system. A great deal of business analysis and, in particular, computer systems analysis is concerned with establishing the existence and role of such relationships.

The boundary of a system does not merely delineate between what is regarded as part of the system and what is not; it also represents the point of contact between the system and the outside world. It is across the system boundary that transactions and exchanges take place, and in information-systems development a concern with the environment has traditionally been expressed in the form of a concern over the definition of *interfaces*.

Consideration of the transfers that take place between a system and its environment allows one of the simplest categorisations of types of systems, between *open systems* and *closed systems* (Bertalanffy, 1950). In closed systems there is no form of exchange between the system and its environment whereas such exchanges do occur in open systems. Bertalanffy originally described as 'closed' those systems which are totally isolated from the environment but such isolation would mean that such a system could not adapt and would not long survive in a changing environment. It is rare to find any part of the real world that could usefully be regarded as a closed system according to such an absolute definition. The open-closed dichotomy is useful however if we consider 'open' and 'closed' as the two limits of a continuum and allow that transfers over the system boundary may include not only material transfers but also transfers of energy and information. We can then think of as relatively closed in terms of information those systems whose behaviour is unaffected to any significant degree by information from the environment and as relatively open in terms of information those systems which have interaction with the environment through information which affects their behaviour.

For example, if we consider a clockwork toy car as a system then that system would be relatively closed with respect to materials, relatively open in terms of energy (think of the winding of the clockwork motor) and relatively closed with respect to information since its behaviour is completely determined and it will not respond to a changed circumstance such as an obstacle in its path. A more expensive toy car might be equipped with simple sensing devices, able to detect when forward motion is blocked and in response reverse the direction of the car. This would have to be regarded as a system that was open with respect to information, for information about the environment has crossed the system boundary and caused a change in the system's behaviour.

### 3.5.2 Boundary and environment defined by system

The location of the system boundary, and therefore the definition of the system's environment, is, of course, entirely dependent upon the definition of the system and its purpose. For example, if we choose to regard a prison as  a system to rehabilitate criminal offenders' then the system boundary will encompass such things as social workers and therapists which, if we regard the prison as 'a system to punish criminals', would not lie within the system, might lie in the system's environment but might be excluded completely from the domain of discourse.

## 3.6 ADAPTATION TO CHANGING ENVIRONMENTS

Whatever is our definition of a system we must recognise that the environment of that system will, as time passes, change. Change is endemic to the world and to all of those things that we might wish to investigate through systems thinking. Any thing which can interact with its surroundings in expected, pre-planned ways but cannot cope with unforeseen interactions is unlikely to survive; examples of this can be seen in every class of system, whether in natural systems it is dinosaurs failing to adapt to climatic changes or in physically designed systems where machinery cannot be adapted to meet new manufacturing tolerance requirements.

Inevitably then, if we wish to use systems thinking to investigate the world, we must include as a basic tenet of systems thinking that open systems must be capable of adaptation to a changing environment, having the capacity to monitor the effects of the environment and control their behaviour in response. By doing so they may achieve dynamic homeostasis, by preserving a basic identity and continuing to pursue the same purposes, albeit in different ways, over time. The possibility of adaptation does not of course provide any guarantee that a system will survive indefinitely, for if the environmental change is too great or too different then the system may be unable to adapt its behaviour sufficiently and will cease to exist. This was recognised early in systems thinking in the form of Ashby's (1956) 'Law of Requisite Variety' which proposed that "only variety can destroy variety", and that continuing survival of a system depends upon the variety of possible responses by the system being equal to the variety of possible changes in the environment.

Emery & Trist (1965) provide an interesting real-life example of how change in the environment may arise from changes both in the behaviour of existing environmental entities and in the arrival of new environmental entities, and of the way in which an organisation may respond. They describe a vegetable canning firm faced by a complex set of changes. The firm had planned investment in new production facilities on the basis that the market environment and their role as manufacturers of the premier brand of a canned vegetable would continue. However, a number of factors changed.

- Retailing methods were changing and supermarkets and grocery chains began to account for a larger proportion of food sales.
- A new market had developed in canned imported fruits and the companies involved in this seasonal trade sought to find other uses for their production facilities.
- Firms involved in producing frozen vegetables, though not regarded as direct competitors, were making available at a low cost those vegetables not meeting their quality requirements.

Canning firms, not previously seen as competitors, which were seeking additional uses for their canning machinery began to buy the vegetables rejected by frozen food manufacturers and sell the canned product at a lower price. Supermarkets began to use these cheaper brands of canned vegetables as house brands, at a cheaper price and in direct competition with the premier branded goods. At the same time the poorer quality of the vegetables now being canned led to a deterioration in the market image of canned foods and more direct competition with frozen foods.

The result of these changes was that

> "... *many upheavals and changes in management took place until a 'redefinition of mission' was agreed, and slowly and painfully the company re-emerged with a very much altered product mix and something of a new identity." p. 24.*

The new company identity and the re-defined missions of the company reflect a different vision of the company. This new view of the company, as a different system, had a different environment to that of its predecessor, one which *could* recognise new competitors and different market forces as environmental entities.

## 3.7  CONTROL

It has already been suggested several times that a system must be able to control its own behaviour. This is necessary by definition if the system is to adapt to changes in its environment and required if the system's organisation is to be maintained and its component parts are to continue to work together towards a common purpose. The classical model of control in systems thinking comes from systems engineering where:

> "*Control is necessary because not all the factors which arise could have been foreseen when the design was optimized. These unforeseen factors are called disturbances in control engineering and have the effect of causing what actually happens to deviate from what should happen. The object of the control scheme is to measure what is happening and then to prescribe some action if performance is not up to plan." Jenkins & Youle (1971) p. 146.*

A monitoring and controlling sub-system regulates the behaviour of other, operational, sub-systems, ensuring that agreed standards of performance are adhered to through the operation of a negative feedback-loop (Figure 3.10).

By sensing the outputs of the system and making comparisons to standards set by a higher-level system, the monitoring and controlling sub-system is able to detect variances from desired behaviour. When this happens then it initiates control action to minimise or eliminate the variance.

There are a number of variations on this model of control. In feedforward-control the monitoring and controlling sub-system anticipates changes in the environment and acts proactively rather than reactively. In positive feedback-loops, the control action increases the discrepancy between desired and actual results. In everyday language we talk of 'vicious circles' to describe examples of this, such as arms races between nations; a nation increases its armaments to improve its security but this prompts its neighbour to

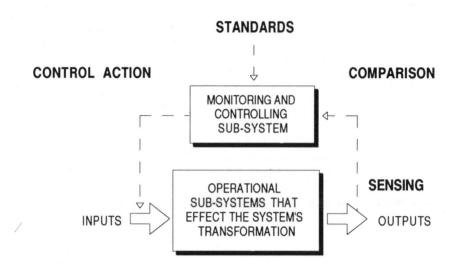

**Figure 3.10**    *Feedback-loop image of control*

add to their weapons, so the first yet again has to add to its stockpiles of weapons and so on *ad infinitum*.

It is though the negative feedback model that is most used and this image of control is often explained by reference to examples of the control mechanisms in physical designed systems, such as the governor in a steam engine or the operation of a central heating thermostat (Figure 3.11). It is however equally powerful as a model through which to understand control and the function of managers in human organisations (Figure 3.12), and is widely used in discussions of management topics; Bedeian (1993), for example, employs the idea of both feedback and feedforward control loops not only to explain organisational control in general but also to make sense of particular issues such as Total Quality programmes.

### 3.7.1  A systemic taxonomy of measures of performance

Adaptation occurs only when it is decided that the existing operation of the system is inappropriate or unsatisfactory, and monitoring and controlling can only take place once suitable measures of performance have been defined. The question of how to define suitable measures of performance is therefore vitally important, but it is also one that has proved very difficult to answer. A useful contribution is offered by Checkland *et al* (1990) who approach the problem from a somewhat different direction. They suggest that we should begin by thinking about how a system might fail and conclude that there are three ways in which a system's performance might be considered to be unsatisfactory or tending towards failure.

First, the intended transformation of the system might not be achieved. In some way the operation of the sub-systems might together not lead to the intended transformation occurring; secondly, the intended transformation might be achieved, but only through an

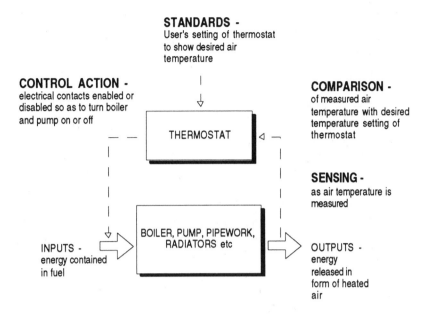

**Figure 3.11**     *Thermostat as a monitoring and controlling sub-system*

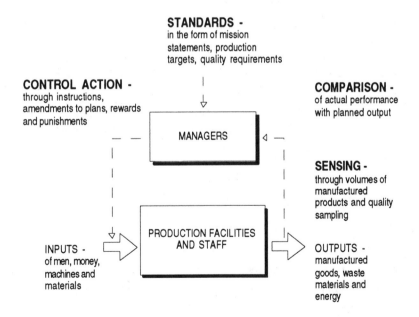

**Figure 3.12**     *Management as the monitoring and controlling sub-system for a manufacturing organisation*

unacceptably high usage of resources; thirdly, the intended transformation might be achieved and resource use might be acceptable, but the system's performance might still be considered unsatisfactory if the achieved transformation contributed nothing to the purposes of the higher-level, wider system.

This suggests three types of measure of performance and the beginnings of a taxonomy of measures of performance for systems (Figure 3.13). Other possibilities such as measures of 'elegance' and 'ethicality' are possibilities but cannot be justified in quite the same way as systemically required.

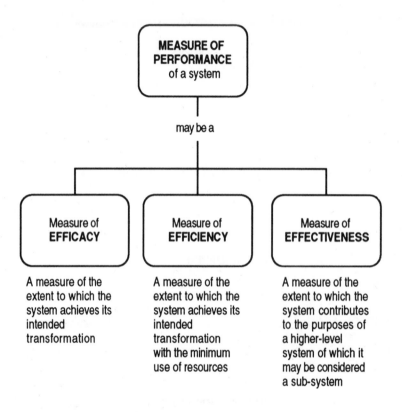

**Figure 3.13**    *A systemic taxonomy of measures of performance*

This provides some guidance to the sort of issues upon which any monitoring and control sub-system should focus, and to the sort of questions that need to be asked in real-world organisations. The managers enacting monitoring and control in Figure 3.12, for example, might seek to answer questions such as:

- "To what extent are the production facilities and staff producing manufactured goods? Is the rate of output good enough?" - questions of efficacy;
- "Are we efficient in our production? Is the rate of use of inputs acceptable? Are levels of wasted materials and energy too high?"- questions related to efficiency;

• "Has the production of these manufactured items helped the organisation pursue its mission? What contribution has been made to profits? Would the production of different products be better to do? - questions concerning effectiveness.

## 3.8 RELATIONSHIPS BETWEEN SYSTEMS

There are many ways in which a system (or sub-system) may be related to another. The most obvious relationship is that one system is a sub-system of another. Others are that one system may regulate another or that two systems are in a symbiotic relationship, with both pursuing their own purposes but the survival of each depending upon the existence of the other.

An important form of relationship is that of two systems being in a master-servant relationship, with the purpose of the first being related to furthering the purpose of the second. In such a relationship the master system could survive alone but its performance, (its efficacy, efficiency and effectiveness) will be enhanced by the existence of the servant system. The servant system however is dependent upon the existence of the primary system; it may receive some necessary resources from the master system but more basically its purpose is defined in terms of, and only meaningful in respect to, the existence of the master system.

This form of relationship is of particular importance with regard to information-systems as this is the relationship between an organisational information-system and the organisation that it serves. An obvious consequence is that it is impossible to analyse the operations of an information-system or design a new one without first having a clear understanding of the activities and the objectives of the business system that it serves. One of the failings of the past is that computer professionals, and the logic of the approaches that they employ, have not taken adequate notice of the importance of this relationship and viewed the creation of information-systems to be an end in itself, rather than as a means to support the business.

# 4 Systems ideas in the field of IS

## 4.1 INTRODUCTION

Having introduced the basics of systems thinking we can begin to apply these ideas to the subject of information-systems. Before we do this however we must consider the extent to which systems ideas are already used, and the effects that this has had upon IS practice. The IS field is, after all, widely assumed to already employ systems ideas and it is not uncommon to find such claims as that:

> "*Systems concepts underlie the field of information systems. Other disciplines may use the term system as an important concept or as a convenient way of describing the phenomena they must deal with. However, knowledge of systems concepts is vital to a proper understanding of the technology, applications, development, and management of information systems.*" O'Brien (1991) p. 11

There are good reasons to believe that such claims are over-stated, for there are some areas of IS in which systems thinking has played no part at all. However, there is certainly also a long and strong inherited tradition of system thinking influencing IS work and we shall concentrate upon how this has affected how we understand the role of information-systems and how they are developed. The most far-reaching of all these is the idea of there being a 'life cycle' for development and we examine both the advantages and disadvantages of IS's adoption of this idea.

## 4.2 INTELLECTUAL FOUNDATIONS OF IS

Histories of the field of information-systems are not yet common, but from Somogyi & Galliers (1987) or Friedman & Cornford (1989) two things are very clear. First, that since the first use of computers in the 1950's there have already been many changes in what organisations seek to achieve with computer-based information-systems and how such information-systems are created. Secondly, those changes have been occasioned by many different factors.

Any purely technological history of the field, which sees the course of events as driven and determined solely by advances in hardware and software, is, in consequence, inadequate as an explanation of either past events or present concerns. A technological view of IS history can only ever allow a single cause for the confusions and dilemmas that have characterised the use of information-systems at different times, namely that organisations and individuals have failed to properly understand or make proper use of the new technology. This is a somewhat impoverished perspective, for it ignores that the path of technological development is, to at least some extent, determined by organisational and social factors. It also has little explanatory value, providing no indication why some technological advances (such as graphical user interfaces) become widely adopted whilst others (such as touch sensitive screens) have little or no impact. Even its descriptive value is limited. The increase in the capabilities of all forms of information technology has certainly been impressive but many managers, whose primary concern has been with the contribution that computerised information-systems have made to organisational performance, might feel that progress has been haphazard and not always satisfactory. A 'technological progress' description of the past would not accord well with many managers' own experiences.

So whilst technological progress has undoubtedly been an important factor in determining the past use of information-systems in organisations there are certainly other equally important factors to consider. As this has become recognised so interest in the subject of computer-based information-systems has widened. It is now a multi-disciplinary subject, one that is of interest to, and researched within, many different disciplines and to which ideas from a number of different fields may be usefully applied.

This multi-disciplinarity causes some disagreement over the theoretical foundations for IS work. Culnan & Swanson (1986) suggest three foundation disciplines - computer science, management science and organisation science - while Liebenau & Backhouse (1990) make claim for only two, sociology and semiology. Ahituv & Neumann (1990) however name no less than six 'exact' sciences, four technologically oriented disciplines and nine social and behavioural sciences as the foundations of the field of information-systems and Zwass (1992) opts for seven contributing disciplines including accounting, sociology and cognitive science.

If one examines what has genuinely influenced practice in the IS field though one must conclude that some of these claims are largely unjustified. One may search in vain for truly influential articles from social scientists, semiologists or the like. Like it or not, in the past it has been computer scientists, with a concern for the technology, and management writers, with a concern for the organisational impacts of the technology, whose ideas have dominated the literature and shaped practice. This would appear to support the contention of Hirschheim & Boland (1989) that the IS field is a combination of two *primary* fields, computer science and management, with a large number of *supporting* disciplines such as psychology, sociology, statistics, political science, economics, philosophy and mathematics.

The interests of computer scientists and management have been so closely entwined that disentangling their effects is, admittedly, difficult. For example, one might argue that it was only when large-scale databases became technically feasible that attention was paid to how such databases might be efficiently structured and that management of a 'corporate data resource' became a subject for discussion. In response one could identify the organisational problems and inefficiencies (duplication of data, redundancy etc) caused by separate file-based data processing as the motivation for developing database management systems in the first place. If we adopt Vickers' (1983) view of history as 'a two-stranded rope of events and ideas' then the history of information-systems has been created by the concerns of both these primary disciplines, each drawing at times inspiration and insight from many other disciplines (Figure 4.1).

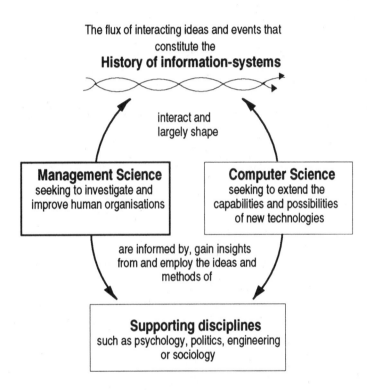

**Figure 4.1**   *History of IS determined by interactions between the concerns of many disciplines*

Since systems thinking has provided the basis for so much of management science it is not then surprising that in the IS field both the methodologies used to apply technology and the conceptual frameworks for understanding the use of that technology display an inheritance from systems theory. The language of the computer professional, composed as it is of systemic terms such as 'environment', 'interface', 'data flow' and 'sub-system', is evidence of this historical legacy. Furthermore, the fundamental legitimacy of IS work, the grounds for claiming it to be a soundly based discipline rather than a mere collection of craft knowledge, is, as we have seen, frequently based upon it being a practical application of 'a systems approach'.

That systems ideas should have been readily assimilated into the field of IS is not surprising. When organisations were first seeking ways in which to employ computer-based information-systems the computers were large, costly and unreliable machines and it was essential that this expensive new resource was employed in the most efficient way. The problems of organising data processing were seen as being in many ways no different from the problems of organising the flow of raw materials and products in manufacturing and process industries. It was perhaps inevitable then that guidance was sought from the methods of RAND style systems analysis and systems engineering which had proved so successful in these areas. It is these which continue to influence IS thinking.

One should not though accept too readily claims that all work concerning information-systems is based upon a systems approach. There is much about the way in which IS development is presently conducted that is quite antipathetic to the conscious application of systems ideas. The IS field certainly employs much of the vocabulary of systems thinking and in some cases terms have been so deeply associated with the IS field that earlier uses have become mostly forgotten; the job title of 'systems analyst' is just one example of this. However, borrowing the occasional idea or piece of language does not alone justify the claim to being a systems approach and one must question the depth of understanding of systems ideas when we find the most basic terms misused. Even when one is accustomed to find the term system used in less than precise ways it comes as a shock to find Ashworth & Goodland's (1990) definition:

> **"System** *Whatever is within the boundary of a study"* p. 272.

In fact there are vast areas of IS in which systems thinking has had no impact whatsoever. In programming, database work, testing or any of the implementation-related subjects of IS there is no real use of the concepts or principles of systems thinking. It is only really in business analysis, computer systems analysis and the management of development projects that there is an inherited tendency to use systems ideas. Regrettably, even here the ideas have become confused, used only intermittently and it is an out-dated version of the systems approach that is to be found.

## 4.3   A HARD SYSTEM THINKING INHERITANCE

To get a clear picture of the basic ideas of a discipline it is instructive to turn to the most basic texts, those by which newcomers to the field learn the language and principles of the field. Many of the introductory texts written for students of information-systems include chapters entitled 'The systems approach' or 'Systems thinking', but their content is usually disappointing, for it is the systems thinking of the 1950s that is described therein. Consider Figure 4.2 which shows the stages of the systems approach as described by Ahituv & Neumann (1990) and Reynolds (1992). Compare these with Jenkins' (1983) stages of systems analysis or Hall's (1962) stages of systems engineering (described in Chapter 2) and it is obvious that the systems approach used within IS and described in the majority of IS texts is a very close relative of the classical 'objectives, alternatives and ranking' systems approaches of the past.

| Stages of the systems approach to problem solving, (Ahituv & Neumann, 1990) | Stages of the systems analysis approach to problem solving, (Reynolds 1992) |
|---|---|
| 1. Defining the problem<br>2. Gathering data relevant to the problem<br>3. Identifying alternative solutions<br>4. Evaluating the cost and effectiveness of the alternatives<br>5. Selecting the best alternative<br>6. Implementing and monitoring the selected alternative | • Define the problem<br>• Define scope of system to be studied<br>• Break down system into basic components<br>• Gather data about each component<br>• Identify and evaluate alternative solutions<br>• Identify best solution<br>• Evaluate interactions among components of selected alternative |

**Figure 4.2**     *Stages of the systems approach as described in the field of IS*

## 4.4  LIFE CYCLES IN IS

The most pronounced of all the influences of hard systems thinking must be the idea of 'life cycles' for information-systems and for development projects. The idea of a life cycle has been used in many ways within the IS field. It has been suggested that organisational use of IT will always go through certain stages (most notably by Nolan 1973, Gibson & Nolan 1974), that particular information-systems have their own life cycle from 'birth' to 'death' and that there is a standard life cycle through which we may understand and organise all development projects. The last of these has become so ingrained in IS thinking that it is now only rarely questioned.

The concept of a development life cycle (which is sometimes also called the 'project life cycle' or 'waterfall model of development') has been at the heart of the thinking about information-systems for many years and regards the development process as consisting of a sequence of inter-related but distinct phases. These phases are time ordered and the 'ideal' project will proceed through these stages in a well managed, ordered and uneventful sequence. Figure 4.3 shows one of the earliest representations of this idea by Royce (1970). There are innumerable versions of the life cycle but Miles (1985) shows that despite differences in terminology these have the same basic structure and the basic notion has remained remarkably stable. The idea is ubiquitous in IS work and through it hard systems thinking has had great influence upon IS practice.

The idea of a life cycle is sometimes properly introduced as a thinking tool, as a conceptual device by which one may understand the world. For example, Lucas (1986) introduces the concept of a life cycle for the information-system by saying that it is:

*"...helpful to think of a system as having a life consisting of different stages"* p. 261

Similarly, Wood-Harper *et al* (1985) say that the life cycle idea:

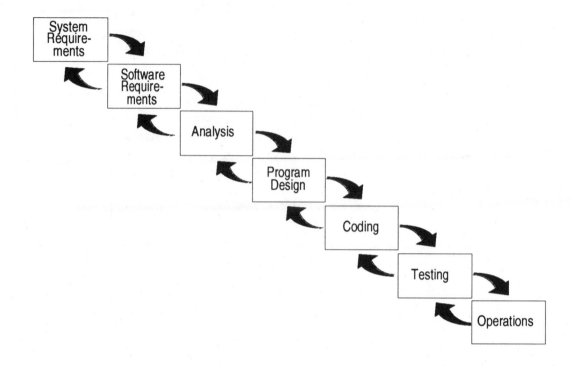

**Figure 4.3**     *The waterfall systems development life cycle of Royce (1970)*

> "... *covers all the steps that a system is thought to go through from the time that the users decide that they have a problem which needs to be tackled to the point where the system is live and running.* " *p. 5.*

The life cycle idea is though more commonly introduced as descriptive of reality, and *as a fact* about systems development that the aspiring systems analyst or designer must know, much in the same way as a chemist should know that hydrogen and oxygen combine to make water or an aviation engineer should know that gravity pulls things earthwards. Hicks (1984) for example states categorically that:

> "*The development of a computer-based system typically goes through seven major phases. These seven phases are called the systems development cycle.*"

Others emphasise even more strongly the normative nature of the idea, that these stages must always occur, categorically stating that:

> "*Structured systems analysis and design is keyed to the system life cycle. As a system moves from concept to implementation, it must pass through each of these steps.*" *Davis (1983) p. 8.*

> "*Once a project has been chosen, the systems development cycle commences. Every project passes through a series of phases in much the same way as a building is conceived, designed, specified, constructed and finally fitted out for occupation. Within each phase there are a number of tasks which must be performed before it is possible to proceed to the next phase. The various phases in the system's*

*development cycle are frequently referred to as the systems lifecycle." Brookes et al*
*(1982) p. 13*

### 4.4.1 Life cycle models of development

It has been claimed that such life cycles had been identified as early as the 1950s.
McNurlin & Sprague (1989), for example, credit the first mention of an IS life cycle as far
back as Canning (1956, 1957). Although the idea did not become truly important in IS
work until the 1970s it is certainly the case that authors throughout the 1960s had
differentiated between the tasks that were carried out during development and seen those
tasks as falling into more general types of activity. As can be seen in Figure 4.4 the names
given to these were similar to the names later used in life cycle models.

Such differentiation was partly born of practical experience and observation of what
practitioners did, and partly inherited from the hard systems methodologies which
distinguished between different stages of problem solving. Thus Graham (1972) presents,
as a framework for discussing the work of the computer systems analyst, a structured set
of system development activities based primarily upon then current practice; Prince's
(1970) 'information systems approach' however, which identifies five phases in the
planning and implementation of information-systems, had declared roots in systems
theory and management science.

### 4.4.2 The shift in IS thinking

The important change that occurred at the start of the 1970s was that a number of authors
began to argue that certain types of activity were *logically required* by the nature of the
development process itself. This was justified by the bringing together of two, closely
related ideas. The first of these was that information-systems, like plants and animals, had
their own natural and inevitable life cycle. The second was that the process of developing
new information-systems should be, not merely systematically arranged, but seen *as
systemic.*

Given the origins of systems thinking in the work of biologists such as von Bertalanffy
it is not surprising that there should have been a long tradition of drawing analogies
between organised human affairs and the patterns of behaviour displayed in nature. This
tradition found most fruitful expression in the work of the cyberneticists, who sought
general principles concerning control by examining the way in which control was
exercised in natural organisms, and in particular, within the human being. That such
general principles might exist was suggested by the fact that many phenomena, whether
they occurred naturally or as the result of human action, displayed similar characteristics.
Beer (1972), for example, noted that S-shaped growth curves are common to phenomena
in the economic sphere as well as the biological.

The history of an information-system could also be interpreted in terms of such curves.
An information-system, like any other application of technology or product in a
marketplace, will take time to become established and valued. During its development
considerable costs will be incurred whilst no benefits are provided to the organisation.

- Definition of objectives
- Selection of applications
- Analysis of feasibility
- Equipment specification
- Proposal validation
- Equipment selection
- Organization of installation program
- Personnel selection
- Training
- Systems planning and design
- Development of standards
- Logic design
- Coding
- Program testing
- System testing
- Site planning
- Site preparation
- Delivery
- Conversion
- Parallel running
- Maintenance
- Audit
- Documentation

**Brandon(1963)**

Analyze the present system
Develop a conceptual model
Test the model
Propose a new system
Pilot installation of the new system
Full installation of the new system

**Optner (1960)**

Analysis of the Decision System
An Analysis of Information Requirements
Aggregation of Decisions
Design of Information Processing
Design of the Control System

**Ackoff (1967)**

Systems Analysis
Systems Programming
Systems Design
System Equipment Manufacture and Software Programs
Systems Installation and Check-out
Systems Service

**Feigenbaum (1968)**

Identification of the problem
Description of the problem
Design of the system to solve the problem
Programming the system
Implementation of the system
Support of the system

**Fisher(1969)**

**Figure 4.4**   *Data processing tasks and activities identified by authors 1960-1969*

There may be teething troubles as the new system goes into operation. There will then follow a learning period and then, for some time, the system operates successfully and to the advantage of the organisation. Periodic evaluations will identify the need for minor amendments and the system is maintained. But this cannot continue indefinitely:

*"What happens next is fairly alarming. The level of performance, however it may be measured, will continue perhaps for some time. After that, if it does not simply stultify, it may actually decline. Just as senescent people may forget what they once knew, just*

*as the biological organism which was fully grown may begin to shrivel, so markets may decline following saturation, so businesses may fail and become bankrupt. Even successful technologies, considered in relation to competitive technologies, may cease to be economic any longer.* " Beer (1972) p. 23

When this happens, Beer suggested, only superimposing a new growth curve upon the old will suffice. Applying these ideas to information-systems then the implication is that any information-system has only a limited useful life-span, and that at some time a new information-system will have to replace the old and a new phase of system development must begin. So arose the notion of information-systems having a generic 'life cycle'; phases of development, use, evaluation and possibly maintenance, leading to further development and so on, in a recurring sequence (Figure 4.5).

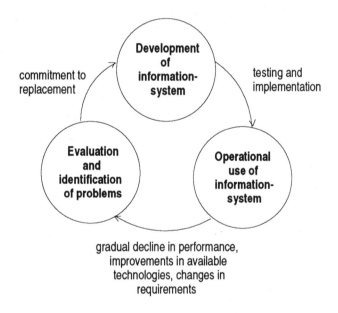

**Figure 4.5**      *The life cycle of an information-system*

### 4.4.3 Life cycles for development

By the time, in the early 1970s, that the life cycle idea entered into IS thinking it was already common practice for the development of new information-systems to be organised through projects, in which an inter-disciplinary team banded together for a finite period of time to achieve some defined goal. This mirroring of the practice in systems engineering gave scope for envisioning, within the more general life cycle of an information-system, other, shorter life cycles. In particular, the process of development might be seen as having its own life cycle.

The idea of a *project* life cycle in addition to a life cycle for the system itself was already well established within hard systems thinking. Kline & Lifson (1971), for example, present both a life cycle for systems engineering, on the basis that all systems have life cycles, together with a definition of the design process which, they argued, occurred during each stage of the system life cycle. Design was here equated with development, being understood as:

*"....an iterative, decision making process for developing engineered systems or*
*devices whereby resources are optimally converted into desired ends" p.18*

This achievement of defined objectives with minimum use of resources was, of course, precisely what was being aimed at during the development of new information-systems. It was natural enough therefore that some writers began to talk not only of an 'information-systems life cycle' but of a 'development project life cycle'. This is the life cycle idea expressed both in Royce's (1970) waterfall model above and underlying in Boehm's software life cycle for software engineering (Figure 4.6).

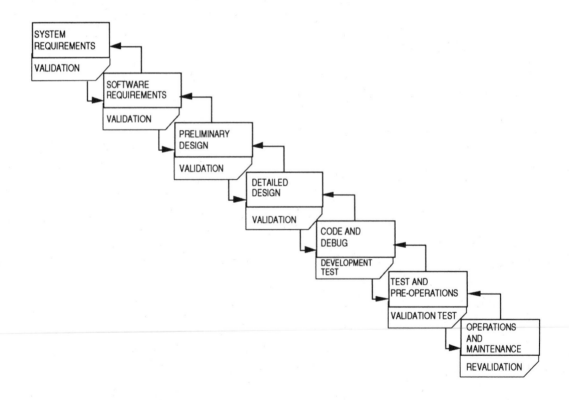

**Figure 4.6**     *The software life cycle of Boehm (1976)*

As suggested by Figures 4.3 and 4.6 most life cycle models of development represented the development process as essentially linear, where each phase must be completed before the next may be begun. Recognising that activities were never truly completed and often required re-doing in the light of new events some iteration was allowed for, but not encouraged. As Brittan (1980) notes:

> *"This serial definition of the project development cycle, known as the linear strategy, embodies one fundamental concept; that one activity follows logically from its predecessor so that each stage is complete before the next begins....*
>
> *....Some allowance is often made for looping back when detailed investigations and analysis reveal problems or when questions indicate that a change in requirement may be necessary, but any extensive looping back is regarded as both unusual and unsatisfactory since it can be held to imply deficiencies in earlier work"* p. 13

### 4.4.4 Development perceived as a system

The widespread adoption of the idea of a development project life cycle in the early 1970s was a significant turning point in the history of development approaches, for it required that development activities be seen as organised together to achieve a given purpose; in short, that the development process itself be seen as a system.

This system displayed hierarchy in so far as the overall process of developing an information-system could be broken down into an ever larger set of increasingly detailed required activities. Even today, the logic of all the modules, stages, steps and tasks of modern development methodologies such as SSADM can be traced back to the principle of there being some form of systemic hierarchy in development activities. Communication between the individual sub-systems of development was to be found in the requirement that each sub-system of development (or, in the language of life cycles, each phase of a project) should have its own required inputs and outputs in the form of defined deliverables and reports. Systemic control was to be found in the emphasis upon project management for many writers favoured the use of a Steering Group for every development project, that group formally and regularly reviewing actual progress against schedules and budgets. A project could not proceed to its next phase until the required outputs of the present phase, usually defined in terms of a document of specified content, had been produced and accepted. The degree to which the specified outputs had been produced thus provided a measure of performance and the basis for systemic monitoring.

This change to viewing the development process as being a system in its own right was immensely significant; it marked a shift from there being some use of hard systems ideas within development to hard systems thinking being used to *understand* the process of development itself. And because of the ontological use of the system concept by hard systems thinking (the belief that systems existed in the real world) it implied that the development process had its own natural structure, a structure that should be respected and reflected in the way that the developers carried out their work. Now, it was possible to offer not merely good advice about how development should be conducted but specify normative models of what *must* be done.

The result of viewing development as a systemic process was therefore a blueprint for conducting development, the core of which was assumed to be common across both organisations and types of project. A complex MIS project might require more time and effort to be spent on some activities than would the automation of an existing manual system but both projects would follow the same pattern of development and, if carried out within the same organisation, might be conducted according to the same, organisationally defined, standards and procedures. Such standards for how development should be conducted soon became common as organisations were eager to manage development in a more organised and controlled way. The result could be sets of development standards of a daunting scale; this author has worked in one large organisation where the detailed prescription of what should be done at every stage of development and what should appear in every required output document occupied twelve large volumes.

## 4.5 ENDURING INFLUENCES ON IS PRACTICE

The argument that all examples of information-system development shared a common natural structure has proved to be a particularly powerful, attractive and enduring one for the IS field. During the 1970s the idea that every development project must pass through certain phases in a certain sequence became part of the mythology of the IS field, one of those ultimately unprovable but powerfully orienting ideas such as are to be found in any means of enquiry. Subsequently all development approaches have been explained in terms of how they address individual life cycle stages. Even though many new development approaches have arisen since the idea was first proposed, these have not threatened its credibility. Prototyping, once seen as an alternative paradigm for development, has become absorbed, being now seen as a way of assisting in design; and the Structured Approaches, argues Friedman & Cornford (1989), continued to use life cycle models as the conceptual framework for development, merely adding detail about how each component activity should be carried out.

Different arguments have been put forward as to why life cycle approaches should be adopted. Sometimes the case is based upon experience; Waters (1974) for example argues that

> *"When a computer-based, information processing system of even moderate complexity has to be developed, experience has shown that it is wise to proceed through an orderly sequence of actions, sometimes referred to as the systems approach." p. 17*

The most influential arguments for a life cycle model of development though rely upon the very practical advantages offered to management. Should there exist a natural structure for all development projects then this would provide a framework against which to plan and control a project, right through from initial conceptualisation to eventual implementation, minimising the risk of costly system development failures. This was the primary justification used for Canning's (1973) influential early proposal of dividing development into ten to twelve standard phases:

> *"There really is no reason why there need be a significant number of failures in EDP projects in the future - where 'failure' is defined as substantial cost overruns, schedule*

*slippage, inability to produce promised benefits, and so on. If a project is failing, that*
*fact should be detected early, and the project terminated or modified. The*
*techniques for information system project management are available. It is a case of*
*pulling them together properly - and then using them." p. 13.*

The IS practitioner's enthusiasm for this facilitation of project management, an acceptance of the life cycle idea as 'natural' and something of a lack of concern for conceptual clarity are all to be found in Hall's (1982) dismissal of criticisms of the life cycle concept:

*"What is a lifecycle? It is a description of the stages through which a system travels*
*from its cradle to its grave. Clearly all systems live out some life cycle.*
*Is there a standard life cycle ? Obviously not. My life has not been the same as yours.*
*Computer systems, like people, do however often go through similar life cycles....*
*What's the point of predicting the systems life cycle ? If you know to where you are*
*travelling before you depart, then you will know when you have arrived. If you know*
*some of the milestones along the road, you will be able to measure your progress.*
*That's it! The use of a life cycle concept enables you to plan the route a system will*
*take from cradle to grave and then you can guide and control it to make sure you do*
*arrive....*
*Life cycles are a good thing. It is pedantic defenders of particular life cycles that are*
*bad. Just as pedantic defenders of particular development methods, or anything else*
*for that matter, are bad." p. 23.*

The criticisms that are periodically made of the development life cycle concept, for example those by Gladden (1982) and McCracken & Jackson (1982) which Hall above responds to, mostly focus on its being a linear, sequential model in which each stage must be completed before the next is begun. This means that it relies heavily on the initial definition of the problem being complete and correct and that the users' requirements will not change in the time taken to progress to final implementation. In the case of modern complex information-systems neither of these assumptions can be safely made and this has set the agenda for much research work in the IS field; the search for better investigative techniques and for formal methods for requirements definition have been responses to the first of these problems whilst the second has been addressed by enabling faster development through CASE tools, fourth generation languages, and re-usable code.

But criticisms can be made at a more fundamental level. The legacies of hard systems thinking, such as the idea of a development life cycle, have become so deeply ingrained in IS thinking that only rarely is note taken of the constraints that they impose upon the way we view the development of information-systems. The result is the paradox identified by Wood-Harper & Fitzgerald (1982), that while the field of IS uses many of the ideas of systems thinking, when it comes to carrying out IS work many of the approaches used adopt a reductionist approach.

The life cycle idea, like others adopted from hard systems thinking, can, if poorly used and unaccompanied by an understanding of the basic principles of systems thinking, actually promote non-systemic practice in IS work. Sadly, it has been the case that many systems ideas have been so used in the IS field and the result has been to encourage the creation of aggregates of individual information-systems rather than integrated information-systems that work together to serve the information needs of the organisation as a whole. Let us examine just a few of the ways in which this has happened.

### 4.5.1 Problem-solving focus to IS activity

We have already seen several examples of how, in the field of IS, the systems approach is understood to be:

> *"An approach to problem solving, which consists of understanding the problem before a solution is attempted, and evaluating several alternate solutions."* McLeod (1990) p. 890.

The development of information-systems has consequently become equated with problem-solving, with information-systems being presented as designed solutions to individual organisational ills. This relegates IS work to a reactive role, with the development of new information-systems being triggered by specific requests from business managers who feel they have a problem. The way in which IS developments were originally funded, with department heads separately providing the funding for those developments that each thought worthwhile, supported this view. Thus from a mimicking of systems engineering practice of the 1950s there evolved a particular pattern for IS work; in this the role of the IS professional is, like the analyst in systems engineering or RAND systems analysis, taken to be to solve particular problems on behalf of an identified client. Emphasis is given to techniques that elucidate a given statement of 'the problem' rather than lead to a wider verstehen of the situation, and attention is focused upon the individual application and the solving of a particular organisational inefficiency or dysfunction.

### 4.5.2 Organisation through projects

The corollary of viewing information-systems development as problem-solving is of course that at some time in the future, when the new information-system is operational and that problem is 'solved', then those working on it will be free to begin working on alleviating other organisational problems. This is reflected in the tradition of organising IS work through a series of separate, one-off 'projects' with staff moving from project to project as their particular expertise is required. When all the stages of development project are completed then it is 'signed off', the project team is disbanded and any later work on that information-system is classified as merely 'maintenance'.

This leads to insufficient consideration being given to the need for adaptation, an essential requirement for all open systems. The demands of a changing environment are acknowledged only indirectly, in so far as the systems development cycle recognises that as when one project finishes another may need to begin; in other words that the 'problems' to be solved keep on coming. The need for adaptation remains though and the concern over the 'maintenance iceberg' (Canning, 1972) that became a major issue of the

1970s was just one symptom of that need. Because of the project focus that dominated IS thinking the response to the problems of an increasing proportion of the IS effort being devoted to maintenance of existing systems was to aim to create (in future development projects) more maintainable systems more speedily. The status of maintenance teams remained low. Had the IS field taken to heart the fundamental principles of systems thinking rather than merely the external characteristics of project organisation then it might have been realised that the maintenance of an information-system is different in kind to maintenance of such designed artefacts as buildings or machinery, and the so-called 'maintenance problem' could never be resolved in this way.

Furthermore, a project-orientation does not encourage the integration of information-systems or the adoption of an organisation-wide perspective. If one starts from the assumption that projects will be initiated when individual managers identify, and are willing to pay for, information-systems to support their own work then the planning of information-systems becomes limited to co-ordinating the satisfaction of individual needs. It is difficult to move towards the strategic planning of information-systems, where system developments are driven by an identification of the strategic information requirements of the business as a whole, that is required by the increasingly competitive global markets of today.

### 4.5.3 Commitment to incremental improvement

The pattern of IS work (a problem-solving orientation, organisation through projects) that was first established during the 1960s and borrowed heavily from the systems engineering practice of the 1950s, remains with us today. It is though not suited to today's needs.

An application-focused and project-organised approach might have been acceptable for the earliest uses of computers in automating manual, well-defined tasks in individual areas of organisations; the individual automating of such things as payroll processing or inventories could then be fully justified in terms of money saved in each area, and could then be undertaken as completely separate projects. Such basic automation uses of computers have though now been mostly completed. As more ambitious uses have been found for computers, as more sophisticated information-systems have been created, the interactions and overlap between information-systems have become vitally important.

The traditional pattern of IS activity though aims towards incremental improvement for it assumes that creating a series of information-systems to meet separate information requirements will result in improvement to the performance of the organisation as a whole. The dangers of sub-optimisation are obvious; individual applications may be, each in themselves, cost-effective but when brought together the overall result may not advantage the organisation as a whole. For example, the development and implementation of a new marketing information-system may lead to the marketing department attracting high levels of orders, but if the production department is unable to fulfil those orders the resulting late deliveries, compensation payments and loss of goodwill will not be to the company's benefit.

It is therefore no longer good enough to create information-systems that serve the needs of individual groups in the organisation alone; those information-systems must be able to share the same stored data and act in concert with the information-systems used by other areas of the organisation or, increasingly, by external customers and suppliers. Organising development through separate project groups, each focusing upon satisfying its own particular 'client', does not facilitate such a wider perspective.

### 4.5.4  Unsophisticated models of organisations

There is considerable evidence, from both academic studies and practical experience, that giving inadequate attention to human and social issues underlies many information-system failures. Hornby *et al* (1992) for example identify a lack of attention to organisational issues such as organisation design, organisational culture and management style within a particular organisation as directly contributing to poor information-system's performance. Despite this most efforts towards the development and introduction of new information-systems are based on a 'task and technology' orientation (Blackler & Brown, 1986) in which human and organisational issues are given scant consideration. The conclusions of Markus & Robey (1983) or Pliskin *et al* (1993) that care should be taken to ensure that an information-system 'fits' its organisational context of use and that their designers should be aware of the *organisational culture* including actual and perceived power relationships are still relatively novel to the field of IS. Few if any IS methodologies specifically address such considerations and the history of many development groups is full of examples where a rationally correct information-system has proved inappropriate to the real-life organisation's needs.

A poor use of systems ideas is not the sole cause of this but has certainly influenced how IS practitioners understand organisations and organisational life. The methods of the hard systems approaches certainly proved most successful where human issues were least important (in the design of artefacts such as buildings or machinery) and least successful when used in situations where human beings played a major role (Hoos, 1972: 1976). And many of the reasons for this have been carried forward into IS practice. In the IS field, as in hard systems thinking, organisations are understood as being goal-achieving mechanisms or 'rational systems' (Scott 1987) in which "... the behaviour of organisations is viewed as action by purposeful and co-ordinated agents" (p. 32) and "... structural arrangements within organizations are conceived as tools deliberately designed for the efficient realization of ends" (p. 48).

The result of viewing organisations in this way is that the techniques by which IS workers investigate the organisation focus almost exclusively upon the formal, designed organisation and ignore the social and political organisational contexts into which new information-systems will be introduced. When the IS developer maps out, using data flow diagrams or other techniques, the organisation's activities they are describing the organisation that was officially planned and not the organisation that is in reality enacted out by its members; the realities of power, the way in which individuals work and informal flows of information are not depicted. In the majority of system development methodologies 'understanding the business' is restricted to documenting the present, formal and officially sanctioned business activities.

Even if the IS field was to use only hard systems ideas then a proper use of systems principles would require that more attention should be given to the constraints of the social and political environments into which new information-systems will be introduced, and to the demands of the wider system that it serves. The 'system' that would be investigated would not be a collection of computing machinery and software but the living system, populated by human beings, that comprises the organisation that the information-system will serve. Furthermore, any awareness of more recent systems thinking would suggest the replacement of the view of organisations as goal-seeking, adaptive-regulatory mechanisms by more complex systems models, of human organisations as purposeful, socio-political systems in which shared meaning and symbolic relationships are maintained and modified through human discourse and interaction. The IS field has though always been rather selective in its use of systems ideas and this has not occurred.

### 4.5.5  IS as engineering

The inadequate attention given to human and social organisational issues may have been encouraged by the adoption of the 'IS development is engineering' view of IS work. The view that developing information-systems is the same kind of activity as that carried out by true engineers is long established. It arose partly from the guidance that was sought on project management from the systems engineering of the 1950s, but also from the nature of the information-systems that were first developed. Friedman & Cornford (1989) note not only the latter influence but also the effect upon the IS developer's view of dealing with human factors:

> "Computer systems, especially early ones, mechanized and automated human systems. This encouraged an engineering view of human relations among system developers. It encouraged a direct control type of philosophy towards the work of users. In order for a system to be computerized it had to be routinized and standardized, especially in the early years of computing when it was difficult to include a wide range of exception conditions." p. 229

Seeing IS work as an engineering activity leads almost inevitably to a focus upon the hardware/software components of the information-system, with a devaluation of the importance of human issues and the social and perhaps moral consequences of information-systems design.

The convention of describing those human beings most intimately concerned with an information-system as 'users' is a linguistic indicator of the emphasis historically given to the engineering of the technical components of information-systems. Labelling human beings in this way makes sense only if one is concerned with engineering the technical components that will be later used by human beings; the term 'user', in fact, defines human beings as lying outside the boundary of the information-system and thus removes any need to give human issues serious consideration during development. This may be acceptable in true engineering, where human beings use a building or bridge but are not themselves part of it, but not in information-systems work. Participative, socio-technical approaches such as those of Mumford & Weir (1979) respond to this danger and encourage the inclusion of the views of the proposed system's users rather than merely those of the owners. Even then, however, little consideration is given to others who might be affected by the information-system's existence and there is no equivalent within the IS field of the 'stakeholder' concept extensively used in other organisational work.

The inheritance from systems engineering means that there are some similarities between IS work and engineering that can be profitably employed in explanation. In discussing the difficulties that may arise in arriving at a specification for a new information-system De Marco (1978), for example, promotes the value of readily understandable specification documents by comparison to the physical models used by marine engineers:

*"If you visit the Royal Naval Museum at Greenwich, England, you will see the results of some of the world's most successful specification efforts, the admiralty models. Before any ship of the line was constructed, a perfect scale model had to be built and approved. The long hours of detail work were more than repaid by the clear understandings that come from studying and handling the models. The success of the specification process depends on the product, the Target Document in our case, being able to serve as a model of the new system. To the extent that it helps you visualize the new system, the Target Document is the system model."*

Used in this way, as a device of explanation and clarification, a comparison between the processes of information-systems development and physical engineering works well but the use of terms such as 'software engineering' or 'information engineering' certainly promotes the idea that there is a closer relationship. In Sommerville's (1982) discussion of software engineering, for example, there is a strong suggestion that the phrase 'engineer' is to be taken seriously, and that the principles, methods and requirements of software engineering are of the same kind as any other form of engineering:

*"There have been a number of definitions of software engineering proposed. Their common factors are that software engineering is concerned with building software systems which are larger than would normally be tackled by a single individual, uses engineering principles in the development of these systems and is made up of both technical and non-technical aspects. As well as a thorough knowledge of computing techniques, the software engineer, like any other engineer, must be able to communicate, both orally and in writing." pp. 1-2.*

Schach (1993), however, points to differences between systems engineering and the physical engineering involved in the construction of bridges and Macro (1990) concludes that:

*"... engineers from other disciplines, and their managers and non-software-expert colleagues, attach a significance to the term 'engineering' that cannot be exactly carried over into the process of software development. Similarities between software*

*development and the more accepted engineering disciplines break down very*
*rapidly, and real engineers are left confused and frustrated, suspecting that some*
*awful inadequacy on the part of software development staff is being concealed*
*behind a smokescreen of special pleading.*
*I have, in fact, found very few engineers who - if they have also developed extensive*
*and complex software systems - support the incorporation of software 'engineering'*
*into the corpus of real engineering subjects, except in one respect. The term*
*'engineering' carries with it a strong connotation of planning and control - of*
*managing, in fact. In this respect we have, over the past decade and a half, sought*
*to make software development a more manageable activity."* pp. 24-25.

That final comment is perceptive, for very often in the IS field the term 'engineering' is used only to denote that some systematic, organised approach is being used. For example, the influential work on information engineering by Finkelstein (1989) promotes a systematic approach employing data-focused analysis and automated support tools; but there is nowhere the suggestion of any debt to, or close similarities to the engineering profession.

Ultimately, whether or not one believes that the creation of the technical components of an information-system (the computer, peripherals and controlling software) is engineering, the creation of an information-system is certainly not. An information-system is a social artefact composed of human as well as technical components and these have properties that are quite different to those of designed physical systems. Its creation therefore requires skills and methods that are not necessary for the design of buildings or bridges.

### 4.5.6  A tendency towards conservative design

In the previous chapter we saw how the term 'system' is used in varying ways in IS. The result of a hard systems inheritance, poorly understood, is that it is used almost exclusively ontologically as a label for some part of the real and objective world, most usually describing a collection of hardware and software or systematic, defined procedures. Whether talking of 'a physical description of the existing system' (as in Curtis, 1989) or 'building a logical model of the current system' (De Marco, 1978) it is assumed that the object of study, 'the system' which is being modelled, is some part of the real world. This has consequences upon the way in which information-systems are created.

First, it leads the analyst and developer to ignore the possibility of alternative, possibly equally valid interpretations of a situation. Returning to the example used in an earlier chapter, a prison might equally well be seen as a means of punishing or rehabilitating offenders. To fail to recognise this and to begin one's analysis from the assumption that a prison *is* one of these possibilities will lead to the creation of an information-system that, at best, serves the information needs of only some interested parties.

Secondly, at a stroke, it obviates any need for consultation with all interested parties. If one begins with the assumption of a single, objective reality then there will seem only limited advantages to be gained from acquiring many different accounts of the same situation. One is not encouraged to explore the views of many different stakeholders (such as employees or potential customers of the information-system), believing that the views of the managers and powerholders, who will most likely have a fuller view of the situation, will be sufficient.

In both these ways there arises a tendency towards conservative design, where new information-systems closely resemble their predecessors, where existing power relationships are maintained and the information-system's relationship to ever-changing business activities is unchallenged.

# Part II

## Decisions, support and data

# 5 Decision-making

## 5.1 INTRODUCTION

We have seen in previous chapters how two complementary strands of systems thinking, the 'hard' and 'soft', developed and how hard systems ideas influenced IS thinking. In this chapter we examine in detail another of the inheritances of hard systems thinking, the use of rational models of decision-making. We suggest that by ignoring the role of social and political factors in decision-making these impose further constraints on our understanding of the complex social situations in which information-systems development occurs. An important contribution which the 'soft' strand of systems thinking can make to IS work is in providing a richer model for understanding decision-making, based upon Sir Geoffrey Vickers' concept of appreciation. This 'appreciative model' emphasises the importance of the decision-makers' perceptions of the organisation and its situation in the interpretation of data, provides the basis for making a clear distinction between 'data' and 'information', and has implications for the ways in which computerised information-systems are developed.

## 5.2 DECISION-MAKING AND INFORMATION-SYSTEMS

The subject of decision-making is important in IS work not merely in relation to the development of those applications specifically designated as decision support systems but to the development of all forms of information-system. For the most common definitions of information-systems, and justifications for the costs of their development, are based upon the service that they may give to decision-making. Figure 5.1 shows the results of examining a number of commonly used introductory texts on the subject of information-systems, and it can be seen that those authors who define information or information-systems at all do so primarily by reference to decision-making.

The emphasis given to decision-making as a raison d'être for information-systems is clear in such statements as:

*"Information is data that has been processed for a purpose. That purpose is to aid some kind of decision." Curtis (1989) p. 5*

*" Information is useful to a manager if it helps in the manager's choice of a course of action. To be precise, information is said to have value if, and only if, it reduces the uncertainty in the manager's decision problem." Harrison (1985) p. 14*

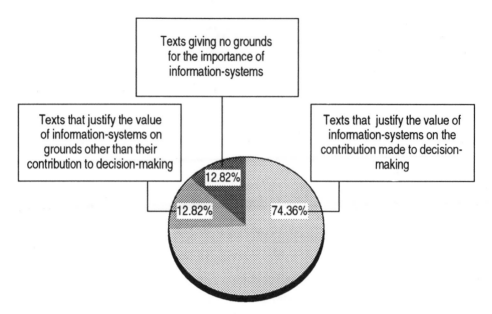

**Figure 5.1**  *Declared justification of information-systems in introductory texts source : Lewis (1991)*

Decision-making is traditionally associated with the work of 'managers' and 'executives', and IS professionals have concentrated most attention in providing support for the decision-making of these groups. The disregard for the decision-making of 'non-management' personnel may be because the decisions that they make are generally governed by well-understood rules and the complexity of the information processing required is low. Both Anthony's (Anthony, 1965; Anthony & Dearden, 1980) hierarchical model of decision-making within organisations and Galbraith's (Galbraith, 1973; Galbraith, 1974) view of the organisation in terms of information processing, though, emphasise the ubiquity of decision-making at all levels of an organisation; decision-making is thus a central concern for all forms of information-systems development.

Of course, if information-systems are seen as giving service to decision-makers then the view which one adopts about how decisions are made will colour one's view of the type of information-systems required. It is therefore important to consider critically the models of the decision-making process which are used in relation to information-systems.

## 5.3   MODELS OF THE DECISION-MAKING PROCESS

In order to talk meaningfully about a process of decision-making one must have some implicit or explicit notion of what decision-making is, in other words a model of the decision-making process. The oldest models regarded the decision-maker as 'economic man' who, utilising a purely rational and objective cost-benefit analysis of every possible option, chose between alternative courses of action in order to maximise attainment of an organisational goal. These proved to be of limited practical use as they simply did not match well enough against experiences of real-world decision-making, where the assumptions of a clear and defined organisational goal were not evident and where maximisation was not always a practically possible option.

Numerous alternatives to the classical model, both descriptive and prescriptive, have been proposed (see for example March & Simon, 1958; Lindblom, 1959; Cyert & March, 1963; Cyert & Welsch, 1970; Vroom, 1974; March, 1982; Forester, 1984; March, 1988). But thinking about decision-making within the field of IS has been dominated by the work of H.A. Simon (1957, 1960, 1965a, 1965b, 1969, 1976). In a survey of introductory texts 84% of those texts which provided any discussion of the nature of decision-making included Simon's three-phase model of decision-making (Simon, 1960) and 53% presented this as the *sole* conceptual framework through which to understand decision-making (Lewis, 1991).

### 5.3.1  Simon's model of decision-making

Simon conceptualised the process of decision-making as consisting of three phases, as shown in Figure 5.2.

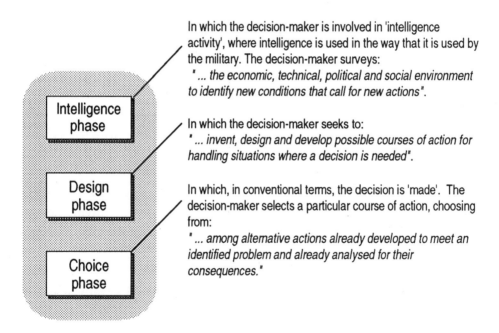

**Figure 5.2**     *Simon's three phases of decision-making*

Simon's perspective on decision-making is a 'bounded rationality' approach in that organisational goals are regarded not as targets but as constraints upon the decision-making process, defining a 'solution space' within which may lie a number of acceptable decision outcomes. As the model allows that multiple goals may exist the desirability of any alternative action may have to be evaluated in terms of a number of different criteria;

a goal of profit making might, for example, have to be reconciled with goals of social responsibility or organisational harmony. The aim of the decision-maker is one of 'satisficing', not necessarily attempting to achieve the greatest possible rewards but merely those which are 'good enough' and acceptable within a given situation.

### 5.3.2  Use of quantitative models

In practice most attention has been given to the last of Simon's phases, in which the executive chooses amongst alternative courses of action. The most widely used approaches to making this choice rely upon the creation and manipulation of quantitative models.

The first step is to create a quantitative model of the situation and identify some criteria for deciding whether one state of the model is better or more desirable than another. These criteria, representing as they do the goals held dear by the organisation, are then combined into some criterion function which reflects the relative importance attached to each goal. When the decision-maker is satisfied that the model mimics the real world as closely as possible then the model may be manipulated and the effect of each alternative course of action upon the model may be discovered and measured in terms of the chosen criteria. The 'best' course of action can then be identified, it being defined as that which shifts the model to the most desirable end state, that is to say, provides the highest value for the criterion function This course of action may then be applied to the real-world situation.

Adoption of this approach requires that a number of assumptions are made, namely that:

- A quantitative model can be created which will do adequate justice to the complex nature of human organisations.
- An objective criterion function may be formulated to evaluate a given state of the organisation. This requires both that the choice of what is, or is not, relevant may be logically deduced from knowledge of goals and that some common denominator, usually financial, can be found that will allow many different variables to be measured and compared.
- Data or 'hard facts' about the situation may be obtained with no subjective interpretation by the decision-maker. The underlying philosophy is therefore that of positivism.
- The decision-making process is unaffected by the prejudices and biases of those involved. Two different, equally rational decision-makers faced with the same situation would, it is assumed, arrive at the same decision result.
- The results of the decision-making process will be universally acceptable because of the rational nature of the way in which they were arrived at.

These assumptions may give rise to some difficulties in practice. First, there is the view of an organisation as a 'goal-seeking machine' with coherent and non-antagonistic objectives. In reality organisations are far more complex entities, with different participants having different perceptions of the nature of the organisation and its aims.

Any single view of the organisation therefore represents only one of many possible perspectives and only one perspective upon what are 'relevant' variables to be included in the quantitative model. The consequences of this may not be too serious if there is widespread agreement amongst stakeholders about the nature of the present situation and the nature of the organisation, but where there is little such agreement then there is unlikely to be acceptance of the decision results. If a group does not recognise the model as a true reflection of the situation (from their own viewpoint) then they can hardly be expected to accept or act upon the results of manipulating that model.

Furthermore, even if an acceptable quantitative model could be created then rational choice-making requires that alternative states of the model be valued according to some criterion function which relates all the relevant variables. Even ignoring the enormous problems of deciding what should be included in such a criterion function there remain great practical difficulties in doing this, for it is unlikely that all the variables in complex human organisations can be adequately quantified in terms of any single denominator. How, for example, should one quantify the value of better working conditions or job satisfaction within a manufacturing organisation? Although one might expect some increase in the value of production and reduced absenteeism a financial measure of these would hardly do justice to the real effects and certainly would not be how their value would be assessed by the workers themselves. There are, in fact, similar problems in applying any of the assumptions of rational decision-making to real world-situations and to base our understanding of information-systems upon such views would appear to be fraught with dangers.

### 5.3.3 Grounding in hard systems thinking

Despite the qualification of its basis as 'bounded' rationality, Simon's work remains essentially positivistic, relying upon that which Scott (1987) calls the 'rational system' view and Gouldner (1959) describes as the rational model of organisations, in which:

> " ... *decisions are made on the basis of a rational survey of the situation, utilising certified knowledge, with a deliberate orientation to an expressly codified legal apparatus. The focus is, therefore, on the legally prescribed structures - i.e., the formally 'blueprinted' patterns - since these are more largely subject to deliberate inspection and rational manipulation.*
>
> *This model takes account of departures from rationality but often tends to assume that these departures derive from random mistakes, due to ignorance or error in calculation. Fundamentally, the rational model implies a 'mechanical' model, in that it views the organisation as a structure of manipulable parts, each of which is separately modifiable with a view to enhancing the efficiency of the whole. "*
> Gouldner (1959) pp. 404-405

It represents decision-making as an explicit and consciously rational process, enacted by a neutral decision-maker, which involves the organisation and processing of information in order to carry out an intentional and rational act of choice. This is used not merely as a description of a necessary process within decision-making, a quality to be found within good decision-making, nor as metaphor for thinking about the process of decision-making, but as a description of what human thinking actually *is*.

Simon's three-phase model of decision-making is clearly consistent with the methodologies of systems engineering, systems analysis and operational research discussed previously. Simon (1960), like Miles (1973a), acknowledges the similarities to Dewey's (1910) description of problem-solving as answering the three questions: "What is the problem?", "What are the alternatives?", "Which alternative is best?". It is perhaps therefore not surprising that the field of IS, which has borrowed greatly from the traditions of both systems analysis and systems engineering, should so readily accept Simon's model of decision-making as a basis for IS thinking.

Simon's work has certainly been one of the major contributions that hard systems thinking has made to the IS field but, as we have already seen, that strand of systems thinking also imposes certain constraints upon IS thinking. The great weakness of Simon's work as generally presented in the literature of information-systems is that whilst it provides an approach to decision-making well suited to the operation of a *machine* it does not do justice to the subtleties of the way in which *human beings* make sense of their world and approach decision-making. Any experience of real organisational decision-making, in which conflict and the struggle for authority and power are, to say the least, not unknown, shows the difficulty of using rational models as an explanation for anything other than the most simple decision situations. Studies of real-world decision-making for example reveal that there is often no clear point at which a decision is 'made'. In one study (Checkland, 1990) of the events which occurred when a major chemicals firm considered whether or not a new production facility should be built it was found that there was no single moment at which the decision to build was made. Instead, gradually and over time, all the participants began to accept that it would be built and the necessary actions were taken.

In such cases no description of the decision-making process would be complete or make any sense without consideration of the social and political factors which surrounded the decision-makers. The simplistic way in which Simon's work is employed in IS thinking, however, allows no role to such factors other than as undesirable interference or 'noise' in a supposedly objective and rational decision-making process. This gives rise to several practical dangers.

First, there is the danger of developing information-systems to serve the decision-making which it is thought should be happening (value free, politically neutral and objectively rational) rather than the decision-making which actually occurs. Due to the status which rational, logical action is accorded, few users might resist this during development for fear of being thought 'irrational ' or 'illogical'; but in practice the information-systems developed would not be truly serving the organisation's needs. In such cases the information-systems might be less used and less effective than they might have been.

Secondly, there arises the danger of ignoring the important differences in organisational culture and history which make organisations unique. This might lead, for example, to the provision of information-systems which emphasised quantitative and financial data to organisations which valued qualitative, non-financial information.

Thirdly, IS analysis will ignore the important contribution which norms and standards make to the organisation's understanding of the world and to the way in which mere data becomes perceived as meaningful and relevant to a decision. The result may be to concentrate upon the development of data storage and retrieval systems rather than genuine information-systems.

These problems have led some authors (for example Ciborra (1984)) to reject decision-making perspectives to IS on the grounds that they are too cybernetic and to propose alternative non-systemic behavioural approaches. However, Simon's work has proved to be a powerful explanatory device and it is not necessary to abandon Simon's work entirely nor to seek remedies from outside the systems paradigm. The presentation and application of Simon's work within the IS field has undoubtedly been too simplistic. However, if it is too often presented without qualification as both a description and prescription for how decisions are made and appears to give too little attention to the political and social conflicts and complexities of organisations, then one of the contributions which soft systems thinking may make to IS is to enrich that thinking through the concept of appreciation.

## 5.4   AN ALTERNATIVE VIEW OF DECISION-MAKING

We have seen so far that most thinking about information-systems accepts with little questioning a rational view of decision-making and that this, with its underlying logical-positivist philosophy, relies upon certain assumptions about the world. The rational models of decision-making are prescriptive accounts of how decisions should (in their authors' opinions) be conducted but do not equate well with much experience of real-world decision-making. It would seem clear that the decision-making done within an organisation will be an unsound basis for planning information-systems if such an impoverished view of the decision-making process is used.

Recent attempts to aid decision-making through decision support software has emphasised the importance of the internally generated, mental models of the organisation and its objectives which managers use in decision-making. Rational models of decision-making may, as in Simon's three phases, implicitly recognise the effect of such constructs but fail to address their nature. The importance of such mental constructs is recognised though in the work of Sir Geoffrey Vickers (Vickers 1965, 1968, 1970, 1983, 1984) where it is explained through the concept of 'appreciation'.

### 5.4.1 Vickers' concept of appreciation

A lifetime's experience of management and policy making at the highest levels convinced Vickers that the view of organisations as goal-seeking machines was both fraudulent and dangerous because:

> *"As all policy makers know from experience, policy does not consist in prescribing one goal or even one series of goals; but in regulating a system over time in such a way as to optimize the realization of many conflicting relations without wrecking the system in the process. Thus the dominance of technology has infected policy-making with three bogus simplifications, just admissible in the workshop but lethal in the council chamber. One of these is the habit of accepting goals - states to be obtained once and for all - rather than norms to be held through time, as the typical object of policy. The second is the further reduction of multiple objectives to a single goal, yielding a single criterion of success. The third is the acceptance of effectiveness as the sole criterion by which to choose between alternative operations which can be regarded as means to one desired end. The combined effect of these three has been to dehumanise and distort beyond measure the high human function of government - that is, regulation - at all levels."* Vickers (1970), p. 116.

Central to Vickers' work is the idea that an understanding of events, the things which an organisation does, or the decisions which it makes, cannot be arrived at in the absence of an understanding of the ideas and notions which shape the organisation's own understanding of itself and its environment. For Vickers:

> *"..human history is a two-stranded rope; the history of events and the history of ideas develop in intimate relation with each other yet each according to its own logic and its own time scale; and each conditions both its own future and the future of the other."* Vickers (1965), p. 15.

A 'problem situation' which calls for a decision to be made is therefore the result of both past events and those ideas which lead to the perception of a 'problem'.

A consistent thread of Vickers' work is that management or 'governance' is primarily concerned not with the organisation of *things* but rather with the maintenance of *relationships* over time, both within the organisation and with the outside world. In order to maintain relationships the organisation is constantly required to adapt in response to changing circumstances. Central to this adaptation is what Vickers describes as the 'appreciative system' of the organisation, which at any moment in time has an 'appreciative setting' which Vickers defined as a

> *"... readiness to see and value things in one way rather than another"* Vickers (1984), p.160.

These appreciative settings, born of past experiences, organisational history and mythology, consist of standards, norms and values which lead the organisation to recognise as important only certain features of the situation in which they exist. In particular, to recognise only certain data as 'relevant' or 'important' and only certain actions as 'possible alternatives'.

Checkland & Casar (1986) explain the operation of an appreciative system as a number of recursive loops as shown in Figure 5.3, where the organisation exists within a constantly changing and interacting flux of events and ideas. The process of appreciation is an on-going process through which the organisation perceives some part of this flux at a point in time, making judgements about what is perceived and, where necessary, attempts to maintain or elude relationships by actions.

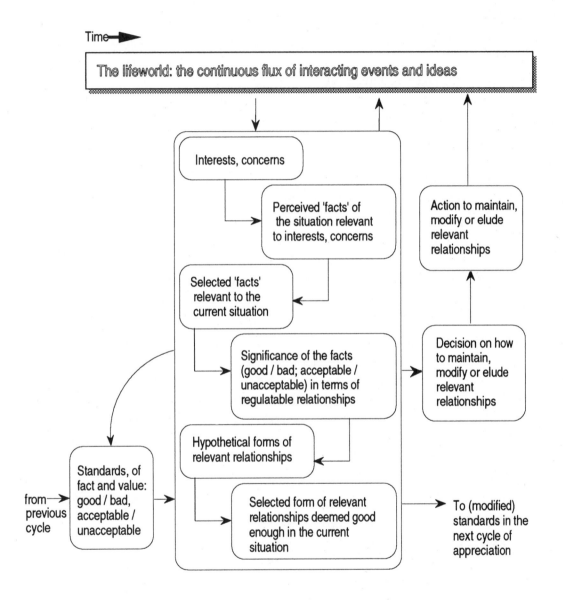

**Figure 5.3**     *Appreciation, decision-making and action*
*{after Checkland & Casar, 1986}*

Appreciation is a complex process whose component sub-processes inter-act with each other. One of these sub-processes is concerned with collecting data from the world and making what Vickers describes as 'reality judgements' about the present situation, whether 'the present situation' is that which appertains now or is a future possibility. This it does based upon sets of norms. Norms is the term which Vickers uses to describe the ideas which allow organisations or individuals to understand facts and give meaning to raw data. They cannot necessarily be written down or described in detail but reveal themselves through their operation. They guide what the organisation 'sees' and what it considers as relevant. The results of this process are compared with standards in order to make value judgements about whether or not the present situation is satisfactory. A third sub-process is concerned with making instrumental judgements about what should be done in the light of the value judgements.

Organisational adaptation therefore occurs through managers making reality judgements and establishing facts about their situation, attributing meaning to these facts through a value judgement, comparing the resultant view of the organisation's position with some normative standard and finally taking some action to minimise the disparity between the two. This might at first seem a re-statement of the notion of a feedback loop, and indeed Vickers had during his life been greatly impressed by cybernetic ideas (Blunden 1985). However Vickers' notion of appreciation is considerably more sophisticated than this, for Vickers hypothesised that each of these sub-processes was profoundly influenced by the others and each component of appreciation was itself changed by the occurrence of the appreciative process. Judgements might be based upon standards of what is acceptable or unacceptable but these standards themselves are part of the flux and are changed through their use. As shown in Figure 5.3, the source of the appreciative system's standards lies in the previous history of the appreciative system itself, and every operation of the system may modify those standards.

Appreciation therefore acts not as a mechanism of control which merely maintains the status quo but as a mechanism for organisational learning. As the appreciative system is the result of past experiences as well as current interests there are interesting similarities between Vickers' notion of an appreciative setting and the notion of psychological expectancy or 'set', where

> "A person's psychological 'set' towards some task, situation, or communication event depends upon his past experience, upon a host of preceding events which have led up to that moment. Such a 'set' is considered to influence his formation of associations, by bringing to bear certain 'determining tendencies', and hence influencing his way of organising or executing the task, or affecting the degree to which he recognizes signs, or forms perceptions, in a communication event. " Cherry (1957), p. 273.

As we shall see in later chapters, this similarity is not coincidental, and is of particular importance in relation to the process of interpretative data modelling.

## 5.4.2 An appreciative model of decision-making

Vickers' work is closer to the phenomenological school of philosophy than to the positivism which underpins rational models of decision-making and it therefore avoids many of the pitfalls which arise from that. It also explicitly rejects naive goal-seeking as a basis for understanding organisational behaviour and allows for multiple perspectives of reality.

Vickers' work does not, however, provide an alternative model of decision-making of the same kind as that of Simon; it is not a prescription of intentional activities which should be carried out but a description of a continuous social process. One could not, for example, talk prescriptively of three stages of decision-making consisting of making reality judgements, making value judgements and making instrumental judgements. These are not activities which the organisation or individual purposefully chooses to do but rather a framework for understanding a social process which occurs at the individual as well as the organisational level.

Vickers' work does, however, allow us to understand the more intentional and prescriptive models in a way that is enlightening; for regarding individual decision-making as occurring *within* a context of appreciation leads us to an essentially different and more humanistic interpretation of the decision-making process. The appreciative model, in effect, subsumes the rational models of decision-making since they may be seen as special cases, describing decision-making in highly structured situations where there is considerable consensus over what decision should be made and how it should be decided. It provides a more useful model for understanding decision-making *behaviour* since it provides an explanation for the subjective content of decision-making and of some of the problems encountered during real-world decision-making; it provides a reason *why* decision-makers, even faced with the same decision in broadly similar situations, vary so much in their interpretation of the situation and arrive at so widely varying decisions as to what should be done.

Integrating the notion of appreciation with Simon's three-phase model of decision-making also enriches Simon's model, for Simon's three phases of decision-making imply that each phase must be provided with certain inputs, as shown in Figure 5.4.

The 'surveying of the current situation' in the Intelligence Activity, for example, implies that the decision-maker is in possession not only of facts about the current situation but also some notion of the organisation and its environment which allows those facts to be interpreted. This Intelligence Activity may lead to something which in Simon's language would be described as the need for a 'decision', and which is reflected within Vickers' epistemology as the need for action in order to establish or maintain a desired, or elude an undesired, relationship.

Given that a need for action is perceived then the Design Activity must receive some input (whether it is searched out or already exists from previous experience) as to what possible courses of action are possible or appropriate and about what would be a suitable strategy for deciding between alternatives. The actual operation of the chosen decision mechanism in the Choice Activity requires the processing of certain facts, selected according to the rules defined by the chosen decision mechanism.

It is the appreciative system of the organisation and its decision-makers which leads to the recognition of the need to take regulatory action (Simon's Intelligence Activity) and

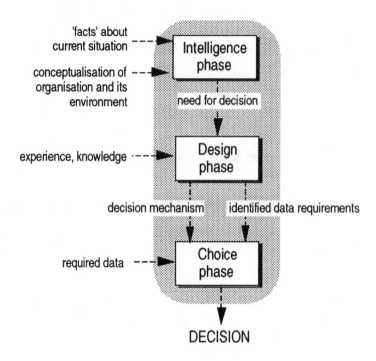

**Figure 5.4**     *Information inputs in decision-making*

which constrains the perceptions as to possible alternative courses of action (Simon's Design Activity).

Furthermore, in Simon's third phase, Choice Activity, the process of appreciation has effects at two levels. First, there is the need to decide how the choice between alternatives will be made. This is itself a decision which will be influenced by the appreciative system and by the particular history, norms and standards of the organisation; particular organisations may thus favour mechanisms which emphasise financial or social factors, deterministic or consultative methods. Secondly, whatever mechanism is chosen, the appreciative system will have effects upon the operation of that mechanism since it acts as a form of filter through which 'facts' about the situation are perceived and interpreted.

The appreciative system therefore surrounds all three phases of decision-making, not only determining the way in which those activities are carried out but also selecting, perhaps distorting, the inputs to those activities.

An important feature of any appreciative understanding of decision-making is that it leads us to regard decision-making not as a once-only, linear process (as does Simon's model) but as a continuous and on-going learning process in which the process of making a decision is inseparable from the process of deciding that a decision is required. An organisation might, for example, in attempting to determine how to achieve strategic goals acquire data that alters their perception of their present situation and leads it to re-assess and perhaps re-define those goals. Well documented examples of this occurred during the oil crises of the 1970s when a number of large oil companies, faced with radically changed circumstances of oil supply, reconsidered their nature and strategic aims and re-defined themselves as energy companies, diversifying investment into alternative sources of energy.

Thus the appreciative system may guide decision-makers to recognise particular aspects of a situation as relevant, towards a particular view of what data is needed and to a particular view of how the decision should be made. The consequent activities and the collection of data may, however, themselves lead to further understanding, to changes in the appreciative system and possibly to a change in views as to what is relevant or even whether the decision itself is now required.

The term 'decision-making' is now descriptive of a far more complex and comprehensive process than previously. Whereas before it described isolated incidents of choice between alternatives, it is now a convenient shorthand description of the need for individuals, groups and organisations to interact with and adapt to their perceived environments. Understood in this way there can be little disagreement that to understand the decision-making processes of the organisation is the essential prerequisite for planning information-systems.

## 5.4.3 The appreciative system as a cognitive framework

This enriched, appreciative model of decision-making provides an explanation for many of the difficulties encountered when trying to assist decision-making, and for one of the most vexing questions of management science; why have the supposedly rational and universally applicable methods of management science proved so useful in well-defined situations, where there is a consensus over the appreciated content of the decision-making situation, and yet unsuccessful in less well-defined situations. For, within the appreciative model, the appreciation affects the decision process in two ways. First, it provides meaning and allows the observer to 'understand' sensory perceptions or symbolic representations of them. Second, it restricts perception and understanding to only those parts of the total, and ultimately unknowable, reality which can be interpreted through the appreciative system. It acts therefore as a cognitive framework or 'filter' which, as represented in Figure 5.5, recognises certain facts about reality as meaningful data and uses these to create the observer's understanding of reality, but rejects and ignores those facts which are not meaningful in terms of the cognitive framework.

The cognitive framework may, however, be modified in the light of the subjective understanding so obtained; data about the perceived reality may reinforce the framework, making the observer more 'fixed in their views' but inconsistencies or other difficulties in interpretation might also weaken previous convictions and lead to changes and expansions of the cognitive framework.

The 'filtering' and selection of facts which occurs in the appreciative model is of great relevance to thinking about the design of data storage mechanisms such as data bases and we shall return to this subject, when we consider whether it is possible to model the organisation's perceived realities as a precursor to information-systems design.

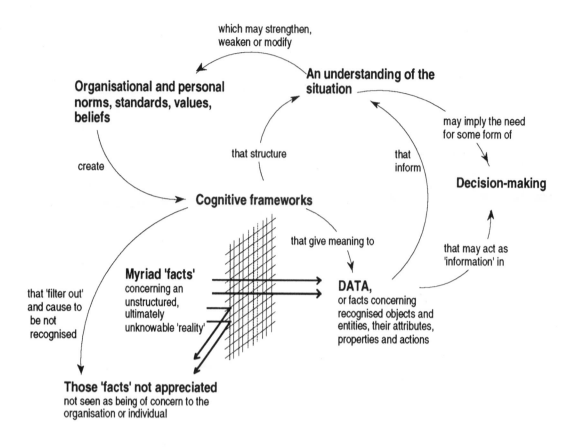

**Figure 5.5**     *The operation of appreciation as a filtering device*

## 5.5   DATA AND INFORMATION

Dretske (1981) has observed that:

> *"It is much easier to talk about information than it is to say what it is you are talking about.. A surprising number of books, and this includes textbooks, have the word information in their title without bothering to include it in their index. It has come to be an all-purpose word, one with the suggestive power to fulfil a variety of descriptive tasks."* Preface.

Such lack of definition is common in IS texts, and the lack of definition or provision of circular definitions is worrying. One learns little, for example, from

> *"Data is the raw material that is processed and refined to generate information. Information is the product that results from processing or manipulating raw data."*
> *Silver & Silver (1989), pp. 6-7.*

The appreciative model of decision-making however provides a coherent basis for differentiating between concepts of 'data' and 'information'. In respect to this model, 'data' are those facts about the world which the organisation or individual appreciates as being meaningful to their interests and concerns; 'information' is data, which may have been processed, that is appreciated as useful within a particular decision-making context.

Remember, though, that in the appreciative model the term 'decision-making' encompasses rather more than the everyday usage of that term. The value of information can only be ascribed retrospectively, in the extent to which it determined the eventual decision choice both through facilitating the operation of a chosen decision mechanism or by providing appreciative learning, and in the extent it provided new insights or reassurance that a previous understanding of the situation remained appropriate. Information is therefore a sub-set of data, and membership of that set is determined by a context for its use. Data are important to the organisation not because, as is so often claimed, they can be processed into information but because they, or processed forms of them, may be *perceived as* and used as information.

## 5.6 IMPLICATIONS OF THE APPRECIATIVE MODEL

This chapter has argued that, since decision-making remains the predominant basis for IS, the way in which the decision-making process is understood has significant consequences for both IS theory and IS practice. It has further argued that such understanding may be enriched by perceiving the predominant Simon model to be a powerful explanatory device which provides a simple, linear interpretation of a more complex, cyclical and social learning process, the operation of which is comprehensively considered within Vickers' concept of appreciation.

Adopting this richer view of the decision-making process, which we have labelled as the appreciative model of decision-making, has a number of implications for the methods and techniques of IS development. These are introduced below and explored more fully in later chapters.

### 5.6.1 Understanding data needs

An important consequence of the appreciative model is that no organisation or individual can ever 'know' the 'real' situation but only *interpret* the situation through a particular set of ideas and expectations. Appreciation acts as a kind of filter, giving a readiness to appreciate certain facts and ignore others. We cannot therefore talk of *the data* required for making a particular decision but only the data which a particular appreciation of the world deems as being required. Any attempts to examine the information needs of an organisation therefore cannot logically be done without at the same time investigating the appreciations which the organisation has of the world and itself. A consequence of adopting the appreciative model is therefore the need for the developers of information-systems to devise new methods and techniques, or perhaps adapt those of other disciplines, in order to carry out such investigations. Since one possible way in which debate concerning such appreciations may be initiated is through comparisons with models of purposeful activity, soft systems thinking provides a readily available means of beginning such explorations.

### 5.6.2 Development methodologies

Adopting an appreciative model of decision-making leads to a distinction not only between data and information but also between a 'data system' and an 'information-system'. A data system is concerned with acquiring, storing and making accessible facts which are meaningful to the organisation; an information-system however actively provides decision-makers with the data which they perceive as information, in a way which is conducive to their needs and chosen decision-making mechanisms.

Unfortunately the difference between data systems and information-systems is often ignored and 'information-system' is used as a synonym for 'database system' or 'data processing system', both types of data system. If one is interested in the collection, storage and provision of data then inevitably there is a concentration of attention upon finding the most efficient means of doing this and technical questions will become predominant. These are certainly important but answering them will not by itself lead to an information-system, nor will it necessarily benefit the organisation. To truly serve their needs organisations require information-systems, and the creation of such systems requires an understanding of the cognitive frameworks by which organisations and individuals perceive the world and themselves. Only when this is done and genuine information needs are understood may the data needs be defined and technical issues be considered.

If then one is concerned with developing information-systems rather than data systems then what Methlie (1980) describes as infological perspectives, which concentrate on 'the outputs of the information-system and how the information is used in the organisation', are to be preferred to datalogical perspectives which do not.

### 5.6.3 Analysis of data requirements

Data-oriented development methodologies which take data, rather than information, to be the corporate resource are methodologies for developing data systems rather than information-systems. This does not lessen their importance, for mechanisms which facilitate the efficient storage and retrieval of data are a vital component of information-systems. However, the first stage of such methodologies is to identify entities or those 'things' which are of importance to the organisation. But this cannot be done without investigating the cognitive framework which identifies certain 'things' as meaningful entities and ignores others. At present data analysts investigate the cognitive framework only implicitly, through discussions and debates with the users as to what is to be included in the set of entities and the nature of their definition within the data dictionary. A consequence of adopting an appreciative view of decision-making is the need to carry out this exploration more explicitly, and in Part III of this book we discuss these issues in detail.

### 5.6.4 IS development as organisational adaptation

Since appreciative systems are never static it follows that what is 'relevant' may change over time. A change in the appreciative setting may give rise to new decision-making contexts or affect what is considered as relevant to existing decisions. For example, it is unlikely that data about public attitudes to the environment would have in the past been perceived as relevant to manufacturing decisions. New knowledge about the effect of certain pollutant gases upon the ozone layer however has led to changes not only in the purchasing decisions of consumers but also in the appreciative settings of manufacturers, and data about the 'greenness' of the public is now clearly extremely relevant to many manufacturing decisions.

This implies the need for IS to constantly adapt over time. So the tradition of organising IS development through once-off, problem-solving 'projects' , as we saw in Chapter 4, is inappropriate and artificially distinguishes between development and maintenance activities.

### 5.6.5 End-user involvement

The uniqueness of appreciative systems means that, even for a given decision, what is 'relevant' for one organisation or decision-maker may not be relevant for another. Three decision-makers may disagree over the factors that 'are important' in making a decision; what is 'information' for one manager may be only 'data' for another and not recognised as at all relevant by a third. This emphasises the unsuitability of generic solutions applied across organisations and the importance of tailoring information-systems to specific organisational requirements and, particularly in the area of decision support, to the cognitive style of the user. The appreciative model therefore provides a logical argument for participative methods (Mumford *et al*, 1978; Mumford & Henshall, 1979; Mumford and Weir, 1979) in that the close involvement of end-users in the development process becomes therefore not merely a 'good' or moral thing to do but essential in order to provide information (which is relevant and meaningful to the user) rather than mere data.

### 5.6.6 Social and political components to IS analysis

The appreciative model recognises human beings as autonomous rather than purely functional components of information-systems. This implies the need for a shift in emphasis in IS work away from the purely technical towards the social and political environment in which ISD takes place. Systems analysis methods which concentrate solely upon the existing business processes and decisions but take no account of the social, historical and political factors which surround them will ignore many important aspects; social and political analysis skills are therefore essential skills for the analyst. Yet such skills are currently given little emphasis in the training of IS professionals or within commercial development methodologies. Within soft systems thinking this is remedied to some extent for there is not only a requirement for analysis of the political and social aspects of the problem situation but also for conscious planning of the intervention process. This remains however an area where techniques are sadly lacking and much remains to be learned from other disciplines.

# 6   Supporting the organisation

## 6.1   INTRODUCTION

We have seen that decision-making is widely accepted as the rationale for expending time and resources upon the creation of information-systems for, the argument goes, if decision-making is to be taken as the central function of management then it is essential that decision-makers are provided with the information that they require. We have also seen though that decision-making encompasses more than a simple choice between alternative courses of action. The concept of appreciation enriches our view of decision-making so that the need to make decisions becomes merely the most visible expression of a more basic need: that for organisations and individuals to maintain desired relationships or avoid undesired ones, in an ever-changing environment. And the enriched view of decision-making, because it allocates a central role for values and interests, allows a clear distinction to be made between 'data' and 'information'.

This chapter continues with this line of thought by considering how information-systems may support organisational activity. We shall see that both different types and different levels of support are possible. We will then consider the different types of decision-making that occur within organisations, the different types of data that these require and the different types of support that information-systems may provide.

## 6.2   SUPPORTING ORGANISATIONAL ACTIVITY

Although there are very many different views of organisations there is little question that all organisations must carry out activities of some kind. This provides us with the starting point for using systems thinking to investigate how information-systems may assist organisations.

First, let us conceptualise a system that carries out a particular activity, the manufacture of a product (widgets) from a number of raw materials. We may represent this system in the most basic way by showing the material flows that are input and output from the system (Figure 6.1).

Let us now assume that some form of support will be provided through the use of new, information technologies (computers, telecommunications etc). This leads us to conceptualise a second system, a system to provide support to the first system. What form might that support take?

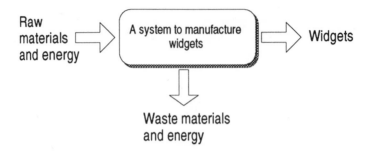

**Figure 6.1** *A physical, input-output representation of a widget manufacturing system*

Systems thinking tells us that there is some set of basic activities that the widget manufacturing system must perform if it is to be genuinely regarded as a widget manufacturing system. So within the 'black box' of Figure 6.1 there will be a host of required activities that must take place if the transformation of raw materials and energy into widgets is to happen; there might well, for example, be activities concerned with obtaining the required raw materials. Each of these required activities will have its own inputs and outputs, not only in terms of physical flows but also in terms of required data.

The first way in which an information-system could conceivably be of assistance is, then, to provide those activities with the data that they require. It might, for example, provide better, faster access to more comprehensive data about the different sources from which raw materials could be obtained. This is, of course, exactly the line of thinking which leads most systems development methodologies to employ data flow diagramming and other forms of process analysis. In data flow diagramming (Gane & Sarson, 1977; De Marco, 1978) a complex, multi-faceted real-world organisation is perceived as being a set of inter-related activities connected by flows of data. The skill of the analyst lies in choosing to 'partition' complex reality into a usable set of activities and sub-activities and in defining the required flows of data between these. The weaknesses of the way in which this is attempted need not concern us here.

We would wish to distinguish the most basic activities, required if our widget manufacturing system is to be a widget manufacturing system, from other sorts of activity. Let us therefore continue to use the terminology of systems thinking and describe these as the operational activities of the system. So, one form of support that may be given to the widget manufacturing system is to facilitate the required operational activities (Figure 6.2). This facilitation is most commonly done by better provision of the data that each requires but, as we shall now see, there is a range of possibilities for the support that might be given to operational or other types of activity.

## 6.3 LEVELS OF SUPPORT

The support given to an activity by information technologies can in principle take many

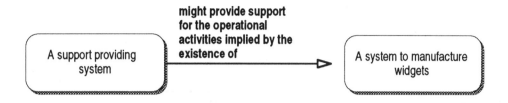

**Figure 6.2**    *One form of support that may be provided*

forms, these being on a continuum between where no support is given, to the other extreme where the level of support provided entirely removes the need for any human involvement in the activity. Between these two extremes lie an infinity of possibilities, but it is useful to consider there being, in all, seven levels of support.

- The **first level of support** is that no support is given at all.
- In the **second level of support** the information technologies are used to mimic previously existing data support. Records previously kept on paper documents within filing cabinets may now be held on a different medium, perhaps as electronic images on magnetic disk. Even though the data is stored and retrieved inflexibly, and may be retrieved in precisely the same format as it appeared previously in the paper document, advantages are gained from the change. Storage costs may be reduced and the data can now be accessed equally readily from many remote locations.
- The **third level of support** is achieved when the users of the data are able to retrieve it in formats other than that in which it was originally stored. They may be able to retrieve only selected records, chosen against some criteria, or selected parts of individual records. There is the ability to perform simple manipulations of the data, for example counting of records, totalling of fields or other arithmetic or statistical functions. The users' freedom to 'play in the data' is, though, restricted: whilst a wide range of reports and retrieval routines may be possible the range and format of the output is pre-defined by the designers of the support system, and by *their* expectations of the needs of the users.
- When we reach the **fourth level of support** this restriction is removed. The provision of high-level command languages and flexible storage mechanisms allow ad-hoc querying of the stored data. The user is able to decide both how to access the data and the format of the output. It is once this level of support is required that technologies such as databases and design techniques that ensure a flexible storage structure of the data, such as normalisation, come into their own.
- It is at the **fifth level of support** that there occurs a qualitative shift. Up to this point the role of the information technologies has been merely to provide the human being with the data that is required to carry out the activity. From this point forward the technologies begin to play an active role in carrying out the activity. A shift therefore

occurs from passive support through data provision to active support of the activity, with some level of participation.

A point-of-sale terminal at a supermarket checkout may now be the mechanism by which details and prices of the customer's purchases are known and by which change is calculated and delivered to the customer. Or the manager seeking to decide between alternative courses of action may now be provided with simulation and modelling facilities that allow them to forecast the results of each alternative. In each of these cases some part of the task that was previously the responsibility of the human being has been handed over to the support system.

- By the time we reach the **sixth level of support** the support system is becoming the primary means of carrying out the activity. Based on stored knowledge of previous carrying out of the activity and of the way in which a human expert would do that activity, it is able to provide suggested actions for each case that occurs. It may act as adviser to the human being carrying out the activity, as in the case of expert systems, or carry out the activity, referring only exceptional circumstances to the human supervisor, as in the case of the automatic navigation and flight computers on board aircraft.

- At the **seventh level of support** we achieve the level of automation where full responsibility for the activity resides with the support system. Human fears concerning safety and reliability mean that this level of support is rarely reached. Only when the situation that surrounds the activity is stable and well-defined do we find genuine examples of this level of support, as in robotic car manufacture or 'dark-room' computer operations.

These levels of support can provide an axis against which we might attempt to make sense of the plethora of (arbitrarily named) types of information-systems described in the literature (Figure 6.3).

To understand how computer-based information-systems can aid the organisation it would be more useful though if we could provide a second axis, that of the type of support being given. We have so far identified only operational support, so let us return to our conceptualisation of a system to manufacture widgets and see in what other ways support might be given.

## 6.4  SUPPORT FOR MONITORING AND CONTROL ACTIVITIES

One of the basic concepts of systems thinking is that of control; therefore conceptualising the system to manufacture widgets means that we must at the same time allow for the existence of a second system, one that monitors and controls the operation of the first. This system will obtain data about the performance of the first, compare these with expectations of how it should perform and issue instructions that modify or maintain the current operations. A second way of assisting the manufacture of widgets could then be to support not the operational activities of widget manufacture but the activities required to do this monitoring and control (Figure 6.4).

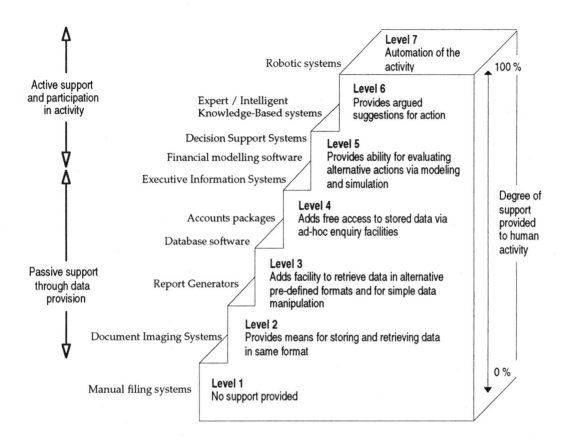

**Figure 6.3**   *Some common types of information-system mapped against the seven levels of support*

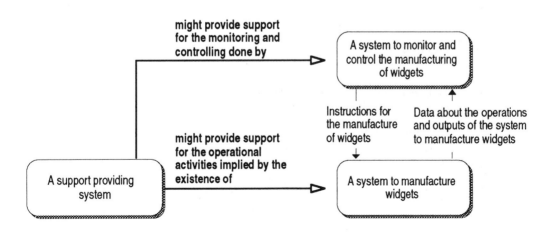

**Figure 6.4**   *Two ways in which support may be provided*

We might, for example, think of an information-system that provides the monitor-and-control system with a more accurate picture of the way that the manufacturing system is operating, or provides suggestions for how performance could be improved.

## 6.5 SUPPORT FOR MANAGEMENT ACTIVITIES

The next stage in our modelling of the widget manufacturing system is to ask how the second system is able to decide whether the performance of the first system requires amendment. The answer to this is that it must have been provided with some expectations of what the manufacturing system *should* be doing, in order to detect if there is any variation that requires control instructions to be issued. These expectations can only come from some higher-level system, so we are led to conceptualise another system, one that prepares plans, budgets and schedules for the making of widgets. We therefore have scope for assisting widget manufacture in yet another way, by improving the *planning* of widget manufacture.

Finally, we may reason that if there exists a system that plans the manufacture of widgets, then there must exist a yet higher-level system, one that has initiated that planning by deciding that widgets should be made in the first place. This system might itself be assisted by an information-system that provides it with the data it requires to make such decisions. Thus our original conceptualisation of 'a system that manufactures widgets' leads us to conceptualise other systems, and reveals that providing support through information-systems may take several forms (Figure 6.5).

This means that we cannot simply talk of using an information-system to support an organisational activity as if this might be done in only one way. We have seen that we may support the making of widgets by providing the lowest-level manufacturing system with operational support; alternatively we could provide management support, aiding and abetting the monitoring and controlling of the manufacturing system or the planning and control activities required by the manufacturing of widgets. The same arguments can, of course, be applied to any other activity of the organisation.

## 6.6 DIFFERING TYPES OF DECISION

It is the desire to provide support to the management activities of organisations that has led to such emphasis being placed upon decision-making. The reader will recall that the more conventional view of decision-making considers it to be the central function of management, and the enriched view of decision-making places it at the centre of all organisational activity. We turn now to considering how decision-making might be categorised.

It seems intuitively obvious that decisions differ. My personal decision on whether to drive or walk to work and a government decision to privatise a national industry are not only absurdly different in the size and scope of their impacts upon the world, but also of qualitatively different kinds.

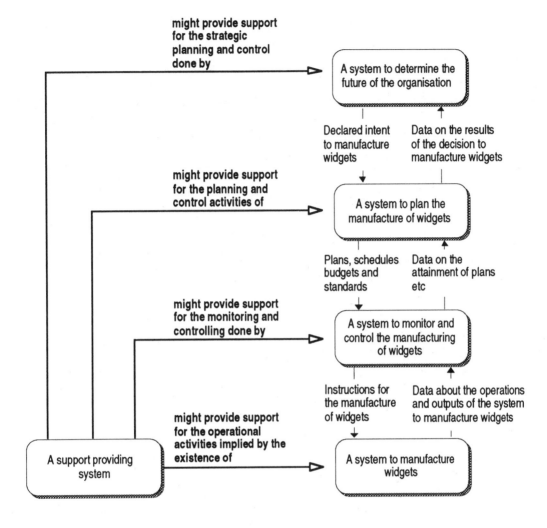

**Figure 6.5**    *Support may take several forms*

Consider also the decisions made by a doctor in treating patients as compared to those made by a clerk involved in order processing within a commercial organisation. The clerk will have a clear set of criteria for deciding whether or not any order is acceptable and consequently a precise definition of what data are required to check whether a particular order meets those criteria. If one of the criteria to be used is that the customer sending the order should not already owe the company money then this defines some of the data needed, namely the amount of money currently owed by the customer. The decision-making is then deterministic since if the amount owed is greater than zero the order will be rejected. And the decision result does not depend upon who is taking the decision; given the same decision situation, the same order and the same data then the order will always be accepted or rejected.

The doctor, in contrast, works with far more uncertain data. First, even that a person is 'sick' is not easily determined, since what might be considered abnormal and symptomatic in one patient may be normal for another. Secondly, a particular group of symptoms might be suggestive of a disease, but might equally well arise from another disease or a combination of unrelated diseases. For these reasons the doctor cannot merely examine the patient but must consider the past medical history and events prior to the appearance of the symptoms in order to make a probabilistic judgement as to what is wrong and what will the best course of treatment.

The variety of decision-making experienced by each is also different. The range of decisions required of the clerk is low, as almost every decision made by the clerk is of the same kind and made upon the same criteria. The variety of decision-making carried out by the doctor is, in comparison, very high, for each patient's case is unique and the doctor may never have experienced anything similar previously. Different too is the time period over which decisions must be made. For the clerk this is short; each order is accepted or rejected as it is received. The doctor however may have to consider likely developments and treatments over a number of years in the future.

If not all decisions are of a uniform type, then it may be that the needs of each type of decision-making are different. If so, and if the decisions made within an organisation are to be used as a guide towards the information needs of the organisation, then we require some way of categorising decision-making. A number of ways have been suggested for doing this.

## 6.7  PROGRAMMABLE AND NON-PROGRAMMABLE DECISIONS

One way of categorising decisions might be to consider the extent to which 'rules' or established procedures exist for making the decision. Simon (1960, 1965) categorised decisions in this way, by their position upon a continuum of decision types ranging from programmed decisions to non-programmed decisions The term 'program' is used here to describe

> "... *a detailed prescription or strategy that governs the sequence of responses of a system to a complex task environment*" p. 6.

Programmed decisions are repetitive and routine and, because they have already been faced before, a definite, routine procedure has been established for tackling them. Examples would include the work done by the order processing clerk above or decisions as to whether a new customer should be allowed credit facilities. If the latter is a decision that an organisation has to make repeatedly it is likely to establish formal procedures and rules for making such decisions, for example, by awarding points for the various factors that are regarded as indicative of a reliable credit risk. Because the decision-making procedures are clearly defined, the data required to make the decision is specifiable in advance.

Non-programmed decisions are by contrast novel, unstructured and the organisation will have no previous experience of how to tackle such decisions. This may be because they have never been taken before or because the nature of the decision is sufficiently complex to distinguish it from any predecessors. The organisation has

*"... no specific procedures to deal with situations like the one at hand, but must fall back on whatever general capacity it has for intelligent, adaptive, problem-oriented action. In addition to his specific skills and specific knowledge, man has some general problem-solving capacities. Given almost any kind of situation, no matter how novel or perplexing, he can begin to reason about it in terms of ends and means." Simon 1960, p. 6*

Examples of non-programmed decisions might be the appointment of a senior executive, deciding the direction of research and development or the formulation by government of a new economic policy.

The identification of these two extremes of a range of decision types was used by Simon to discuss the limits to which computers could, at the time of writing, assist with organisational decision-making. Its subsequent use has though been somewhat different; it has, as we shall see, been most commonly used to facilitate understanding of another idea, that of a hierarchy of organisational decision-making

## 6.8  HIERARCHY OF DECISION-MAKING

The single most widely used basis for classifying decision-making must be Anthony's (1965) suggestion that differences between the decision-making typically done by senior managers, middle managers and workers at lower levels of responsibility could be explained in terms of three types of planning and control activity. These were strategic planning, management control and operational control.

There exists within Anthony's distinction between the three types of planning and control activity an implied hierarchy of management activity, for management control is done within the context of the objectives and policies set by strategic planning and operational control takes place in the context of plans created by management control. For this reason the three types of activity are often presented in the form of a pyramidal structure as in Figure 6.6.

Strategic planning is defined by Anthony as:

*"... the process of deciding on objectives of the organization, on changes in these objectives, on the resources used to attain these objectives, and on the policies that are to govern the acquisition, use, and disposition of these resources." Anthony (1965), p. 16*

It is therefore concerned with establishing long-term goals for the organisation and deciding upon strategies by which the organisation will seek to achieve those goals. Because of the long time horizons involved strategic decision-making must involve a great deal of uncertainty.

Decision-making of this kind is the most difficult to assist since it is largely non-repetitive and probabilistic. A recent development has been attempts to provide some assistance for strategic decision-making in the form of Executive Information Systems (EIS). These may help by presenting the data in a way that is easily assimilable by senior

**Figure 6.6**     *Conventional pyramidal representation of the relationship between three types of planning and control activity implies hierarchy*

managers but, nevertheless, strategy formulation is a process requiring much intuitive feel and external data. Much judgement is required in the interpretation of the outputs of the information-system.

Management control should, Anthony points out, really be called 'management planning and control' since it encompasses both these activities. It is:

> "... *the process by which managers assure that resources are obtained and used effectively and efficiently in the accomplishment of the organization's objectives.*"
> Anthony (1965), p. 17

Management control thus takes place within the context already set by the objectives and policies decided upon by strategic planning, and generates plans for action. The criteria for judging those planned actions are effectiveness and efficiency in the use of resources. Examples include scheduling production and budget allocation.

Operational control is primarily concerned with controlling the everyday activities of the organisation, with monitoring what is actually done and ensuring that the plans originated at the tactical level are carried out in the best possible way. Decision-making at the operational level is primarily centred around ensuring the minimum variance between actual performance and planned targets. Anthony describes operational control as being:

> "... *the process of assuring that specific tasks are carried out effectively and efficiently.*" Anthony (1965), p. 18.

Decisions made at the operational level tend to be routine, frequent and made according to well-defined procedures. Examples of operational-level decision-making would include ensuring that customers' orders are fulfilled, that payments are made and received, that stock records are kept up to date and that raw materials are obtained.

These three types of activity provide a framework into which may be placed the majority of business activities, though it is recognised that the distinction between them is not absolute and there may be situations that do not fit exactly in a single category.

An important feature of Anthony (1965), and perhaps the reason that it has been so influential upon the field of information-systems, is that it distinguishes two other topics which are related to, but distinct from, the area of planning and control. Not only is financial accounting considered separately but so too is information handling, with the latter having a support relationship to all other areas. The discussion of the three types of planning and control activity also includes specific discussion of the types of information (we might prefer to say data) required by each.

### 6.8.1 The use of Anthony's work in the field of IS

The reader will surely by now have recognised similarities between this hierarchy of decision-making and the conclusion reached earlier, that whenever we conceptualise a system to do some activity, such as manufacture widgets, then we must also take account of systems that monitor and control that activity, plan that activity and decide to do that activity in the first place. These similarities do not arise by accident, for Anthony's analysis is rooted in systems thinking, albeit of a 'harder' kind than we have used.

But we should also note that Anthony's work is often, wrongly, considered to delineate the complete range of decisions made within organisations. This misconception arises primarily in respect to the question of Anthony's operational control. As we have seen Anthony describes this as being 'the process of assuring that specific tasks are carried out effectively and efficiently', and this coincides well with our idea of a system that 'monitors and controls' the operation of another system that carries out a particular activity. It is, though, regrettably easy to confuse the process of *monitoring and controlling* an activity with the process of actual *execution* of the activity, and this confusion is often to be found within the literature of IS. For example, we find statements that:

> "Anthony (1965) suggests a convenient organizational model consisting of three levels of decision making ... Operational decisions include the everyday decisions required to carry out the overall firm and individual mission requirements determined by strategic and tactical management" Martin (1991) pp. 35-36.

As Anthony's work is so widely used, and decision-making has been given so central a role in the determination of organisational information requirements, such confusion has had serious consequences for the field of IS. There is not scope to discuss all of these here, but we may note that:

- Confusion over whether Anthony's work is a model for the organisation as a whole, rather than a framework for understanding planning and control activities, means that thinking about the information needs of the organisation may be restricted to a consideration of the needs of planning and control. There will be a consequent tendency to emphasise the satisfaction of the needs of management rather than of other participants or the organisation as a whole.
- Wrongly interpreting operational control as equivalent to carrying out operational activities means that an important set of activities, those concerned with monitoring and control, are given little attention.

- Anthony (p. 67) suggests that staff and top management are the people primarily involved in strategic planning and it is line and top management that are primarily involved in management control; but not that there is an exclusive division of kinds of decision-making throughout the organisation. If, as is commonly done in the IS literature, we confuse epistemology and ontology and talk of there being clearly defined levels of management, each exclusively concerned with a different kind of decision-making, then we over-simplify the problem of providing organisational support and do little justice to the rich and complex realities of real-world organisations.

## 6.9  STRUCTURE IN DECISION-MAKING

The impact of Simon's and Anthony's works in the field of information-systems has been greatly increased by bringing together both ideas to create a further framework for understanding the types of managerial activity which information-systems have been asked to support.

Gorry & Scott Morton (1971) combined Simon's idea of there being a continuum of decision types (programmable through non-programmable) with Anthony's classification of planning and control activities to create a framework:

> "... *designed to be useful in planning for information systems activities within an organization and for distinguishing between the various model-building activities, models, computer systems, and so forth that are used for supporting different kinds of decisions.*" p. 56

The continuum of decision types (here bounded by 'structured' and 'unstructured') provides a way of looking at the way the decision-making is conducted, whilst the classification of planning and control activities provides a way of looking at the purpose of the management activity. The resulting framework is of managerial activity and Gorry & Scott Morton are able to locate common decision topics within it (Figure 6.7). It should be noted that the title of the work in which these ideas were first expounded was 'A Framework for Management Information Systems', thus emphasising that it was, in the terms of our systemic model for support, the support of management activity that was under consideration.

The importance of Gorry & Scott Morton's work lies in their belief that distinguishing between different types of decision was important if an organisation was to be successful in its use of information-systems. They argued that:

- Supporting structured decision-making was primarily a technical issue, since the way in which the decision was to be made was well-defined and 'support' here meant primarily supplying the manager with the data required.
- There were different requirements of managers, and the analysts seeking to help them, in structured and unstructured decision-making; for example, in unstructured, strategic planning decision-making the manager will be required to take a more active role in defining the problem and identifying the key relationships than would be the

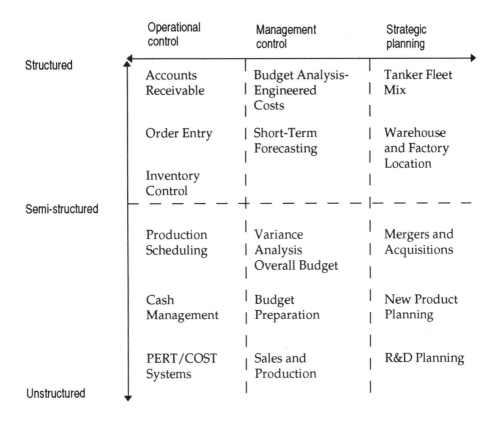

**Figure 6.7**    *The Gorry & Scott Morton framework of decision areas
(Source: Gorry & Scott Morton, 1971)*

case in well structured, operational control decision-making. For the information-system developer this means that the methods and technologies that prove effective in supporting decision-making of one kind might well be inappropriate to decision-making of another type.

In a retrospective commentary upon the original work, Gorry & Scott Morton (1989) remind us that their thinking employed Simon's phase model of decision-making but that they later believed that a richer model of problem solving would accord better with reality.

*"Such a view adds richness to the decision-making perspective by recognizing the crucial learning that takes place during the complex iterative process of moving towards a solution in anything but the simplest situation." p. 59.*

The enriched model of decision-making based upon appreciation that was introduced in Chapter 5 emphasises both learning and the need for an on-going process of accommodation with a changing environment. The implications of this regarding classifying types of decision-making are discussed below.

## 6.10 STABILITY OF APPRECIATION

The three frameworks for categorising decision-making that we have so far looked at include little direct consideration of the context that gives meaning to the need to make a decision. The appreciative model for the decision-making process makes it clear that this is a crucial omission since appreciation affects not only every part of the decision-making process, including the rules and procedures for decision-making and the information used, but also the consideration of whether or not a decision is required at all.

One way in which we might redress this omission is to refine the notion of structure in decision-making by introducing the idea of stability of appreciation. As we have seen, the notion of structure in decision-making used by both Simon (1960) and Gorry & Scott Morton (1971) is defined by a single continuum between 'programmable and non-programmable' or 'structured and unstructured' decision types. We may expand this view by considering how stable are the organisation's appreciations, both of the current situation and of what would be considered desirable in future.

The enriched model of decision-making is based upon the idea of an organisation having a continually evolving appreciation of both the world and its place, actual or wished for, within it. In some organisations those appreciations are less susceptible to change, alter more slowly, or we may say are more stable, than in others. Religious organisations, for example, tend to operate within very stable appreciations of the world and the future. Some of their norms and values may gradually change over time (divorce may be sanctioned, women may be admitted to the priesthood) but their view of the world and of an ideal world remain remarkably constant over long periods of time. If a worshipped God does not destroy the world on the day predicted then this does not weaken belief in the God but merely confirms belief in the mercifulness of the God.

Appreciation of the current situation will tend towards non-stability where:

- the organisation is very sensitive to its environment and has a readiness to note new threats or opportunities;
- it has previously employed low quality data, in which case the likelihood of obtaining data which gives a different picture of the current situation is high. This is particularly likely to occur where the organisation is focusing upon future events and as time goes by more and more uncertainty is removed;
- the organisation is facing a novel situation that it has not dealt with before and understanding of cause-effects relationships, and of how to influence events, is uncertain.

The organisation's appreciation of 'what is desirable' will be affected by its understanding of itself and its purposes. Such basic standards are much less likely to change than are the norms or values but changes are possible and organisations do on occasion 're-think their basic missions'. The oil companies that re-defined themselves as 'energy producers' in response to the OPEC producer nations' demands for greater control of oil supply during the 1970s underwent just such a radical self-examination.

The stability of the two appreciations, of what the current situation is and of what the organisation might consider to be a desirable situation, combine to define the level of structure of any particular decision-making context (Figure 6.8).

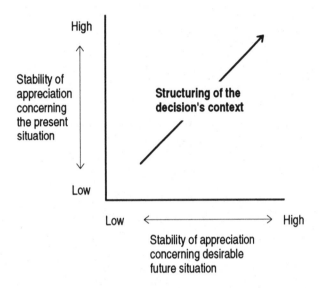

**Figure 6.8**     *Structure of decision context related to appreciative stability*

## 6.10.1. Four types of decision context

Dividing up the body of Figure 6.8 produces four basic contexts within which decision-making may take place, as shown in Figure 6.9.

In highly structured contexts there is a shared and stable understanding of the present situation and what would be considered desirable. It is therefore possible for there to be clear and unambiguous rules for how the decision should be made and what data are required to make the decision. There can be agreed rules for how the data should be processed and how these precisely relate to a known range of possible decision outputs. The values of the data used therefore determine the final decision made.

Within this context Simon's programmable decision-making is possible. The stability of both appreciations, though, makes the likelihood of organisational learning low.

Non-structured contexts occur when there is a lack of stability in the appreciations of both the current situation and what is desirable. Such contexts are characterised by novelty, the lack of a clear understanding of how the decision should be made and therefore of what data is required, and the absence of clearly defined rules about how the data should be processed. Decision-making therefore occurs at many levels, for decisions must be made about whether and how to make the decision.

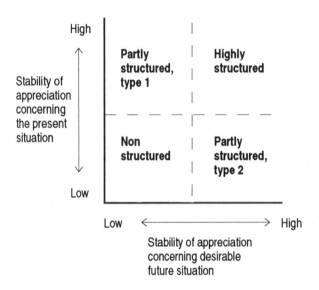

**Figure 6.9**     *Four types of decision context*

In such contexts, where we might expect to find 'unprogrammable' or 'unstructured' decision types, the changing appreciative system of the organisation will have a large effect upon the decision-making process but there is, in turn, a high likelihood of organisational learning resulting from the process of making the decision.

Partly structured contexts arise when there is reduced stability in either of the two appreciations. There may be some similarities with previously experienced decision contexts that are suggestive of ways in which decision-making may proceed but some interpretation of the results of processing will be necessary and the decision-making process is likely itself to be educational for the organisation.

In partly structured contexts of type 1 there is stability of appreciation about the current situation, with possibly high quality data available about everything that is currently or will probably be in future perceived as relevant. But there is a lack of stability in the organisation's appreciation of what is desirable, so the rules for decision-making cannot be entirely defined and, unlike the above case, the values of the data cannot determine the final decision made.

In partly structured contexts of type 2 there is stability of the organisation's values and purposes so that given a clear idea of the present situation the organisation's response would be clear. However exactly what the current situation is remains unclear. This may be because the organisation is attempting to make decisions for the future and the data available is probabilistic, estimated and not certain. In such cases there may well be doubts and uncertainties about the situation or the cause-effect relationships that lie within it.

## 6.10.2 Stability of appreciation and levels of decision-making

The notion of a hierarchy of decision-making can be related to the stability of appreciation by considering the type of decision-making context with which each is most likely to be concerned (Figure 6.10).

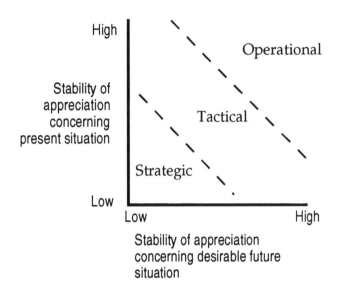

**Figure 6.10** *Frequency of occurrence of decision contexts at differing levels of organisational activity*

Decision-making of the operational control kind is primarily concerned with the execution of programmes and tactics decided upon previously. There is therefore a relatively stable basis for knowing what is considered a desirable future situation. The decisions made tend to be repetitive and focused upon the present, which gives a tendency towards a stable view of the current situation. This kind of decision-making therefore takes place within highly structured decision contexts where the range of possible decision results is known, there is confidence in the data used and the way in which the decision will be made.

Strategic planning, in contrast, focuses upon the, always unknowable, future and the type of decisions made are often novel and of a kind not before encountered. It therefore primarily occurs within non-structured decision contexts where the reliability of the data is uncertain, and where the possible decision results and how they might be arrived at are unknown.

Relating the different levels of decision-making to different decision contexts in this way is undoubtedly a gross generalisation, and there will be cases where, for example, strategic planning and control decisions are made within a well-structured context: but it does give some insight into why a particular historical pattern of information-systems use has occurred. Most approaches to developing information-systems require both a clear specification of the current situation and of what is required in the future. It is not therefore surprising that, to date, most information-systems have provided data support for the decision-making of operations, operational monitoring and control or management control. Support for the decision-making of strategic planning, in the form of executive information systems (EIS), remains in its infancy.

### 6.10.3 A new basis for categorising information-systems

We may now bring together the ideas that we have discussed so far to create a framework through which the reader may understand the nature of the information-systems in place in their own organisation. Figure 6.11 shows such a framework.

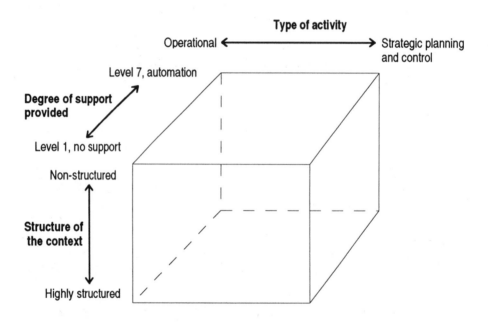

**Figure 6.11**  *A framework for categorising information-systems*

This takes the form of a cube, defined by three axes. The axes are concerned with:

- the type of activity supported
- the structure or stability of appreciation that surrounds the activity
- the degree of support provided to the activity.

Within this cube the reader may attempt to locate some of the information-systems currently used within their own organisation. For example, a computerised catalogue within a library may provide only limited data support, supports the operational activities of the library (helping readers to find books) and is used in a highly structured context. It would therefore be located somewhere in the nearside, bottom-left hand corner of the cube.

Indeed, we would predict that most of the information-systems that the reader is familiar with will be located somewhere in that area, for the challenge with which the developers of information-systems are still struggling is how to create information-systems that can be located towards the other extreme, the farside, top, right-hand corner.

## 6.11 CHARACTERISTICS OF DATA

Many different suggestions for categorising data and information are to be found in the literature of information-systems. However, these often confuse the separate questions of:

- What determines if data may be regarded as information?
- What, given that some particular data is useful to an individual in decision-making, makes one set of data more valuable to that individual than another?
- How may the use of the data be described?
- What characteristics does the data have independently of the use to which it is put?

Our enriched view of decision-making allows us to restrict our discussion to the last of these questions, and disqualifies some of the more common suggestions for the characteristics of data. We cannot for example consider 'relevance' to be a characteristic of data (as do authors such as Martin, 1991; Martin & Powell 1992; Reynolds 1992). The enriched model of decision-making tells us that the 'relevance' of some fact is determined by the appreciative settings that lead to a readiness to see and value that fact in one way or another. There is, for example, an almost infinite range of data that *might* be collected about a real-world event such as a sales transaction but only some of this is usually considered as relevant or useful. One might for example collect not only the obvious data such as details of the product or service sold and the value of the sale but also the colour of the customer's eyes. No organisations however currently record the latter datum about sales because it is not appreciated as 'relevant' to any decision that they may need to make now or in the future. The mutability of the appreciative system may of course change that appreciation of relevance; thirty years ago the customer's sex was unlikely to be seen as relevant to any decision-making whereas today that datum would be appreciated as very relevant to many marketing decisions. Relevance is therefore not, for us, an inherent characteristic of the datum.

Nor may we consider a datum to have in itself any 'surprise value', for, clearly, what is unknown and 'surprising' to one person may be already familiar and uninteresting to another. Any surprise value can only be descriptive of a relationship between the datum and a potential user.

Another set of suggestions centre around the way in which data is used. Such things as 'the frequency of use' may guide us towards a judgement of the importance of particular data to the organisation at a particular time. But once again it is clear that the frequency with which a datum is used is determined by the frequency with which particular decision-making contexts occur and not by the intrinsic nature of the datum itself.

Frequent, repetitive decision-making will, obviously, lead to the need for frequent access to a given datum.

We may however sensibly talk of data having some characteristics that are independent of the context of its use. These are the internal characteristics of: focus, concern, time perspective, structuring, and quality. In addition we may choose to categorise data by particular external characteristics such as the source from which it was acquired and the mode of its acquisition.

## 6.12 THE INTERNAL CHARACTERISTICS OF DATA

### 6.12.1 Focus of data

If data are appreciated facts about the world then the focus of data may be said to be determined by the location of the subject of the data in respect to the data's user. Three such locations need to be considered (Figure 6.12).

**Figure 6.12**     *Three environments for the subject of data*

Internally focused data are facts that concern the entities and relationships which make up the user's immediate area of concern, social setting or organisation. Such data may be generated as a by-product of an individual's or organisation's activities, for example plans, budgets, details of staff employed, or they may be descriptive of those activities, such as number of orders processed or products produced each day.

Externally focused data concern entities and relationships that lie outside this immediate boundary of concern, but with which continuing and important interactions occur. For a formal organisation this might be considered as the organisation's operating environment.

Environmentally focused data concerns entities and relationships that lie in the wider economic, social and political environment. The actions of governments, central or foreign monetary mechanisms or changes in social behaviour might all be the subject of environmentally focused data.

### 6.12.2  Concern

The concern of a datum is whether it is descriptive of a single instance, a particular set of such instances, or a generic class of thing. For example:

| | |
|---|---|
| *Order No. 1234 was placed on August 1<sup>st</sup> of this year* | is a datum that concerns only one part of the world, namely that which is recognised as the order with the identifier of '1234'. |
| *The value of orders placed in the last quarter is £5 million* | is a datum concerned with a particular set of such orders, namely those placed within a particular time period. |
| *Orders placed by government agencies are treated differently from other orders* | concerns a generic class of things that are perceived to exist in the world, namely 'Orders placed by government agencies'. |

### 6.12.3  Time perspective

Any datum is a fact relating to some part of the world at a given moment of time. A further characteristic of data must therefore be whether it is descriptive of the past, present or (expected) future state of that thing. Examples of data with a past focus are last year's sales figures; an example of data with a present focus might be a list of current employees; projected sales for next year would have a focus of the future.

### 6.12.4  Degree of structuring

Where data are always associated together in a regular, expected way then we may consider the data as being more structured than where the data may be associated in many alternative ways. My date of birth, for example, is a relatively structured datum in that you may always expect it to consist of a day-within-month, a month and a year; the relative positions of these components may vary though between the US and UK. My view of the probable state of the UK housing market in ten years time is though unstructured data for, until I give it to you, you will have no idea of what it will contain or how it will be presented.

Internally focused data is usually associated together in a highly ordered form; for example data about members of staff is usually organised in such a way that all the data about a particular individual is associated together in a standard way. This may be on a Personnel Record Form or held within computer files in a defined record format. Environmentally focused data, by contrast, is commonly obtained from textual or spoken media reporting, in forms that have inconsistent content and organisation. It is therefore mostly of an unstructured kind.

### 6.12.5 Quality

The quality of data is a rather nebulous concept, but we suggest that it may be discussed in terms of three dimensions, namely correctness, completeness and currency.

Correctness is a measure of the closeness with which the symbolic message contained within the data reflects 'the truth' about a real-world situation. For example, if a datum concerns a transaction worth £10,000 then the closer the data reflects the event the more accurate it is. Therefore data which represents that transaction as being £1,000 is less accurate than data which reflects it as worth £9,000.99.

Completeness is a reflection of the extent to which the data tells 'the whole truth' about the real-world situation. Data about the sale of £10,000 worth of goods would be accurate but incomplete if it did not also tell that a discount of 40% had been allowed.

Currency is a measure of the extent to which the data reflects the most recent available knowledge about the situation. This is quite different to whether or not the data has a past, present or future orientation and it is quite possible to have very current data concerning a past event.

Although we do not consider it to be an inherent characteristic of data, we should note that closely related to a user's perception of quality is the confidence which that user has in the data. If the data comes from an unimpeachable source or if the same meaning is confirmed by data from many sources then the user will have high level of confidence in the data. If however the 'surprise value' of the data is high, i.e. it communicates an unexpected meaning that no other data has led the user to expect, then although the potential value of the data is high the user's confidence level would be low.

Of course, not every situation requires data of the highest quality in terms of all the above dimensions and a trade-off between the various quality dimensions may be made. For example, the importance attached to the currency of data varies greatly. In operational activities great importance is often placed upon the currency of data; the travel agent attempting to reserve an airline seat, for example, will be very anxious that the data used in the airline's reservations system shows how many seats are available now as opposed to how many were available an hour ago. The airline's management, however, in deciding whether to purchase more aircraft might need to know how many seats have been booked over the last two years but having details up to now, rather than a week ago, will not be of great importance. A passenger travelling on one of the aircraft would of course hope that the data about the aircraft's height being used by the pilot was very current indeed!

## 6.13 THE EXTERNAL CHARACTERISTICS OF DATA

As well as thinking about the characteristics of the data itself we may consider where, from the perspective of the organisation, a datum has been obtained and the level of effort required to obtain it.

### 6.13.1 Source

We have already discussed the focus of data and whether the data relates to entities and relationships within or outside the organisation. Whatever is the focus of the data, the data itself may be obtained either internally or externally. For example, data about the past purchases of customers (an external entity) may be obtained by analysing sales records held within the organisation. In contrast, decision-making at the strategic level is centred around the relationship of the organisation to the future economic, social and political environments and often the data used here is that which is only available from outside bodies. Studies of the decision-making of senior executives have revealed that one of the most highly valued sources of data for high-level decision-making is the public media such as newspapers, television and radio reports; news items, political statements and the informed opinion of public commentators might all affect future investment decisions.

### 6.13.2 Mode of acquisition

The collection and storage of any data of course requires some effort and the use of some resources but the amount of effort required may vary considerably. The mode of acquisition refers to the purposeful effort that is required to obtain the data. Some examples of passive and active collection from different sources are given in Figure 6.13.

An important source of data for most organisations is the data collected as part of the normal activities and transactions that occur in the normal course of the organisation's business. For example, the normal sales and invoicing procedures may require a record to be kept of the names and addresses of customers. Even after invoicing is complete this data may prove valuable for decision-making, perhaps providing the basis for analysing the social or geographical spread of customers. Using this type of data requires only relatively passive acquisition mode, since the data is already available for use within the organisation and very little effort is required to obtain it.

Where the data source is external an active mode of data acquisition may though be required. For example, market surveys may have to be commissioned to obtain data concerning patterns of consumer spending or the reaction of potential customers to a new product.

## 6.14 USE OF DIFFERENT DATA

Bringing together the above discussion of the characteristics of data and the different types of activity that information-systems may support we can suggest that different activities may be more or less likely to require data with particular characteristics than others. Figure 6.14 suggests some of these differences in data requirements.

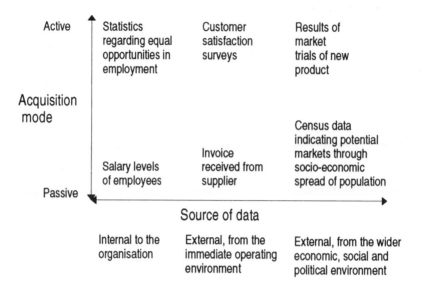

**Figure 6.13**     *Examples of data with different sources and modes of acquisition*

| | Operational | Monitor & Control | Management Control | Strategic Planning |
|---|---|---|---|---|
| **Focus** Internal | VERY HIGH | VERY HIGH | MODERATE | LOW |
| External | NONE | LOW | HIGH | MODERATE |
| Environment | NONE | VERY LOW | LOW | HIGH |
| **Perspective** Past | VERY LOW | LOW | MODERATE | LOW |
| Present | VERY HIGH | VERY HIGH | HIGH | MODERATE |
| Future | VERY LOW | LOW | HIGH | VERY HIGH |
| **Structure** Structured | VERY HIGH | VERY HIGH | HIGH | MODERATE |
| Unstructured | VERY LOW | VERY LOW | LOW | VERY HIGH |
| **Quality** Accuracy | VERY HIGH | HIGH | MODERATE | LOW |
| Completeness | VERY HIGH | HIGH | MODERATE | VERY LOW |
| Currency | VERY HIGH | HIGH | MODERATE | LOW |
| Confidence | HIGH | HIGH | MODERATE | VERY LOW |
| **Concern** Individual | VERY HIGH | HIGH | NONE | NONE |
| Set of individuals | LOW | MODERATE | HIGH | LOW |
| Generic class | NONE | NONE | LOW | HIGH |

**Figure 6.14**     *Probability of importance of different characteristics of data to different forms of organisational activity*

This varying pattern of data characteristics at differing types of decision has important consequences for the physical design of information-systems to serve them; if strategic planning and control makes greater use of unstructured data it is likely that information-systems to support that type of activity will require a greater variety of storage methods than would an information-system that supports operational activities, where most of the data used is highly structured. An order processing system for example might deal exclusively with customer orders in a pre-defined format that can be easily be stored and accessed using a database management system (DBMS). Although an executive information system might also use a DBMS for the retrieval of some of the data it requires it might also require hypermedia, statistical software and text analysis packages capable of accessing less structured data.

# Q & A: CHAPTER 6

**Q.**  **Are the issues of decision-making only relevant when we try to support the work of managers?**

**A.**  No. The important change that arises from both the enriched model of decision-making and from the systemic view of support is that we understand decision-making in a rather different way than previously, and that management support or operational support can be provided at any level of the organisation's hierarchy of status.

It is, of course, much more likely that management support will be provided to those activities traditionally thought of as the domain of 'white-collar' staff; but we could, in principle, envisage management support being provided to shop-floor workers and operational support being provided to the chief executive.

**Q.**  **I receive many mailings from software manufacturers attempting to sell me their latest products. These are variously described by terms such as 'decision-support systems', 'geographic information systems', 'office automation systems' and many, many more. Do the ideas introduced in this chapter allow me to make sense of all these and decide if they will be useful?**

**A.**  Sadly probably not, because of the ways in which such labels are given to different types of software product. For example, the distinguishing feature of those things that are lumped together as 'geographic information systems' is the subject of the data that they hold. The distinguishing feature of 'office automation systems' is the type of activity that they support. The distinguishing feature of 'decision support systems' is not that they aid the making of decisions (since many other information-systems do this too) but in the features (simulation, answering of 'what-if' questions) that the package includes. There is also the problem that the producers of software will often choose to describe them in whatever way is 'flavour of the month' and gives greatest marketing advantage; so there have been many disputes over whether particular products described as 'relational database management systems' are really worthy of that title.

So there is no consistency in the way in which such labels are allocated, and it is unlikely that any framework for thinking about information-systems will be able to inject consistency into an already chaotic labelling. The best which one can do is to accept such labels as that, merely labels, and try to understand how a particular product may be relevant to your particular organisation and its needs. The ideas of this chapter are intended to help with doing this; as we saw, you might understand a particular product according to the support that it provides to a particular activity. *Caveat emptor* must though remain your watchword. A vendor's description of their product may help guide you towards determining its possible utility but you will always need to evaluate it against a specific organisational need.

# 7 Problems with data analysis

## 7.1 INTRODUCTION

Within the IS field the term 'data analysis' refer to the process of investigating the nature and structure of the data used in a problem situation. This type of investigation has come to be one of the most important parts of information-systems development and a battery of different data analysis and modelling techniques now exist. Descriptions of these are so commonly available that the mechanics of their use need not be discussed here; readers not already familiar with the techniques of data analysis and modelling will find good descriptions provided by Date (1990), Benyon(1990), Loomis (1987),Rumbaugh *et al* (1991), Kroenke (1992) and many others. In this and later chapters the value of data analysis in the design stage of creating new computer-based information-systems is not questioned; we do suggest that difficulties arise when the same techniques are used in earlier stages of development.

Little attention has been given in the extensive literature concerning data analysis to the essential nature of the process of investigation being done or to the assumptions that underlie its techniques; assumptions concerning the world and how it may be investigated. This omission has allowed a curious situation to develop: whilst the *practice* of data analysis demands a large degree of subjective choice on the part of the data analyst, the espoused *theory and philosophy* of data analysis is not sympathetic to this need. This chapter considers the discrepancy between the theory and practice in data analysis and the problems caused by a poorly defined underlying philosophy. We shall see both that the theory of data analysis embodies objectivist assumptions of an independent reality composed of entities, attributes and relationships, and that its techniques rely on there being a high level of agreement as to the nature of the present situation, what is 'the problem' and what any new information-system should do. This can cause many problems and makes them particularly unsuitable for use at the earliest stages of analysis, where it is just such things which are undecided, and which form the major subject for investigation and debate.

However, alternative forms of data analysis and modelling are possible, ones more suited to the requirements of early investigations of a problem situation. In the later part of the chapter we describe how such an alternative, interpretative form of data analysis can employ the idea of appreciation and later we shall see how it might be brought about using soft systems thinking.

## 7.2 DEVELOPMENT OF DATA ANALYSIS

Spending time and money on data analysis can be justified on three main grounds:

First, data are an important resource of the organisation and failing to investigate data will lead to a vital aspect of the situation being ignored. If an understanding of the organisation's data is desirable in any form of intervention in the organisation's affairs, then it is essential when the intervention concerns information provision. Whether one believes data to be a raw material from which processing can produce information or, as we have suggested, a selected set of facts that may be given meaning so as to be perceived as information, some understanding of the organisation's data is an essential step in deciding how to satisfy information needs.

Second, effective management of an organisation's data resource requires a complete and consistent description of that data, in a form that is independent of any specific storage mechanisms, hardware or software. Such descriptions have proved to be invaluable in the strategic planning of information-systems, to enable more productive application development and to aid in the task of maintenance. Those descriptions may only be produced through data analysis.

Finally, and most importantly, data analysis is required if data are to be stored, organised and used in the most effective way. The way in which the data are physically stored, whether in computer files or manually, has a large impact upon the efficiency with which the data may be retrieved and processed, and therefore upon the performance of any information-systems using that data. Modern methods of data storage such as databases provide for great flexibility in how items of data can be stored and subsequently later retrieved, but their advantages will be lost, it is often argued, if the design of the database does not reflect the 'true' structure of the organisation's data. This data structure is thought to remain relatively stable over time; unless the organisation moves into an entirely new line of business then the type of data required tomorrow will differ little from that required today. The processes which go on within the organisation(the procedures, job definitions, the way of doing things) are however more volatile and change much more frequently. If therefore analysis and design is based upon discovering what the organisation's true data structure *is* then the resulting information-systems and data storage designs will be relatively stable solutions to the organisation's information requirements. They should be capable of meeting both present and future requirements with minimum alteration.

It is probably the last of these reasons that has led to data analysis becoming a component of almost every approach for the development of information-systems. The widely used SSADM methodology (Cutts, 1987; Ashworth & Goodland, 1990; Downs *et al*, 1992; Eva, 1992; Weaver, 1993), for example, prescribes that an analysis of the data, its use and storage be done by using the several techniques of logical data modelling, normalisation and entity-life histories.

The emphasis given to data analysis by modern development methodologies is though absent from earlier suggestions for how to develop information-systems, especially those that pre-date the advent of database management systems. Methodologies such as ARDI

(Hartman *et al*, 1968), though extremely detailed prescriptions for the development of new information-systems, gave surprisingly little attention to data at all. There was no analysis of the nature or the structure of data and no consideration of the inter-relationships between separate items of data: data were discussed only *en-passim*, in respect to the processing that would be done upon them by programs and the file structures in which they would be physically held.

The change to the present situation where an understanding of data is seen as central to information-systems development could be attributed to a number of factors. Some are organisational, as with data becoming seen as a corporate resource requiring management and, more recently, capable of being used to gain competitive advantage. The single most important factor though was probably a purely technical one, in that large-scale databases become technically possible and products such as IBM's IMS software became commercially available. Large investments were made in purchasing software and the hardware that the resource-hungry packages required, so that organisations became very concerned to ensure that these were used efficiently and questions of how to organise data in the best possible way immediately came to the forefront of the concerns of IS. The pioneering work of Codd (1970) regarding the normalisation of relations and Chen's (1976) exposition of entity-relationship modelling therefore soon provided the basis for an extensive new literature, that concerning data analysis and modelling. This differed from previous discussions of data *storage* for it focused upon the intrinsic structure of the data itself, rather than the organisation of files, records or other physical mechanisms for holding data.

The early attempts to use database technology were not always successful, most notably when the ambition was to create organisation-wide management information-systems (Somogyi & Galliers, 1987). But there were many success stories and the attractions of a data-oriented approach to information-systems development have proved to be enduring. Well-structured organisational databases offer the ability to integrate separate processing requirements, to introduce control over the data resource and promise release from the fear of changing requirements. The 1980s and 1990s have therefore seen many more organisations adopting the 'database approach' and employing database technology as the basis for all of their data processing activities. And it seems unlikely that there will be any diminution of the importance of data analysis in the future; the emergence of object-oriented databases and the consequent search for object-oriented analysis methods suggest quite the opposite. The question of how to investigate the data components of a problem situation is therefore likely to remain a critical issue for the field of information systems.

## 7.3 NEW CHALLENGES

Despite the practical importance of the subject and its extensive literature, a weakness exists in that very little attention has so far been given to the process of inquiry that data analysis represents, or to the essential philosophy of that enquiry. This omission is of increasing importance as data analysis begins to be used earlier in the systems development process, and as thinking in the field of IS increasingly emphasises the social nature of organisations.

### 7.3.1 Changing use of data analysis

The world and the demands placed upon the IS developer have changed considerably since data analysis first emerged in the late 1960s. Data analysis techniques were originally used late in the development process and concentrated upon how to best physically store data. By the time they were employed the development process was well advanced and the data analysts already knew what data items were to be used by the information-system and the meaning of those data items was not in question. Over the last twenty years though the situation has changed.

The growing sophistication of data storage technologies very soon allowed a separation of discussion of physical design issues and the way that data would be used from discussion of 'conceptual data models'. These concentrated upon the essential nature and meaning of the data items and their inter-relationships, and would only later be translated into physical designs. The ANSI/SPARC three-level architecture for database systems formalised this distinction during the early 1970s in terms of the data models that might be provided at the internal, conceptual and external levels, and consequently between the data analysis activity producing each type of model.

Analysis of the essential nature and structure of data thus became 'de-coupled' from the detailed design of particular data storage mechanisms. One could begin to think about the type of data that was to be stored and what links existed between items of data well before one knew what hardware or software would eventually be used to store it or how it would be used by programs. At first this meant that data analysis might be used in systems analysis, rather than later in systems design, but over the years the techniques have gradually begun to be used still earlier in the development process. Their use is now being suggested at its very earliest beginnings: analysis of the organisation's data is used to create the enterprise models required by approaches like IBM's Business Systems Planning (BSP) and authors such as Ward *et al* (1990) and Olle *et al* (1991) suggest the use of data analysis in information-systems planning and business analysis.

When data analysis is used at the earliest stages of systems development the intent is often to produce high-level, abstracted and general data models of the organisation as a whole. Such data models are sometimes called 'enterprise models'. The value of such models lies in their stability and robustness with respect to change. They describe data requirements at a high level of abstraction, independently of any considerations of how the model might be reflected in physical data storage mechanisms or what use individual applications may make of the data stored within those mechanisms. Even though the organisation may purchase newer and better database management systems, may find new data processing requirements and introduce new applications, the enterprise model will remain valid and be useful as a blueprint against which change may be planned and considered.

But if data analysis techniques are used in such early stages of development they are being employed for different purposes than previously. Rather than being used to decide the best way of storing the data required to satisfy largely known requirements they are being used to demarcate and define the problem domain. And in the early stages of development, analysis encompasses fewer defined technical problems and many more social and political issues. The focus shifts from addressing questions of how to store data efficiently inside the computer to questions of what it is that the organisation wishes to achieve and how a balance may be achieved between the interests of different involved parties. Here a data model may easily become infused with political meanings and be used to legitimise or discredit a particular view of the organisation. These differences pose serious new challenges to data analysis.

## 7.3.2 New thinking in IS

The desire to use data analysis in the early stages of development has been fuelled by new ideas that are emerging in the field of information-systems. Of particular importance are those ideas which concern:

- The role of information-systems with respect to the business that they serve and the need for the development of information-systems to be closely linked to strategic planning of the organisation;
- The complex social and political nature of human organisations, including the construction of meaning that takes place within any human situation and the interpretative and communicative action that takes place in business and information-systems planning.

## 7.3.3 Linking of IS and business planning

Desiring a closer alignment of the planning of information-systems and the planning of the business is perhaps an inevitable consequence of recognising the importance of information-systems as a factor in strategic planning of the business. The work of such as Ives & Learmonth (1983), Wiseman & MacMillan (1984) and Porter & Millar (1985) has led to wide acceptance of the idea that information-systems do not merely facilitate existing business practices but may themselves shape the business, be used to secure competitive advantage or required through competitive necessity. They may, of course, also restrict freedom of action, for otherwise attractive business plans may be ruled out by the inability to create new, or modify existing, information-systems to support them. An example of this occurred in the late 1980s when it was widely reported that a planned merger between two UK mortgage lenders had to be abandoned due to the incompatibility of their computer systems.

It may well be that we are entering a new era of IS use, where businesses are critically dependent upon their investment in information-systems, and IS/IT planning:

> ... has crept unerringly away from the computer room, through the IS department and is now clearly a process that depends on users and senior management involvement for success. It has become difficult to separate aspects of IS/IT planning from business planning. Hence, it is important to use the tools and techniques of business strategic analysis and planning to cement that relationship. More specific IS/IT planning approaches have to be knitted into this pattern of business strategic management.
> (Ward et al, 1990 p.37)

If, though, a closer linking of business and information-systems planning is often called for, surveys of the practice of strategic information-systems planning (SISP) suggest that to achieve it is not simple. As Galliers (1991) reports:

> *While it is invariably argued that SISP should be closely associated with the business planning process (if only one part of it), it is still too often the case that the link is tenuous at best, with the two processes being undertaken in isolation from each other and with little business planner involvement in SISP and vice versa. p. 60.*

Part of the reason for this may be that information-system professionals and business planners often view the organisation through different mental models. A closer linking of information-systems work with planning of the business may require IS practitioners to abandon not only long established though outmoded models of organisations and decision-making but also the certainties that exist when IS work is envisaged merely as the satisfaction through technology of given data processing requirements. They may now have to embrace instead the uncertainties and value-laden questions that are more familiar to the social scientists. This is already happening to some extent, as IS thinking begins to take greater account of the social and cultural contexts in which information-systems are placed.

### 7.3.4 Concern for organisational cultures

Gaining an understanding of the organisation and the business that an information-system is to serve has, of course, long been seen as a prerequisite for development. For development to be more closely allied to strategic planning though 'understanding the served business' must mean more than just investigating the present business procedures. IS professionals must be able to comprehend and perhaps contribute to the debates about what the organisation might or might not aim at, and how it might strive to achieve those objectives in the future. The need therefore arises for IS practitioners to understand the images which organisations have of themselves and their environment and IS thinking is becoming increasingly influenced by the models of organisations and organisational behaviour used in the social sciences. The simple, 'hard' systems thinking model that has influenced IS thinking so strongly in the past is that organisations can be fully understood as being goal-seeking, adaptive-regulatory mechanisms. This is now being rejected in favour of more complex systems models of human organisations as purposeful, socio-political systems in which shared meaning and symbolic relationships are maintained and modified through human discourse and interaction.

A good example of this is the literature concerned with improving the 'organisational fit' of information-systems. This means ensuring that information-systems are designed to be not only technically efficient but also appropriate to the power structures and culture of the organisation that is to use them. The conclusions of such as Markus & Robey (1983) or Pliskin *et al* (1993) are that care must be taken to ensure that an information-system 'fits' its organisational context of use and that their designers should be aware of the *organisational culture* including actual and perceived power relationships.

Such thoughts are still relatively novel to the field of IS and one would find it hard, perhaps impossible, to identify an IS methodology that includes such considerations. Other management disciplines have, though, long discussed the importance of cultures, the way in which they become enshrined and reflected by language and the extent to which they guide both management thinking and the observable structures and actions of the organisation. Pettigrew (1979), for example, identifies symbol construction as :

*... a vehicle for group and organizational conception. As a group or organization at birth represents its situation to itself and to the outside world it emphasizes, distorts, and ignores and thereby attaches names and values to its structure, activities, purposes, and even the physical fabric around it. The symbols that arise out of these processes - the organization's vocabulary, the design of the organization's buildings, the beliefs about the use and distribution of power and privilege, the rituals and myths which legitimate those distributions - have significant functional consequences for the organization. pp. 574-575.*

An information-system developer who makes no attempt to understand the culture and symbol construction, present and historical, within a problem situation would then be at a loss to understand the context of a new information-system. In failing to empathise with the way in which potential users understand their world they might easily design information-systems that breach particular, perfectly rational in their own terms, norms or taboos.

Pfeffer (1981) argues that organisations can be legitimately understood not only in terms of a functional purpose (the manufacture of cars, the sale of products and services) but also both as political arenas in which power is exercised and as:

*... social systems populated by individuals who come to the system with norms, values, and expectations and with the necessity of developing understandings of the world around them so there can be enough predictability for them to take some action. p. 4*

Pfeffer concludes that gaining an understanding of organisations therefore requires two distinct levels of analysis. One is concerned with the organisational actions and decisions that have observable, substantive outcomes such as inventory levels or the average time taken to satisfy an order. The other is concerned with understanding how such organisational activities are perceived, interpreted and legitimated. Information-systems development techniques have traditionally concentrated upon the former, identifying task responsibilities, charting the flow of materials, data, etc. An important consequence of the new thinking about information-systems is that they should also attend to the latter.

## 7.4   DATA ANALYSIS AS A MEANS OF ENQUIRY

How this might be done with respect to data analysis is not obvious, for the literature is remarkably bereft of attempts to ally data analysis with any sociological paradigm or to justify its techniques in terms of the nature of social reality or how human beings make sense of their world.

Data analysis and modelling are widely assumed to be 'neutral' or value-free. This arises from the claim that data analysis merely uncovers an independently existing, objectively true, structure of the data in a problem domain, recording this structure through some form of conceptual data model. Whether this model is a relational model (Codd, 1970), entity-relationship model (Chen, 1976), RM/T model (Codd, 1979) or object-oriented (Schlaer & Mellor, 1988; Coad & Yourdon, 1990; Rumbaugh *et al*, 1991; Kim 1990; Hughes 1991) it is usually presented as descriptive of what Cutts (1987) describes as the generic underlying structure of the organisation's data. When combined with an ontological use of the concept of 'system' this leads to representations of data analysis as an uncomplex (though admittedly sometimes complicated) process concerned with the creation of models that describe precisely the real-world. The commitment to creating data models that reflect the real-world is extremely important, for it suggests a particular philosophical location for data analysis as an organised means of rational enquiry.

When data analysis is used as part of systems development it is being employed as a means of enquiry, and can therefore be considered in relation to the general model of organised enquiry shown in Figure 7.1. This is based upon the model of research and enquiry proposed by Checkland (1985) and identifies three major components to enquiry. These are: an intellectual framework of ideas through which any investigation will be conducted; a methodology which will allow that framework of ideas to be applied and used; a specific application area to which use of the methodology will be directed.

The intellectual framework will always include both a 'philosophy' which will orientate the enquiry in a particular direction and a set of concepts through which understanding of a particular situation may be structured and discussed. The philosophy of enquiry is itself composed of several parts. Ontological assumptions are beliefs concerning the nature of the physical and social world, whilst epistemological assumptions relate the way in which that world may be validly investigated and what will be considered as valid knowledge about the world. Ethical values may also be made explicit, constraining the ways in which enquiry is conducted, the purposes for which it may be used and the kind of changes that the enquiry may attempt to engender in a situation.

The philosophy will be made extant through certain concepts or ideas, through which particular problem situations may be understood and discussed. Particular disciplines may have, in addition, what we shall call their own 'mythology', consisting of untestable assertions about the way things work or happen which provide coherence to the ontology and epistemology.

All of these conceptual components will then be operationalised through a particular methodology. The methodology will allow for the use of particular methods and techniques, and define the research methods that are considered appropriate and acceptable.

There has been much reflection upon all of these components with respect to the natural sciences and to the various systems approaches (OR, soft systems etc) described previously. It is therefore relatively easy to consider them in the terms of Figure 7.1. Comparing data analysis, whether as found in composite methodologies or as used in its own right as an approach to development, with the model of Figure 7.1 is not so easy to do.

There is not much difficulty in identifying the methodology, methods and techniques of data analysis for it is these that are widely described in standard texts; indeed, refinement of these has been the main concern of most of the published literature. The concepts used in data analysis are also reasonably easily found, and we can see how the set of these has grown

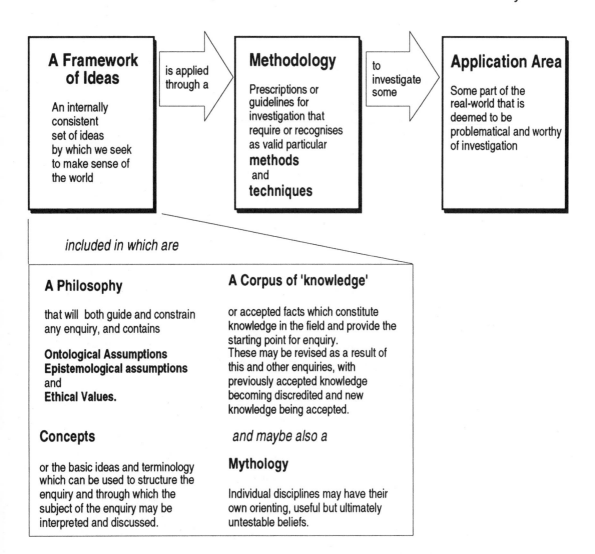

**Figure 7.1**     *A general model of organised, coherent enquiry*

over the years; concepts such as 'file' and 'record' pre-date the computer, concepts of 'entity and 'relationship' have become widely known since their introduction in the late 1960s and the recent interest in object-oriented methods has led to new additions, such as 'inheritance' and 'service'.

The ethics of data analysis may be assumed to be similar to those of IS development as a whole, though these are certainly not clearly defined. The encouragement of participation by users as being a morally correct thing to do (Mumford *et al* 1978; Mumford& Henshall 1979) and the codes of professional conduct of organisations such as the British Computer Society are though some evidence of extant ethical contributions to the field of IS.

Data analysis even has a small, though influential, mythology of its own. Statements such as "Data is a resource of the modern organisation" are not testable hypotheses but are extremely useful in orienting IS work. If we begin to think about data as a resource, as we do for finance or personnel, then this leads us to think that it may need to be protected or controlled. Even the fact that data has, in many other ways, little in common with resources such as men, money or materials may be enlightening. The idea that 'data are a resource' is therefore not a concept of the same kind as 'entity' or 'record' but provides coherence to the use of such concepts, and it is such ideas that we label collectively as mythology. The reader should note however that this term is not used in any pejorative sense; mythology is both useful and valuable for enquiry.

When, though, we turn to considering the philosophical assumptions of data analysis we meet with problems; its presuppositions have rarely been made explicit, few authors declare the basic assumptions of their work and little attention is given to understanding data analysis through social science typologies such as that of Burrell & Morgan (1979). Work such as that reported by Hirschheim & Klein (1989) however emphasises the important effect that the different assumptions made during systems development may have upon its results.

### 7.4.1 Subjectivism and objectivism

A useful starting point is to follow Klein & Hirschheim (1987) in distinguishing between some extreme possibilities of ontology (beliefs concerning the nature of the world) and epistemology (beliefs concerning how the world may be investigated).

For ontology we may identify two extreme positions of realism and nominalism. The realist position assumes that there exists a common external reality with predetermined nature and structure. This external reality, which is the ultimate source of all experience and observations, exists independently of any observer. Set against this is the nominalist position that reality is over-overwhelmingly complex, confusing and constantly changing. No-one (except God) may have true knowledge of its nature, and because it is observed by human beings there can be no single account of reality but only different perceptions of it. Reality does not exist 'out there' separate from the observer, but is a social construct, coloured and distorted by both sedimented and consciously adopted cultural beliefs and values.

With regard to epistemology we may identify two extreme positions of positivism and interpretivism. Positivism is characterised by a belief in the existence of causal relationships and general laws that may be identified and investigated through rational action. In contrast, interpretivism allows that no individual account of reality can ever be proven as more correct than another since we are unable to compare them against any objective knowledge of a 'true' reality. Even when two observers experience the same phenomena the true meaning for each may be different.

This then provides us with two continuums which can be combined (Figure 7.2) to provide a framework for thinking about the philosophy of enquiry used in data analysis, and in particular, whether it follows an objectivist or subjectivist paradigm.

If data analysis lies, broadly, within an objectivist paradigm then the nature of the problem domain would be taken as given; it would be assumed that 'real-world' data structures exist, independent of the data analyst and that causal relationships within these may be identified and investigated. The alternative subjectivist paradigm would hold that,

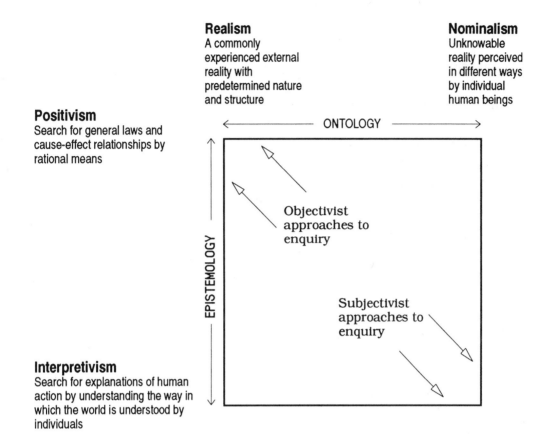

**Realism**
A commonly experienced external reality with predetermined nature and structure

**Nominalism**
Unknowable reality perceived in different ways by individual human beings

**Positivism**
Search for general laws and cause-effect relationships by rational means

ONTOLOGY

EPISTEMOLOGY

Objectivist approaches to enquiry

Subjectivist approaches to enquiry

**Interpretivism**
Search for explanations of human action by understanding the way in which the world is understood by individuals

**Figure 7.2**     *Framework for discussing the underlying philosophy of data analysis*

whether or not there exists any objective 'real-world', this cannot ever be directly cognised by human beings but only ever interpreted through the socially created and transmitted concepts and preconceptions of the observer.

The available evidence does suggest that data analysis follows an objectivist paradigm, characterised by ontological assumptions that are realist and epistemological assumptions that are positivist. Within the literature many of the *en-passim* statements made, and the attempted definitions of such core concepts as 'entity', do suggest acceptance of the existence of a singular, objective reality and hint towards a positivist orientation. This is most evident in the literature when the primary aim of data modelling is taken to be the design of data storage mechanisms which 'mirror' the real-world (the original use of data modelling), as in statements such as:

> "By definition, any database contains representatives of certain real-world entities (e.g., suppliers, parts, and shipments, in the case of the suppliers-and-parts database). Since entities are distinguishable in the real world, their representatives in the database must also be distinguishable." Date (1990) p. 596.

It can though also be found when data modelling is being used as a means of initial problem definition. For example, in SSADM (where the term 'system' is used as synonymous with real-world data processing arrangements) we find the claims that:

> "*All systems possess an underlying generic entity model which remains fairly static in time. The entity model reflects the logic of the system data, not the physical implementation.*"
> (Cutts 1987, p. 23)

> "*SSADM is a data-driven method. This means that there is a basic assumption that systems have an underlying, generic, data structure which changes very little over time, although processing requirements may change. Within SSADM, this underlying data structure is modelled from an early stage.*" Ashworth & Goodland 1990, p. 10.

The contention that data analysis is primarily an objectivist means of enquiry is also supported by the few attempts that have been made to examine its basic assumptions. For example:

- Wood-Harper & Fitzgerald (1982) argue that data analysis is based upon a science paradigm (rather than a systems paradigm) on the basis that its objectives are analysis rather than problem-solving and that its unstated assumptions are essentially reductionist. This taxonomic classification accords well with the general perception of data analysis as one of the more rigorous and precise techniques of ISD; whereas techniques such as data flow diagramming may be intuitively attractive and have proved to be practically useful, the claim that various forms of data model are based upon the axioms of mathematical set theory (a claim partly challenged by Kent, 1978) has imbued them with greater academic respectability.

- Klein & Hirschheim (1987) identify the most familiar and widely used forms of data-focused approach such as entity modelling as following an objectivist paradigm and describing the essential difference between this and the alternative subjectivist position being that:

  > "*The difference is whether one believes that a data model 'reflects' reality or consists of subjective meanings and thereby constructs reality. The implication for subjectivism is that the immediate social milieu and society at large pre-orders what subjectively is experienced as reality...*
  >
  > *... From this point of view a data model is correct if it is consistent with the perception of the Universe of Discourse as constructed by institutional programming, sedimentation and tradition. In contrast, the objectivist view holds that language neutrally depicts reality which is the same for all regardless of culture and individual perception.*" p. 9

  Klein and Hirschheim conclude that alternative, subjectivist approaches deserve further attention but have not been developed to a sufficiently practical level.

- A rare discussion of the philosophy of object-oriented modelling is provided by Wand (1989). In this the formal model of objects that is developed is a conservative one, incorporating many assumptions of longer established data modelling practice. The ontology described is realist in that 'object' is used as a label for things of the real-world, where:

*"The world is made of objects. Objects describe concrete beings, that is, specific entities rather than types or classes" p. 550*

*"Objects are viewed here as describing real things" p. 552*

*"... objects gain their importance because they reflect a 'natural' view of the world we are modelling (abstracting) in our software. This being the case, if we view programs as models of some reality, the use of objects amounts to adopting programming and database constructs that are direct mappings of real concepts." p. 538*

Iivari (1991) concludes that the ontology of data-focused approaches includes viewing information-systems as primarily technical systems that manipulate and disseminate data/information, data as descriptive facts, and a formal-rational view of organisations. The epistemology of the data-focused approaches is found to be positivist.

## 7.5  SOME DIFFICULTIES CONCERNING DATA ANALYSIS

The available evidence therefore suggests that data analysis is an objectivist means of enquiry having at its heart the premise that data structures exist, independently of the observer, in the real-world. It is therefore not surprising that the usual starting point for data analysis is identification of existing data stores and real-world things or events, or that when a data model has been created it is checked by comparison to known application requirements. An independently existing reality is thus accepted as both the ultimate source of knowledge for creating a data model, and the means by which the integrity and correctness of a data model may be validated.

This does not rule out the possibility that it could be employed as part of an alternative paradigm, or of a different form of data analysis being employed within a subjectivist approach to development. Before thinking about what such an alternative form of data analysis might consist of, it is worth noting that data analysis is not without a substantial subjective content already. This is realised by most practitioners and by a few authors but it is not admitted by the theory of data analysis. This presents that theory with certain problems and paradoxes. These are not insurmountable in practice, and much of the 'craft knowledge' of the data analyst lies in knowing how they may be overcome. But that they arise at all, and that the means by which they are overcome are incommensurate with ontological assumptions that are realist, indicates problems with the view of data analysis as a necessarily neutral investigation of real-world data structures.

### 7.5.1  Identifying entities or objects

If one takes seriously the claim that during data analysis one is uncovering the 'true' structure of data and that data models reflect an absolute external reality then several questions immediately arise with regard to how a data analyst identifies 'entities' or 'objects' and uses these to categorise and compartmentalise the problem domain. The most obvious of these is how one decides which of all the infinitely large number of entity-types available should be included in, and which omitted from, a data model. Directives to identify those things that are of 'relevance and importance to the organisation' only pose further problems: How does one identify what is or is not 'relevant'? What do we mean by 'relevant'? To whom are they relevant and in what context?

Few texts discuss how the initial identification of entities or objects may be done, and some rather suggest that there is no problem, suggesting that *"... the world being modelled is made of objects ... objects are just there for the picking!"* (Meyer, 1988 p. 51) or that *"Identifying objects is pretty easy to do. Start out by focussing on the problem at hand and ask yourself 'What are the things in this problem?'"* (Schlaer & Mellor, 1988 p. 15). These views are difficult to reconcile with observations of novice and inexperienced data analysts who frequently find great difficulty in initially identifying a set of 'relevant' entities or objects.

When suggestions for how to identify entities and objects are provided in the literature these are drawn from the 'craft knowledge' of experienced practitioners rather than being derived from any theory of how human beings make sense of their world or inquire into problematical situations. Discussions with probable users, investigating the contents of existing data stores, studying written problem statements (who prepared these is not clear) and intuition and experience are certainly all practically useful; in the last resort however the data analyst remains forced to make subjective choices of what are relevant entities or objects.

Of course, if data analysis is being used at a late stage of development then knowledge of what the information-system is to do and how it will do it will enable us to side-step the issue. Then we may define 'entity' pragmatically as being *"... something about which you need to store information, and which has a unique key"* (Longworth, 1992 p. 73). This is not much help though if data analysis is to be used early in development, when its role is to investigate exactly what things we need to store information about.

## 7.5.2 Ontological or epistemological devices

The lack of attention given to the question of how to identify entities, objects and the like might be explained by the original use of data analysis in the later stages of development, where it is relatively straightforward to identify the 'things' about which data are required to be held. It was in this context that entities were first presented as generalised descriptions of real-world 'things', and authors such as Martin (1975) explicitly describe an entity as something which exists in the real-world; entity occurrences are merely particular identifiable instances of the same real-world 'thing'. Chen's (1976) widely quoted paper shares this same perspective in stating that:

> *"The entity-relationship model adopts the more natural view that the real world consists of entities and relationships."* p. 9

As use of data analysis has shifted to earlier stages of development where 'the problem' is less well defined, one would have hoped that proponents of data analysis would be clearer as to exactly what they meant by terms such as 'entity', and to declare in particular whether they are used as ontological labels for parts of the real-world or as epistemological devices through which the nature of the real-world may be explored. Unfortunately, this has not occurred and there has been continued reliance upon pragmatic, 'common-sense' definitions.

Many authors merely add to Chen's (1976) rather loose definition of an entity, as *"a 'thing' which can be distinctly identified"*, the requirement that knowledge of that thing is important to the information-system or of interest to the organisation. Maciaszek (1990), for example, defines an entity as:

> *"...an object which can be distinctly identified and is important to the information system of the organization" p. 31*

whilst Downs *et al* (1992) describe entities within SSADM as:

> *"...things of interest to the organization. They may physically exist, such as Borrowers. They may be transient such as Loans or even represent aspirations, such as Reservations. Unfortunately there is no simple or precise definition of an entity. In practice, if it is something that you want to store information about, it is likely to be an entity. " p. 123*

## Common to object-oriented thinking

The recent interest in object-oriented analysis has led to some re-interpretation of the nature of data analysis and at least some suggestions that a data model might be an epistemological device, a coherent means of investigating the problem domain rather than being a description of the real-world. Schlaer & Mellor (1988), for example, talk of a data model being:

> *"...a thinking tool used to aid in the formalization of knowledge. It helps us work out how we want to think about a problem: the terms we need to define, the assumptions we make in selecting those terms, and the consistency of our definitions and assumptions." p. 7*

Odell (1992) too emphasises that:

> *"Object-oriented (O-O) analysis should not model reality - rather it should model the way reality is understood by people. The understanding and knowledge of people is the essential component in developing systems." p. 45*

Unfortunately, there are also signs that the literature concerning object-oriented analysis is inheriting some of the lack of conceptual clarity of its predecessors. The comparison of different object-oriented analysis approaches made by de Champeaux & Faure (1992) compares different approaches only in terms of technical details such as whether the influence of re-use (desirable from an implementation perspective) affects the definition of classes, the diagramming conventions used and whether or not the different approaches allow multiple inheritance. Fundamental questions of ontology and epistemology are, significantly, not considered at all. And in much of the O-O literature the concept of 'object' is merely *described*, in that objects have identity, state, behaviour and properties and can be characterised by the set of operations that can be performed on it or by it and its possible states. However, it is not *explained* in terms of any meta-level model of human sense-making, so that what an object is or what an object model represents remains somewhat ambiguous.

When object orientation is being applied at the implementation level of database design and programming then, as before with previous data analysis approaches, the problem domain is so well defined that this may not be too serious. To define object as *"..a named representation of a real-world entity"* (McFadden & Hoffer, 1991 p. 189) or state that *"Any real-world entity is an object, with which is associated a system-wide unique identifier"* (Kim, 1990 p. 13) is at these stages not likely to affect the investigation's outcomes too much. More serious consequences result if we assume that there exists a one-to-one correspondence between the objects within the computer or data model and parts of external reality during the earlier stage of problem definition; the likelihood of such assumptions being made for object models seems to be greater than for other forms of data model, and we cannot but agree that:

> *"The confusion between objects in the system and objects in the world, and the lack of an intermediate conceptual model, are cause for concern. The idea that object-oriented systems are a 'natural' representation of the world is a seductive but dangerous over-simplification. In reality, the fact that the object model seems so close to reality makes it far easier to misuse it than other modelling techniques which do not purport to represent the world so directly." McGinnes (1992) p. 13*

### Need for clear distinction

Whether working with object-oriented ideas or more established forms of data modelling, the danger that arises from not being clear whether core concepts such as 'entity' or 'object' are epistemological or ontological devices is that one is forced to fall back upon 'common-sense', example-led definitions that may be inconsistent. For example, Rishe's (1988) definition of an abstract object is as:

> *"...a non-value object in the real world. An abstract object can be, for example, a tangible item (such as a person, a table, a country), or an event (such as an offering of a course by an instructor), or an idea (such as a course)." (p. 5)*

One must question whether 'a country' is a tangible item in the real-world or rather an idea shared by many individuals. Consider, for example, the aspirations of many Middle Eastern and East European citizens for regional independence. Did a real-world thing called Slovenia exist in December 1991 when some inhabitants of Yugoslavia had declared its independent existence? Did it exist in January 1992 when the European Community but not the United Nations or the government of Yugoslavia officially recognised its existence? The answers, of course, depend on how we define 'a country', and this is socially and politically decided; it is not an absolute characteristic of something existing in an independent 'real-world'.

## 7.5.3 Dealing with multiple views

If data analysis is rooted in objectivist assumptions then these include a realist belief in a common external reality with predetermined nature and structure, existing independently of any observer; if two observers provide different accounts of reality, then this can only be due to imperfect observation tools, failure to fully observe some aspects or wilful distortion of their findings. The theory of data analysis does not therefore allow for the possibility of multiple perceived realities and many, equally valid, perceptions of a problem domain.

The consequences of this may be given form by rendering into IS terms a classification problem originally identified by Law & Lodge (1984). This concerns the predicament faced by a data analyst charged with the remit of producing a conceptual data model of the flora and fauna of New Guinea. The task may not be accomplishable if the theory of data analysis alone is used, for that theory does not recognise that the situation might be perceived in fundamentally different ways; the anthropological study of Bulmer (1967) suggests that this will cause insurmountable difficulties concerning the flightless creature called, in the West, the cassowary.

Europeans and the Karam natives of the region perceive and classify the creature in very different ways. Europeans, seeing similarities with creatures such as emus and ostriches, classify the cassowary as a type of 'bird'. The Karam people though reject including the cassowary in their class of 'yakt', which covers flying birds and bats, placing it instead in an alternative taxon, that of 'kobtiy'. This is in no sense a perverse or foolish decision, for the Karam recognise as important a different set of similarities by which to classify the cassowary, and their classification is perfectly respectable in terms of its coherence and its usefulness to them. Their rejection of the cassowary being 'a bird' lies partly in questions of behaviour and habitat; for the Karam something is only a bird if it can fly and inhabits the air; cassowaries are virtually wingless, flightless and inhabit the forest. But it is also based upon cultural factors. The Karam eat the brains of birds and mammals and whereas birds have fragile skulls the cassowary has a large bony casque protecting a disappointingly small potential meal. Furthermore the religious beliefs and mythology of the Karam provide the cassowary with special status. so that the killing of cassowaries is surrounded with a significant number of taboos that govern how the kill should be made and the subsequent behaviour of the hunter.

Clearly then the data model that our data analyst produces will be very different depending upon whether it shows the reality perceived by the Karam or the westerner. The generic classes of which the cassowary and other creatures are considered sub-types will differ, the attributes associated with particular classes would vary and one data model could contain a whole range of classes that the other would not consider to be 'things of interest', for certain types of creature have religious significances to the Karam that are unrecognised by the Westerner. Any data model produced in this situation will encapsulate many subjective and inter-subjective choices, some deliberate and some unconsciously accepted, about how the situation is to be seen.

### 7.5.4 Compartmentalising the problem domain

A data analyst must, in choosing the entity-types for modelling, define boundaries and compartmentalise the real-world into separate 'things'. This is not always easy, and any reader with practical experience of data analysis will recognise the type of problem posed by Figure 7.3.

The interesting point is that such questions do not present insurmountable difficulties in the real-world. Somehow, people do manage to create library databases. The reason is that the sort of questions raised in Figure 7.3 are soon resolvable in *a given context*. If we know the use that will be made of the data model there is a basis for making decisions about what to include and how to divide up the problem domain. For example, a public library is unlikely

## What is a book ?

Imagine that the task is to create a data model of a library. An obvious candidate for one type of 'thing' which should be included in the data model is 'book'. But what exactly is meant by 'a book'?

Write your own a definition of 'book' and then consider the following questions:

- ❏ *Is the 'The Tempest' by William Shakespeare that resides on the bookshelf in my office a book ?*
- ❏ *Is the 'The Tempest' that I have at home also a book ?*
- ❏ *Are they the same book?*

This may cause you to amend your definition of 'book'. Very probably you will want to differentiate between such things as 'book' and 'copy of a book'. Now use your amended definitions for the following questions:

- ❏ *I also own 'The Collected Works of William Shakespeare', part of which contains the same text as my bookshelf version of 'The Tempest'.*
  *Are those pages a 'copy of a book' in their own right ?*

- ❏ *If I photocopy 'The Tempest' from my bookshelf, have I created a new book or a new copy of a book?*

- ❏ *If the bookshelf version, my newly created copy and an elegantly leather bound, first folio edition are all examples of 'copy of book', then why is the latter so much more valuable?*

By now more complicated ideas such as 'published opus' , 'personal copy of text' and attributes such as 'rarity' will probably have arisen.

Did these things exist in the real world all along or have we just created them by defining the terms and understanding the world in terms of their existence ?

Can we claim to still be creating a 'true' model of the world?

**Figure 7.3**     *An exercise to illustrate the problem*

to have a first folio Shakespeare in its collection, and is only interested in knowing of the existence and whereabouts of the type of things which it owns. If the library supervisor is asked "Do you have 'The Tempest by William Shakespeare'?" they will readily interpret this as a request to know whether they have some physical artefact containing the text of Shakespeare's work. It does not really matter, for *the purposes of the library*, whether those physical artefacts are described as 'books' or as 'copies of books'. Here the context gives meaning to the way in which reality is perceived, and provides the basis for drawing boundaries between parts of reality in any data analysis exercise.

The potential for experiencing difficulties and constraining the future course of events in undesirable ways is greatest where there is no clear context for use. And there is least of such a context for use in the early stages of development and in information-systems planning. Here the aim of data analysis is often to create very high-level 'enterprise' data models of the organisation as a whole. Although these are intended to be independent of any design considerations, and unaffected by later data processing requirements, we must remember that this type of data model will eventually be translated into data storage mechanisms that will be used by a very large number of different users, and employed for many different purposes. The meanings and world-views that are captured within them will therefore influence greatly what is done later.

Kent (1978) points out that where data are employed within a single context, such as being used within a single application, then semantic ambiguities are manageable; human beings have the ability to resolve differences in meaning in a largely automatic and unconscious way through understanding the context of use. But when the same data storage mechanism serves many different users and many different applications then any ambiguities must be identified and resolved. This principle is practically recognised in that the automated generation of large shared databases is usually done using the set of definitions of the meaning of each entity, object attribute etc in the data dictionary. The technologically imposed requirement for such definitions to exist does not though guarantee that those definitions will be well thought out. The meanings encapsulated in enterprise data models and their data dictionary definitions will subsequently affect the design of many shared databases. How more vital it is, then, that data analysts be aware of the import of, and the essentially subjective nature, of their decisions. How more important it is that they give consideration of the process by which meaning attribution takes place, of the system of enquiry that is being used to investigate the problem domain, and of any constraints imposed by its underlying philosophy and the concepts that it employs.

### 7.5.5  Continuing identity over time

In the everyday world human beings regard parts of the world as maintaining the same identity over time, of being 'the same thing', even though many of their characteristics may change. The unfortunate amputee is no less a human being and in no way a different individual despite the loss of a limb or certain physical abilities. The river which I see today is no less the same river as I saw yesterday, though its level, course and chemical composition may have changed and even the water molecules within it are not the same molecules which composed it yesterday. The Greek philosopher Heraclitus was factually correct in his observation that we can never step into the same river twice, but it normally serves us quite well to believe that we may. In data analysis though the conservation of identity as a particular instance of an entity is more problematical.

Difficulties about the maintenance identity have long been recognised in philosophy, as exemplified through the conundrum known as the Ship of Theseus. Figure 7.4 presents this, together with our own updated version entitled 'the database administrator's dilemma.

---

### The Ship of Theseus problem

Theseus sets sail from Athens in a ship. As the voyage progresses so various parts of the ship are lost at sea and replaced, until, eventually, none of the original components of the ship remain.
A sailor following Theseus collects all the lost parts of Theseus' ship and later re-assembles them in their original positions.

*Which of the two ships now existing, the ship containing Theseus or the re-assembled ship, is the ship that sailed from Athens ?*

---

### The Database Administrator's Dilemma

A database administrator is in charge of a database storing records of motor cars.
One car is severely damaged in a crash, and many panels and parts of the car are replaced, and the car is repainted in a different colour.
In what way is this the same vehicle as the one that existed before the crash?

*What changes should the database administrator allow to the database?*

---

**Figure 7.4**     *Classical and modern versions of the problems of maintaining identity*

The dilemma for the database administrator is whether the stored details of the crashed car should be amended (in which case we lose data concerning the car before the changes) or there should now be two records held in the database referring to the same car, one describing the car before the crash and a second describing the car after its re-build. In this latter case the stored data no longer reflects the real-world as such, for we are now building a history of the past and present states of certain things in the world. And since we may need to introduce a new entity such as 'accident' or 're-registration' to link related records together, are these being included as a requirement of reality or as a requirement of our modelling?

In practice such problems are resolved by reference to defined rules. One might for example in the case of the vehicle database obey the rule that if the registration number of two vehicles is the same then they are considered to be one and the same vehicle for the purposes of the database. Such rules are though arbitrary, however sensible or practically useful they might be. They are choices of the designer, not imposed by any aspect of an external reality. After all, if we re-register a Ford saloon and a Porsche sports car such that each now has the vehicle registration that previously belonged to the other, then we do not normally consider the Porsche of the present to be 'the same car' as the Ford of the past; the essential identity of each is the same as before, they merely have different registration numbers to those they had previously. It is important then that we understand that a data model never reflects an absolute reality but only shows a chosen way of understanding reality.

Questions regarding conservation of identity are clearly related to the subjective way in which the problem domain is compartmentalised, what entities were first identified as important and relevant and how those were defined. As Kent (1978) says

*"There is no neutral set of categories. The set of categories to be maintained in an information system must be specified for that system " p. 13.*

So long as we remember this and understand the conventions used in a particular data model then it may be useful to us, just as many other forms of model are usable and useful even though they do not reflect reality. In road atlases, for example, we expect that the spatial relationships between London and other cities to be represented in a way that is analogous to the position of those cities in the real world that is experienced whilst driving a car. Road atlases though often represent London as a large red area; this does not mean that we expect to find the streets and pavements of the real-world conurbation of London to be painted red. We understand the conventions used and the purposes for which the road atlases may be used.

### 7.5.6 Attribution of identity

A final problem, again related to identity, concerns when we may attribute or deny identity, recognising that some example of an entity has been newly created or has ceased to exist. For example, do we recognise an example of an order as having come into existence when placed by the customer or when received by the supplier? Or to take a more extreme example, if our categorisations include 'human being', then when do we recognise the existence of a new human being? Most data storage mechanisms, and therefore most data models, adopt the moment of birth as the deciding event. The arbitrariness of such identifications can be seen though by considering the difficulty raised by the rights of embryos of differing ages during debates concerning abortion.

Once again, there can be no 'right' answer to this problem of when an example of an entity becomes an example of that entity; a subjective choice must be made. Part of the task of defining the categorisations which will be used to examine the problem domain will be to decide *what we want to define* the life-history events of those categorisations to be.

## 7.6 POSSIBILITY OF AN ALTERNATIVE FORM OF DATA ANALYSIS

From the previous sections it should be clear that, in practice, data analysis must include a large degree of subjective choice. This subjectivity exists whether or not the philosophy of the data-focused approaches uses the concept 'entity' (or 'object') to be an ontological device.

If entities *are* taken to have real-world existence then the analyst must be choosing, from the infinitely large number of entities that exist and might in principle be included in a conceptual data model, only some entities as being 'relevant' and suitable for inclusion. Over twenty years worth of literature provides no suggestion that this is done other than subjectively, as a choice of the analyst. This means that, however well researched and rigorous are the techniques for manipulation and refinement of the conceptual data model, they ultimately rely upon a subjective and interpretative identification of entities or objects. Consequently, the process of creating such a model is not value-free and the resulting data model is not 'neutral'; it will be affected very much by the values, beliefs and expectations of those creating it.

If real-world existence *is not* assumed then conceptual data models are epistemological devices and entities or objects are, by definition, subjectively created by the analyst in order to understand the world. In either case, the conceptual data model cannot be described as a model *of* the real-world but only as an *interpretation* of reality.

The subjective content of data analysis has been admitted by the more thoughtful writers on the subject. For example, authors as early as Chen (1976) emphasised the importance of making conscious *decisions* about what is or is not a thing of relevance to the organisation, and of what should be included in, or excluded from, discussion. Kroenke (1992) captures the essential point well in stating:

> Sometimes, when evaluating alternatives, project team members engage in discussions and arguments about which data model best represents the real world. These discussions are misguided. Databases do not model the real world, though it is a common misconception that they do.
>
> Rather, databases are models of users' models of the world (or, more to the point, of their business environment). The question to ask when evaluating alternative data models is not 'Does this design accurately represent the real world?' but rather 'Does this design accurately represent the users' model of his or her environment?' The goal is to develop a design that fits the user's mental conception of what he or she wants to track." p. 117

Unfortunately, for every statement of this kind the literature provides ten or twenty others that commit data analysis to the objectivist paradigm. This is perhaps due to there being in the theory of data analysis no declared model of human sense-making and none of the techniques of data modelling assist by making the required subjectivity explicit and open to debate.

As we begin to use data analysis for new purposes, earlier in development and in more socially and politically turbulent settings, then this becomes increasingly unacceptable. It becomes then increasingly important to provide data analysis with a theory of human sense-making, of how human beings understand and interact with the apparently chaotic reality that surrounds them.

### 7.6.1 Understanding data analysis differently

Having looked at the problems that arise from believing that the world may be understood in a neutral, value-free way we should perhaps begin to consider data analysis from a different perspective. If we try to understand the process of data analysis against a phenomenological model of human sense-making then data analysis may be interpreted in an altogether different way.

Let us remind ourselves of the point made back in Chapter 5 that appreciation acts, in effect, as a form of cognitive filter; it enables organisations and individuals to 'understand' the world but also restricts understanding. It allows certain facts about reality to be recognised as meaningful data and uses these to create the observer's understanding of reality, but filters out those facts which are not meaningful in terms of the cognitive framework that it creates.

So a business organisation may, for example, in the normal course of events not recognise the existence of those things called 'hospital' and hold no stored organisational knowledge about them since they have no relevance to the company's interests. If however the company enrols its employees in a private medical insurance scheme then decisions may need to be made which require knowledge about local hospitals and hospitals then become relevant to the organisation's interests. Attribute values of individual hospitals such as their location, number of beds etc. then become data for the organisation.

Against the background of such a model of human sense-making much of the present practice of data analysis becomes explicable. For example, in practice most effort in doing data analysis is expended, not upon operating the relatively mechanical operation of techniques of normalisation but upon building a rich understanding of an often novel business situation and *negotiating the meaning* of data items with the business users. The hours spent with the users to formulate definitions of entities and attributes to include in a data dictionary are not, as is sometimes arrogantly implied, about rationalising the users' ambiguities and confused terminology but about arriving at a shared interpretation of the problem domain. This may be understood in terms of the appreciative model as being necessary, as the data analyst strives to understand the appreciative settings of those in the problem situation and so define the problem domain for data analysis.

The appreciative model thus seems to provide an explanation of the activites of data analysts. But more than this, it alerts us to the possibility of a different form of datas analysis, one which pays far greater attention to the subjective ways in which reality is understood in any particular situation. We shall look at this alternative, interpretative form of data analysis in more detail in later chapters.

# Part III

## *Using soft systems thinking*

# 8  Soft systems methodology

## 8.1  INTRODUCTION

There are many ways in which systems thinking might be employed in the IS field, but the most important of these relates to answering the most crucial development question of all - what information-system is it that is needed? As Brookes (1987) says:

*"The hardest single part of building a software system is deciding precisely what to build. No other part of the conceptual work is as difficult as establishing the detailed technical requirements, including all the interfaces to people, to machines, and to other software systems. No other part of the work so cripples the resulting system if done wrong. No other part is more difficult to rectify later." p. 17*

This is also, sadly, the question that has, so far, been least satisfactorily addressed by the IS field. As we have seen, thinking about how to create information-systems has been strongly influenced by systems engineering and RAND style systems analysis. In these approaches the nature of the problem is taken as given, and carried over into IS thinking has been the same assumption that what is to be done has already been decided.

Soft systems thinking has an important contribution to make here, for it permits a defensible sequence of analysis, leading to an identification of what information-systems are required. Using SSM we can explore in detail the way in which an organisation understands itself and its world, creating models of systems relevant to the organisation and identifying necessary activities. From these we may move to identifying the data that seems to be required, both for the direct enactment of the organisation's activities and for the support of those activities. Then, last of all, may we discuss alternatives for providing that data and decide what information-systems should be developed. It is only when this sequence of analysis has been completed that we can turn to deciding *how* the identified new information-systems should operate and how to create them.

In the following chapters we examine this sequence of analysis in detail, and necessarily begin by describing the soft systems methodology (SSM). The brief description of SSM given in this chapter cannot do full justice to the subtleties and power of the methodology but should serve to indicate the usefulness and practicality of the systems ideas that we have so far introduced only as theory. Fuller descriptions of the development, principles and use of SSM can be found in Checkland (1981) and in Checkland & Scholes (1990).

## 8.2 SSM

SSM is a methodology that employs the concepts of systems thinking to tackle ill-defined, 'messy' real-world situations. Like other systems approaches, it uses systems concepts such as emergence, control and hierarchy, but is distinctive both in employing the concept of a human activity system and in embodying a phenomenological approach.

The 'track-record' of SSM is impressive. It has been successfully used in several hundred interventions of different kinds and found to be a particularly flexible form of the systems approach: it has been found to be equally useful to the external consultant as to the manager seeking to resolve their own difficulties, to the small voluntary organisations as to multinational commercial organisations, and applicable to a wide range of problem situations. This flexibility can, though, be a vice as well as a virtue. Because it is capable of being tailored for use in particular situations and used in many different ways it is often difficult for someone seeking to learn about it to make sense of what it actually is and how they might employ it.

To overcome this problem we describe SSM in a stage-by-stage manner, as if there were a prescribed sequence of activities to be carried out in using SSM, and a single, definitive way in which it should be applied. This is an inaccurate representation of the nature of SSM, for we shall be describing only one of many ways in which the methodology might be applied: not every use of SSM will involve the activities being done in a strict sequence and on occasion the activities may be done in a different order or some may be omitted. Describing SSM in this way, as being the same kind of prescribed procedure as most information-system development methodologies, does though allow us to give a broad overview of the approach and the kind of activities that it involves.

## 8.3 A PROCEDURAL DESCRIPTION OF SSM

In the first expositions of SSM (Checkland 1972; Checkland, 1975) and in much of the secondary literature by other authors (for example Waring, 1989; Patching, 1990) the methodology is described as consisting of seven stages that together lead to desirable and feasible changes in problematical situations. More recently the nature of SSM has been described more subtly and comprehensively (Checkland & Scholes, 1990) but the seven stage description of SSM has become so well known that diagrammatic representations of it, as in Figure 8.1, have become somewhat emblematic of the methodology. For simplicity we shall base our own discussion of SSM around the stages shown in Figure 8.1, but, even so, must point out that by carrying out these stages we enact only one of *two* streams of enquiry required by SSM.

### 8.3.1 Two strands of enquiry

The user of SSM will always be concerned with two separate, but interacting, types of investigation: to use the language of SSM, they will always carry out both a 'logic-driven stream of enquiry' and a 'stream of cultural enquiry'.

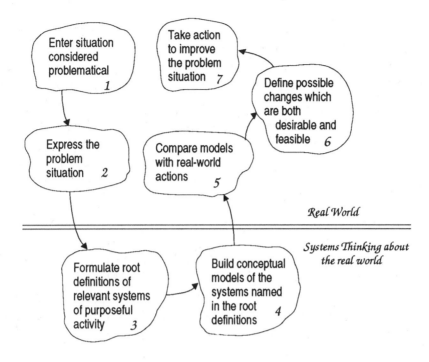

**Figure 8.1**     *The learning cycle of soft systems methodology*
*Source: Checkland 1989, p. 84.*

It is the logic-driven stream of enquiry which was described in the earliest expositions of SSM, to which most attention is usually given and that the secondary literature sometimes wrongly describes as *being* SSM. It is this which Figure 8.1 shows the required activities of, the core premise being that the conceptualisation and modelling of relevant systems can lead to agreement about changes that are both systemically desirable and culturally feasible.

Recently however it has become recognised that this stream of enquiry is always guided by another stream of enquiry. This focuses upon the human aspects of the situation and in particular upon the three areas of:

• The intervention which the SSM study represents: any situation involving human beings is changed immediately it is studied, and continuing attention must be given to the roles which individuals may play, expectations of the study's outcomes and how the study will be carried out.

• The social context in which the study will occur and may affect: in using SSM one must never forget that the organisations studied are human organisations, so that the SSM-user needs to have some grasp of the informal as well as the formal social processes that are operating. Checkland & Scholes (1990) suggest that the ideas of roles, norms and values are a way of making sense of the social context, but techniques from disciplines such as sociology or anthropology might also be appropriate.

- The political context: an essential part of understanding the nature of the problem situation is understanding the politics and the political processes that operate within it. The SSM-user should therefore be always alert to questions of power, authority and influence, the way in which these are exercised and how they may aid or hinder the study.

This cultural enquiry will continue throughout the study, informing and helping to decide the direction of the logic-driven stream.

Some consideration of the cultural context and reflections on how to manage the study must have occurred in all the past several hundred recorded applications of SSM. It is only recently though that what were previously seen as craft knowledge or consultancy skills have become recognised as being just as valid and important as, and just as much a part of doing SSM as, enactment of the logic-driven stream. Little advice has yet been given on to how to carry it out, but even now the SSM-user need not rely solely upon their own social skills and awareness: practical experiences of using SSM have led to a number of helpful guidelines. For example, managing a SSM study and making sense of the social and political contexts in which it takes place is easier if we are clear about certain roles that will be played out during the study.

### 8.3.2 Roles in the problem situation

The term 'role' is widely used in management science to describe the functional tasks carried out by individuals. Such roles may be institutionally imposed and defined in job descriptions and organisation charts, for example in job titles such as 'sales manager' or 'lathe operator': or they may be less formally earned or given, in roles such as 'our ideas man' or 'a good team worker'. The definition of such roles is accompanied by particular norms about how the occupant of such a role is expected to behave and a particular set of values is used to judge the performance of individuals occupying them.

It is the differences in such roles, norms and values that make one organisation so different from another, even when they are in the same industry, and it is the need to learn and adapt to these differences that causes an individual moving jobs to take some time to 'fit in' or 'become part of the team'. In one large building consultancy for example the complicated business of designing and building factory buildings required the interaction of teams of architects, office designers, electrical engineers, plant layout specialists, and construction managers. All group members had an equally vital part to play and the formal organisation chart showed the senior management of each group as being of equal status; officially, decisions were made on a group basis. Yet when one observed these formal roles in action at planning meetings it became quite clear that particular norms existed within this company that determined how the occupants of these formal roles acted. It was thought to be 'bad form' for a member of the 'non-creative' groups such as plumbers or electricians to criticise arguments put forward by designers on terms of the practical difficulties which might be caused. And perhaps because the most senior management had always traditionally been drawn from the ranks of the professional architects, any arguments which that group put forward were seen as having especial weight.

During a SSM study there will be a concern with these kinds of role, both formal and informal, and the norms and values that are associated with them. Understanding such things is essential if the SSM-user is to be able to operate effectively whilst doing the study and avoiding making cultural faux-pas or inadvertently breaking local taboos. In SSM there is though an unusually high level of reflection about the nature of the intervention itself and how it should be conducted. This requires us to consider another set of roles, this time relating to the intervention in the problem situation that the study represents.

### 8.3.3 Roles in the intervention

In most management science approaches the person investigating the problem situation is regarded as being an external observer and the engineer of a solution; their role is analogous to that of a surgeon, who, armed with special equipment, knowledge and expertise, operates upon a patient and makes those changes which they believe will improve the patient's condition.

SSM however emphasises participation and the involvement of individuals within the problem situation in the problem-solving process. This could go to the extent that the main 'deliverable' of a SSM study is a transfer of SSM-using skills, so that the organisation is better able to solve its own problems in the future. An analogy here, then, would be with the psychiatrist who works with a patient to help them achieve their own resolution of their difficulties. As a consequence of this approach the SSM study and the activities of the SSM-user are seen not as external to, but as part of, the problem situation.

The SSM-user must then give careful consideration to the parts played by both themselves and others in the study. This is done by the requirement to specify, and then repeatedly review, who is being taken to occupy the three roles of client, problem-owner and problem-solver.

The role of *client* is usually the most straightforward to identify as this is the person or persons who have authorised or caused the study to happen. A useful 'acid test' of whether a particular person is the client for the study is to ask whether that person is able to authorise payment for its costs.

The role of *problem-solver* is given to those individuals who are seeking to bring about improvement in the problem situation through active participation in the study. In other management science approaches such as Operational Research there would be little confusion about who occupies the role of 'problem-solver'; it is the OR professionals who employ simulation, queuing theory or other OR techniques to bring about change. In a SSM study though there is a much greater variety of possibilities.

In some situations, where the organisational culture is oriented towards deliverables the SSM-user may be simply asked to "Tell us what to do". If there is no interest in understanding how the study is carried out or any willingness to actively participate in it then the role of problem-solver is thrust upon the SSM-user alone and they must act, like the OR practitioner, as the expert advisor. Such cases are surprisingly rare.

Perhaps the most common pattern is that where study is seen as a joint responsibility of the client, the SSM-user and others. In such cases the role of problem-solver is shared by all those individuals and all influence the decisions concerning what is or is not relevant, the choice of systems modelled and the conclusions of the study.

At the other end of the spectrum of possibilities is the case where those involved in the situation wish to learn to use SSM and carry out the study themselves. The role of problem-solver is then properly theirs, with the SSM practitioner merely facilitating, by providing advice on the methodology and techniques.

The role of *problem-owner* is allocated by the problem-solver to those individuals who will benefit from improvements in a problem situation. We emphasise that this role is *allocated* by the problem-solver rather than being a natural feature of the problem situation, and in every study there will be many possibilities for who might be the problem-owner. Since the client is causing the study to happen then whoever is assigned this role will naturally also be a candidate for the role of problem-owner; but others will always exist, and sometimes these may not even be conscious of the problem situation. For example, in a study of a training scheme for unemployed young people the client was taken to be the sponsors of the training scheme but one possibility for the role of problem-owner was the unemployed young people whom the scheme was intended to make more employable: many of these were however unaware of the training scheme's existence.

Experience of using SSM has shown that it is vital to be clear about who is being taken to occupy the above three roles. Less vital, but still helpful to thinking about and discussing the intervention, is the identification of some other roles. *Actors* is the general term used to describe those individuals who populate the problem situation. An actor may be a person with power and authority or be disenfranchised, they may be able to cause or prevent change, they may be affected, for good or bad, by changes in the situation. It may also be useful to distinguish between those actors who are *powerholders*, and can affect the operation of decision making in the situation, and other *stakeholders*, who do not.

Though the stream of cultural enquiry is now recognised as being of vital importance this recognition is fairly recent. There is far more recorded experience available concerning the logic-driven stream of enquiry summarised by the stages of Figure 8.1. It is enacting these stages that was first described as, and which remains most widely perceived as, being 'doing SSM'. Let us therefore look now at what is done in each of these stages.

## 8.4 FORMING AN APPRECIATION OF THE PROBLEM SITUATION

In Stages 1 and 2 of SSM the SSM-user enters into the problem situation, begins to explore its nature and define their own role within it.

The first task of the SSM-user is to gain as complete an understanding (or in the terminology of SSM as 'rich a picture') as possible of the problem situation. Only when this is done can any attempt be made to name various candidates for 'the problem' or begin to think of what human activity systems might be relevant. From the start then SSM differs from those systems approaches and management consultancy techniques which are problem-oriented and driven by an assumption that there exists a particular problem to be solved. This is because official statements of 'the problem' reflect only a single perception of the present situation and of what is unsatisfactory. Accepting these too readily may lead one to treatment of the symptoms rather than the cause of a malaise.

For example, in a manufacturing setting one might be told that the reason that out-of-stock situations frequently arise is inadequate stock control procedures. The 'problem' thus becomes how to improve those procedures and, if one did not question this, the intervention would focus entirely upon amending those procedures. However, it would be wise to confirm that this reading of the situation is the only possible one; if there happened to be a lack of communication and co-ordination between the activities of the sales department and the warehouse then it could be that no amount of improved stock control procedures would improve the situation; one would merely know that one was out of stock more accurately.

SSM takes the possibility of this kind of error very seriously, seeing it as the inevitable result of any situation being interpretable in many different ways. So, SSM starts from the modest proposition that a 'problem situation' exists which is felt by some of those involved to be problematical. The nature of 'the problem' however is not taken for granted, but is to be explored and defined in the SSM analysis.

## 8.4.1 Investigating the situation

A great deal of facts about the situation may be gained by observation, document collection, and in particular by the interviewing and questioning of those involved. It is often useful to consider the facts gathered as relating to the structures and processes of the situation.

### Structures

The structures within the problem situation are those elements which are comparatively stable and slow to change. Physical structures may include the location, layout, capacity of buildings and equipment. Where the study is oriented towards the use of information then the type, configuration and capacity of installed hardware and communications networks will be of particular interest.

Social structures of the situation include such things as: the way in which organisations are formally organised into divisions, departments or work groups; the scope of the authority allocated to these; the defined job roles of individuals; the established administrative and reporting procedures. By investigating these the SSM-user assembles an understanding of the official organisation, as defined and enshrined in official documents, staff handbooks and formal working practices.

Such things as organisation charts, showing the lines of responsibility and reporting, are usually available from the start of a study and are invaluable as an initial 'map' of the new culture which one is entering. One must though always remember that the real organisation will rarely work in quite the way shown in these, and that this picture of the official organisation needs to be used alongside the results of the continuing, parallel stream of cultural enquiry.

Such an understanding of the formal organisation is essential to any management or consultancy work but is rarely discussed as a necessary part of computer systems analysis. Computer systems analysts have however identified the need to learn about a third type of structure, that of the data structures within the situation. Data analysis techniques, such as normalisation or entity life-histories, are powerful tools for clarifying the nature of, and inter-relationships between, the data used in the situation.

### Processes

A different perspective of the situation may be gained by identifying the transformation processes occurring within it and the inputs and outputs of those transformation processes. Of interest will be: physical processes, such as those by which raw materials are transformed into finished products; non-physical processes, such as those changes in intent which occur during planning and management meetings; and data processes such as the transformation of information about customer orders into records of customer indebtedness.

The SSM-user may wish to investigate in detail:

- The tasks carried out by individuals, how they are done and factors that determine whether alternative outputs are produced.
- The relationships between tasks, including how completion of one task may provide the inputs or be the trigger for the start of another.
- The sequence in which processes occur for an individual transaction. In a sales organisation, for example, it may be worthwhile to track the progress of a single customer order as it passes through all stages of processing, from initial placement to final completion and invoicing.

This kind of analysis of tasks and procedures is common to many intervention approaches. Process charting has been done since the earliest days of Frederick Taylor, through the heydays of Work Study to the techniques found in modern computer systems development methodologies: data flow diagramming is now probably the single most widely used method of recording process details. Operation research practitioners would perhaps give greater emphasis to quantitative measurement, recording volumes and frequency of transactions and observing the behaviour over time. Techniques from these or any other fields may be used by the SSM-user in their attempt to build as detailed and complete as possible a picture of the situation.

The use of flowcharting, data flow diagramming or any other techniques that focus upon the formally defined, rational organisation and its procedures should not lead to the informal communication flows and undocumented working practices that arise in human groups being ignored. The case of the London Ambulance Service's computer system demonstrated well the danger of ignoring these informal procedures and other essentially human factors. This information-system, intended to handle emergency calls for over three hundred ambulances, failed after being in service for just 36 hours. Although there were technical problems in its design a subsequent inquiry also pointed to the problems caused by ignoring human factors during design of the system. A redesign of the control room obstructed the close interaction between operators that had previously existed and under the new procedures the operators had no flexibility in allocating emergency calls to ambulances. Even the need to do the most simple, everyday things such as allowing drivers brief rest periods or re-allocating calls to take account of unusual circumstances could not be accommodated.

## 8.4.2 Rich Picture Diagrams

As the SSM-user gathers myriad facts about the situation these will need to be recorded for later use. Gradually, as more facts are assembled and different people raise the same concerns, his or her view of the situation will gain its own structure. As any view of the situation will both shape and restrict subsequent action it is essential that all those involved in a SSM study have a broadly similar appreciation of the present situation and expectations of what the intervention will achieve. If this is not so then, however diligently the rest of the study is conducted, there is little chance that its results will be seen as acceptable or useful.

Preliminary discussions, the negotiations over contractual arrangements and the terms of reference for the study will all contribute to some initial view of the situation and what would be done during the study. Contracts and official terms of reference must though often be worded to give a large degree of flexibility, so, in order to ensure that no large discrepancies exist in how various parties view the situation and what constitutes the 'problem domain', some more explicit technique is required. We need some way of making explicit and open to debate appreciations of the problem situation.

The particular technique often used within (though not required by) SSM is the drawing of Rich Picture Diagrams, in which a pictorial representation of the problem situation is created. A picture often is 'worth more than a thousand words', and drawing such diagrams has proved to be a particularly effective way of representing the issues and concerns of different parties.

Figures 8.2 and 8.3 show two examples of Rich Picture Diagrams drawn during studies using SSM. In each of these is captured a considerable amount of information about the problem situation, which to describe fully in text would require many pages.

Figure 8.2 shows the Rich Picture Diagram of the study of a training scheme for young people, a scheme funded by a government body and the chemical industry. It records the major issues found during the initial investigation of the problem situation. These include:

- A growing shortage of technician level workers in the chemicals and allied products industries

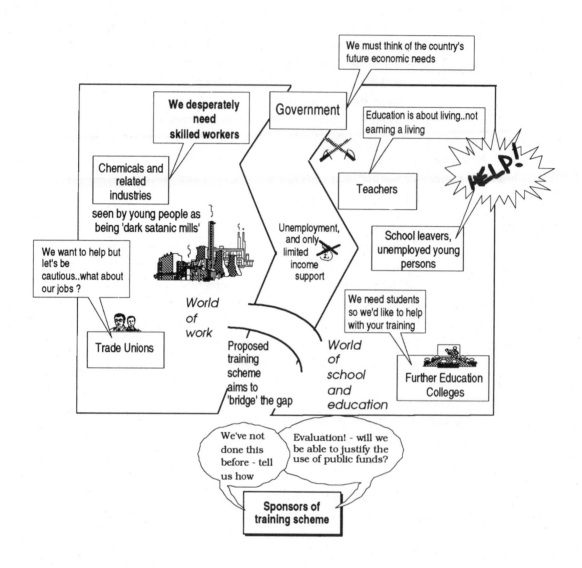

**Figure 8.2**  *Rich Picture Diagram of the problem situation surrounding a training scheme for unemployed young people*

- Unprecedented and growing levels of unemployment amongst school leavers and young people
- The poor image held by young persons of work in the chemical industry being dirty and unsafe
- The gulf which was perceived as existing between the worlds of education and work, which the training scheme was intended to 'bridge'
- The caution with which trade unionists regarded the schemes because of fears concerning job security

- The political debate of the time regarding the aims of the education system and the resistance found amongst many educationalists to vocational training.

Figure 8.3 records the situation found in a study concerned with automating the operations of a university-owned accommodation service.

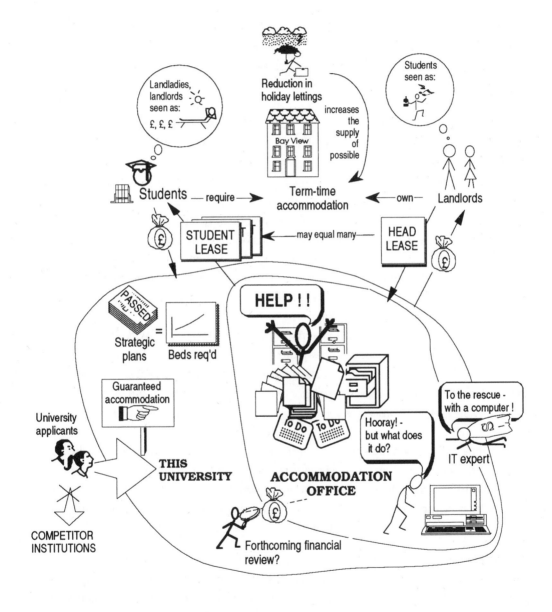

**Figure 8.3** *Rich Picture Diagram of problem situation concerning automation of a university's accommodation office*

The study resulted in the prototyping of a new computer-based office system, as described in Lewis (1989). The diagram captures a number of the issues described as relevant by the staff of the accommodation office and senior university personnel. These include the value of a quality accommodation service to give competitive advantage over other universities, the difficulties of persuading property owners to allow student occupation of their houses and flats, and the need for the service to be financially justifiable.

It is through debating what elements of the problem situation should be shown, and how they should be represented that some alignment of appreciations occurs, or perhaps a greater understanding of the reasons for any disagreement arises. Individual actors may identify what they consider to be 'problems' and problem causes. Inconsistencies between different actors' views can be identified and considered. For every issue raised one may ask questions such as: Is this really a problem or merely a symptom of some other malaise? How serious is this 'problem'? For whom is it problematical? What might be considered to be a solution?

Rich Picture Diagrams can often present facts in an insightful way and be used to generate discussions amongst concerned individuals to a degree that is rarely possible using only written text or tables of figures. The technique of rich picture diagramming has therefore become widely used and has attracted considerable attention.

Inexperienced SSM-users do, though, sometimes over-emphasise its role in SSM; it is a useful technique but there is no requirement that it should be done as part of a soft systems analysis. Indeed, the originator of the technique has found it necessary to emphasise that creating Rich Picture Diagrams:

> *".. is an efficacious way of recording the finding-out phase because relationships and interactions are more briskly captured in pictures than in linear prose. However, the fundamental requirement is to gain a discussable appreciation of a problem situation; pictorial representation is simply one means of doing that which has been found useful. But it is not an axiomatic requirement. " Checkland & Scholes (1990), pp. 156-157*

It cannot be emphasised too strongly that the value of rich picture diagramming lies in the process rather than the product of the process. The requirement of SSM is that the SSM-user builds a rich picture *in their mind* of the situation. Lewis(1992) shows that the novelty of Rich Picture Diagrams has often led to this being forgotten, with the emphasis being placed upon the diagram rather than the process by which it is produced.

### Style and content

There can be no strict rules about how to draw a Rich Picture Diagram for each diagram is dependent upon the particular meaning that those creating it attribute to the figures on the paper. Without discussion between us you the reader can never understand Figures 8.2 or 8.3 in precisely the same way as I, their originator. This is perhaps why examples of rich pictures diagrams are rarely given in published descriptions of SSM studies; the fear is that they might be misinterpreted and their inclusion would confuse the reader. Or the reader might be misled into believing that the diagram shown was somehow 'right' and should therefore be imitated in their own studies. There cannot of course ever be a 'right' diagram, and the only possible answer to the question 'What should I show in my Rich Picture Diagram and how should it be presented?' is simply 'Whatever seems important to you and others in the situation and will be helpful to *your* use of SSM'. This means that the technique is a very flexible one and for example:

- The injection of humour into Rich Picture Diagrams can sometimes be useful. In a study of a financial institution facing the removal of professional entry requirements, the organisation was portrayed as a medieval castle, with the presently qualified members pulling up the drawbridge and pouring boiling oil over would-be new entrants (Crellin, 1988). This intentionally light-hearted depiction of the situation focused attention upon a contentious issue in a non-threatening manner and useful discussions resulted that might not otherwise have occurred. Here an understanding of the politics of the situation (from the stream of cultural enquiry) and the context in which the diagram would be used justified making a joke of a very serious issue. Trying to make a Rich Picture Diagrams humorous for its own sake is, however, pointless.

- The creation of a Rich Picture Diagram may be done by SSM-users alone, being used solely by them to record salient facts and their own view of the problem situation. But it can also be done as a group activity in workshops involving a wide group of concerned individuals. The construction of the diagram then provides the focus for discussions and as a way of arriving at some shared appreciation of the situation.

- It is usually possible to represent the core elements of a problem situation in a single diagram but Avison & Wood-Harper (1990) suggest that where necessary a Rich Picture Diagram might be decomposed, with further diagrams showing individual areas in greater detail.

- If it is felt that some parts of the Rich Picture Diagram require elaboration and explanation, and especially if you wish to use the diagram as a means of organising the materials accumulated in the investigations, then hypertext software packages might be usefully employed.. The Rich Picture Diagram can then be used as the 'home menu', providing the means of navigating through a large amount of accumulated material. Pointing with a mouse device on any part of the diagram will then cause the display of more detailed information about that area.

There is then a large amount of freedom allowed as to the use, style and content of Rich Picture Diagrams. This can be intimidating to newcomers to the methodology and perhaps because of this there have been in recent years several suggestions made for the use of computer support tools for Rich Picture Diagramming and for the use of standard diagramming symbols.

The use of standard symbols is attractive if one does not consider oneself 'artistic' but does have disadvantages. Unexciting, over-stylised diagrams may result and however large is the range of available pictures and symbols there will always be the danger of trying to express subtle and complex aspects of the situation in an over-simplistic manner. If all clashes of appreciation must be signalled by crossed swords then mildly differing opinions may be indistinguishable from wildly antagonistic beliefs.

Additionally, one of the reasons that standard symbols are advocated, to make the 'reading' of Rich Picture Diagrams easier, is based upon an incorrect perception of SSM as a set of techniques used by an external analyst *upon* a problem situation; within such a view the need for the analyst to communicate their appreciation *to* the problem-owners might provide some argument for using a standard language of symbols. But SSM is primarily a methodology for learning through participative action, in which problem-owners, clients and stakeholders may all be part of the problem-solving team working *within* the problem situation. Used in such a way there is less need for a standard set of symbols; each use of SSM will generate its own set of symbols, meaningful to those involved in that particular instance of inquiry.

Lewis (1992) points out too that ambiguity and unintended interpretations may arise from an excessive use of symbols and pictorial metaphors The originators of a Rich Picture Diagram may choose to pictorially depict the role of data administrator as an organisational policeman, having in their mind notions of the friendly British 'bobby' who protects the organisation's data resource for the benefit of all. Others, perhaps of a different generation, might 'read' and interpret such a characterisation rather differently, and understand the role of the data administrator less sympathetically.

## 8.5 THE MODELLING OF SYSTEMS

It could be argued that until this point the SSM-user has done little that might not be done by any experienced and politically competent analyst or consultant. It would be difficult to claim that, so far, a systems approach was being used. That changes as, in stages 3 and 4, the idea of a human activity system is consciously used to make sense of the wealth of facts so far gathered.

The exact point at which the SSM-user moves from finding-out of stages 1 and 2 to the modelling of systems in stages 3 and 4 can never be fully predicted, and need not be. Finding-out about the situation never really stops, for throughout the life of the study more and more facts will come to light, and one's appreciation of the situation will never stop growing and changing. If Rich Picture Diagrams have been drawn then it is worth remembering Frederickson's (1990) description of them as 'evolving diagrams' and continually update them to reflect the changing appreciation of the situation.

When then the time seems right the SSM-user moves on to the modelling of systems. This is not a once and for all move, for the methodology is all about learning and there is always the option of returning and choosing to model other systems later if necessary. Far greater problems usually arise from over-caution, where the SSM-user spends almost all the study in finding-out more and more about the situation without ever feeling confident enough to move on.

From the understanding of the situation built up in stages 1 and 2 several issues of concern will have become evident. If rich picture diagramming has been used then these will often appear somewhere in the diagrams produced. It is unlikely that the SSM study will be able to address itself to all of these, so there will need to be some decision made in conjunction with the client and other concerned actors as to which area of concern should be investigated further. Once this has been done then relevant human activity systems may be identified and modelled.

Now, with a better idea of the concerns which the study might address, the SSM-user can conceptualise several systems which seem relevant to the chosen areas of concern and likely to be of use in discussion of those areas. It cannot be emphasised too often or too strongly that the modelled systems are not high-level abstractions or intentionally descriptive of parts of the problem situation (though they chance to be so), nor are they ideas of what should exist in the future. They are rather systems which it is thought will be relevant and useful in debates and discussions about the situation. So if for example the area of concern in the real problem situation is production planning then we should not be trying to model the way in which production planning is done at present or define new operating procedures. The systems that will be imagined and then modelled are systems that, it is hoped, will allow the nature of the problem situation to be better understood and provoke fresh thinking about what changes might be made in the real world.

### 8.5.1  Radical or conservative modelling

The systems that are chosen may or may not accord well with the status quo or existing organisational groupings. In fact it has been found that more insightful results often arise when deliberately radical views are introduced and firmly entrenched ideas are introduced to 'their worst enemy'. It is even sometimes useful to conceptualise systems whose transformation process is quite the opposite of what would be considered acceptable or helpful in the real situation. If we find that in real life there is a problem of communication between two parts of the organisation, say Production and Sales, then 'a system to co-ordinate the efforts of Production and Sales ' might be a sensible system to model. But useful insight might also arise if we conceptualise 'a system to ensure that Production and Sales act in each others worst interests and operate together to the worst consequences for the organisation as a whole.' Modelling such a system and then seeing the extent to which its equivalent can be found in the real situation may be an excellent way of identifying things that need to be changed.

In some studies a cultural analysis will warn one that a radical approach will not be well received and the systems chosen may need to be conservative and highly constrained. But even when a possible system is dismissed as 'not relevant' because it is too 'absurd' or 'off-the-wall' reveals a great deal about what is, and what is not, meaningful within the critic's frame of reference. Such information is extremely useful both in the later activity of deciding what changes would be culturally feasible and in the continuing process of managing the intervention itself.

Not only the radicality but also the number of different systems that are modelled will be largely determined by the particular circumstances of the individual study: the openness of those involved to new ways of looking at the situation (hopefully by now known from the still continuing stream of cultural enquiry), the willingness of others to participate in the systems modelling and the time constraints of the study will all play a part.

For example, in a study of a training scheme for young people (that for which the Rich Picture Diagram was shown in Figure 8.2) the choice of relevant systems was driven by the different perceptions of the scheme held by the industrialists, educationalists and others participating in its creation. A formal survey and programme of field interviews identified many different reasons for co-operation, so systems were conceptualised for each of these. Maintaining the co-operation of all involved parties was felt to be so important that considerable time was spent upon the modelling and discussion, and even at the end of the study seven systems were still under discussion. This effort was worthwhile, for discussion of the modelled systems and their implications helped to bring about a far closer alignment of expectations about the scheme.

In contrast, in the situation portrayed in Figure 8.3, the systems modelling was done for the benefit of and by the SSM-user alone. The choice of relevant systems was solely theirs and was constrained by the contractual requirement to quickly produce a new computer-based information-system. The range of systems modelled here was therefore much smaller and more tightly focused, for radical changes to existing practices were not an option.

Whatever systems are conceptualised it is important to emphasise that the analyst is not in any sense advocating any of these systems as being right or preferable; all are being examined only in order to give insights into the situation and its possibilities. They are tools for examining the situation rather than representations of 'What Is' or prescriptive designs for 'What Should Be'.

### 8.5.2 Defining conceptualised systems

Given that several relevant systems have been identified and informally named then these need to be formally described. In SSM this is done in several ways. The most important of these is by creating a Root Definition, a concise and precise description of the relevant system. For example, one of the systems used in the training scheme study referred to earlier could be described as:

*A XXXXXX owned and funded system to improve, by means of training and the removal of employment barriers, the chances of selected young people obtaining employment in specified skill areas within the chemical and allied products industries, so as to reduce the local levels of youth unemployment and satisfy the recruitment needs of the chemicals and allied products industries*

In this root definition is described *what* is to be done by the system (improving the employment prospects of selected young people), *how* the system will attempt to do this (by providing training and removing employment barriers) and *why* it is to do this (to lessen youth unemployment and to satisfy industry's recruitment needs).

This sort of root definition was used alone in the first uses of SSM, but such bare descriptions of the system were found to be not always enough. By 1976 SSM had been used in several hundred studies and enough experience had been accumulated to allow conclusions to be drawn about what should be included in the definitions of systems in order to make them more useful. Smyth & Checkland (1976) were able to conclude that certain things needed to be made explicit in any well-formed system definition. This could be done in the root definition, or through an accompanying 'CATWOE' declaration. The six things to be identified were:

| | |
|---|---|
| The **C**ustomers of the system | The beneficiaries or victims of the systems activities, who is advantaged or disadvantaged by the system |
| The **A**ctors | The persons who carry out or cause to be carried out the system's activities |
| The **T**ransformation process | The core transformation process of the human activity system. This might be defined in terms of the input and output of the transformation. |
| The **W**eltanschauung | The basic beliefs or view of the world implicit in the root definition that give coherence to this human activity system and make it meaningful |
| The **O**wners | The persons who have the power to modify or demolish the system |
| The **E**nvironmental constraints | The constraints on the system imposed by its environment or a wider system that are taken as given in the root definition. |

Figure 8.4 shows how the underlying idea of the root definition of the training scheme might be better communicated by giving an accompanying declaration of these 'CATWOE' elements.

### 8.5.3  Building activity models

Having created root definitions and CATWOE declarations for one or more relevant systems then each of these may need to be explored in greater detail. This is done by identifying the activities which must logically be done by that system if it is to pursue its given purposes by achieving the named transformation, and showing the logical dependencies between these. The model that is created is thus, in the words of Checkland(1981):

> "... an account of the activities which the system must <u>do</u> in order to <u>be</u> the system named in the definition." p. 169.

**SYSTEM DEFINITION OF :**

S(3)- A system to improve the chances of selected young people obtaining employment in the chemicals and allied products (CAP) industries

Page ___1_ of _2_

Version _____3_____

**ROOT DEFINITION**

A xxxxxx owned and funded system to improve, by means of training and the removal of employment barriers, the chances of selected young people obtaining employment in specified skill areas within the chemical and allied products industries, so as to reduce the local levels of youth unemployment and satisfy the recruitment needs of the CAP industry

**CUSTOMERS OF THE SYSTEM**

| Advantaged | Disadvantaged | Other Stakeholders |
|---|---|---|
| Those young people selected to receive training and other benefits | None identified | CAP industry firms<br>Providers of training |

**ACTORS**    XXXXXX and others whose co-operation is achieved

**TRANSFORMATION**

Young people ⇨ ( T ) ⇨ Young people with greater chance of employment in CAP industry

**WELTANSCHAUUNG**

Unemployment of young people is undesirable and may be lessened, and industry needs met, if young people are equipped with the skills and expertises required for employment in the CAP industries.

**OWNERSHIP**

The training scheme's originators and sponsors, XXXXXX

**ENVIRONMENTAL CONSTRAINTS**

| Constraints imposed by environment | Constraints accepted in modelling |
|---|---|
| Limited possible funding making the necessity for selection of young people<br><br>Aims can only be achieved with co-operation of CAP industry and others<br>Need for continual monitoring of which areas offer greatest scope for employment and of the prerequisites for, and barriers to, employment<br><br>Legal and moral constraints on what might be done | That other barriers than having required skills may obstruct young people seeking employment in CAP industry<br>That active marketing will be required to inform and attract young people to the benefits offered.<br><br>That use will be made of training facilities and other support offered by parties other than XXXXXX |

**Figure 8.4**    *Root Definition and CATWOE declaration for one system deemed relevant in the study concerning a training scheme*

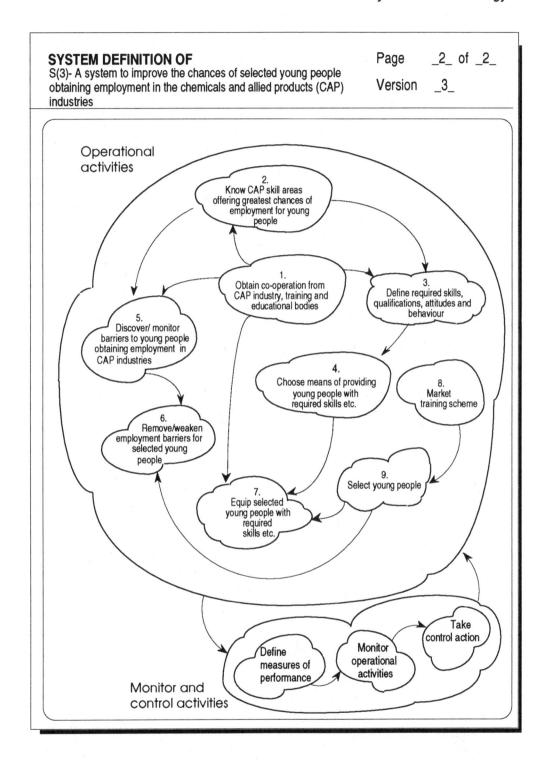

SYSTEM DEFINITION OF
S(3)- A system to improve the chances of selected young people obtaining employment in the chemicals and allied products (CAP) industries

Page _2_ of _2_

Version _3_

Operational activities

2.
Know CAP skill areas offering greatest chances of employment for young people

1.
Obtain co-operation from CAP industry, training and educational bodies

3.
Define required skills, qualifications, attitudes and behaviour

5.
Discover/ monitor barriers to young people obtaining employment in CAP industries

4.
Choose means of providing young people with required skills etc.

8.
Market training scheme

6.
Remove/weaken employment barriers for selected young people

7.
Equip selected young people with required skills etc.

9.
Select young people

Define measures of performance

Monitor operational activities

Take control action

Monitor and control activities

**Figure 8.5** *Conceptual activity model for one system used in the training scheme study*

Such models cannot be verified in an absolute sense but the analyst can check that they are internally consistent and viable in terms of such systemic components as connectivity, sub-systems and resources. Figure 8.5 shows an Activity Model for the system described in Figure 8.4.

### 8.5.4 Taking models to a higher resolution level

We now have, through the root definition, the CATWOE declaration and the model of the required activities of the system together, a formal definition of the system. It may be useful however to explore that system in greater detail, and to do this we take the system modelling to a *higher resolution level*. Just as in microscopy one might increase the magnification of the microscope so as to zoom in on and examine a smaller area in greater detail, so now we may examine parts of the conceptualised system more closely.

For each of the activities shown in the activity model we ask the question "How would we conceptualise a system that performed that activity?", and create new root definitions, CATWOE declarations and activity models to describe this new system(Figure 8.6). This new system is, of course, a sub-system of the one that we began modelling, and so we begin to define a hierarchy of system definitions. As we conceptualise the sub-systems, so we understand better the originally conceptualised system, the wider system of which they are a part.

**At resolution level 'n+1'**

Conceptualisation of systems to enact each of the activities identified at the previous level of resolution

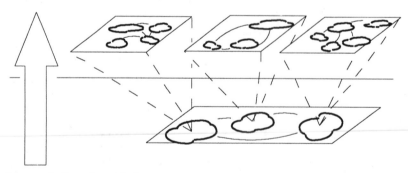

**At resolution level 'n'**

Conceptualisation of some system and identification of the logically necessary activities of that system

**Figure 8.6**     *Moving to higher resolution levels*

In this conceptualising of sub-systems we must make choices, for any activity in the activity model at the first level of resolution could be done in many different ways. The system defined for enacting that activity is thus always only one of many that could have been defined. It is important that we always remember this, and that we make it clear to others. For example, if there is an activity at the first resolution level of 'maintain financial records' but some of the activities at the second resolution level are logically required only because conventional accounting practices are being followed, then this constraint should be identified in the root definition or CATWOE declaration at that level of resolution.

There is always then an element of subjectivity in SSM modelling, which leads us to give two words of warnings. The first is that one should not create models that, deliberately or accidentally, confuse activities that properly belong at different levels of resolution. Checkland (1981) suggests that:

> "Experience has shown that it is best to begin conceptual model building by writing down no more than about half a dozen verbs which cover the main activities implied in the root definitions. ....
>
> ... it has been found best always to complete a model at a low resolution level (little detail) and then to expand each major activity at a higher level of resolution.
>
> ... The art in model building of this kind lies, in fact, in keeping separate the major activities of the system and, in a given model, in maintaining consistency of resolution level." p. 171.

Half a dozen or so activities need not be taken as an absolute limit, but if an activity model contains more than about a dozen activities then it is almost certainly includes activities which should appear at higher resolution levels.

The second concerns the apparent similarities between moving through levels of resolution during such systems modelling and the hierarchical decomposition which is used in data flow diagramming in IS work. This might suggest that activity models are similar to, possibly translatable into, data flow diagrams. It is therefore worth pointing out an essential difference. In data flow diagramming the developer is assumed to be exploring an objective reality. Although it is recognised that the partitioning done by the analyst is arbitrary, the assumption is that, at some very lowest level of decomposition, there will exist a given set of activities no matter what partitioning is done. In SSM's modelling however every time one moves to a higher resolution level one makes a new *choice* about what the system now being modelled actually *is*, choosing between alternative conceptualisations of that system. The results of those choices will never be resolvable at even the highest resolution level.

One consequence of this difference is that data flow diagramming places great emphasis upon ensuring consistency between diagrams at different levels of decomposition. Checks are made for example that diagrams at one level 'balance' with those at the next and, if they do not, then they must be amended. Such balancing checks do not exist in SSM modelling. If a high resolution model implies activities and interactions with some external entities that are unrecognised by the lower resolution level diagram, then this is a result of particular choices which have been made when drawing the higher level diagram. Had some alternative system been modelled at that level then such activities and interactions may not have resulted. To introduce the need for such interactions into lower level models would be to introduce new constraints and change the concept of that system.

This is but a single indication that the two forms of modelling are of a different kind. One attempts to 'map' what is taken to be an objective reality that is the same for all observers, the other is an exploration of ideas. One should be wary of denying those differences too readily.

## 8.6 LEARNING AND CHANGE

In many other methodologies model building would be the prologue to design and the creation of a real-life implementation of the system but in SSM models are built so as to allow, in the next stage, a comparison to be made. The purpose of defining and modelling systems is to express, precisely and explicitly, alternative, perhaps contradictory or antagonistic, views in order to facilitate discussion about them. The hoped-for result of such debate will be an agreement as to how those involved in the debate will choose to perceive the situation, what is to be regarded as problematical and therefore what should be done. This is done in stage 5, where the system definitions are compared with the picture of the problem situation which was previously built up in stages 1 and 2. This may be done in a number of ways, with an activity-by-activity comparison between the necessary activities of the Activity Model of each system and things done in the real situation being perhaps the most common.

It is important to note that where discrepancies are found between the conceptualised system and the real situation the SSM-user does not attempt to modify the system so as to bring it closer to the real situation. This might be the response of the management scientist, who attempts to build models which *mirror* the real-life situation as closely as possible and manipulates those models in order to predict the effects of proposed changes. The SSM-user employs modelling instead as a way of gaining insight. The analyst aims to create a debate in which the people most closely involved in the situation consider the differences between the models and reality and question any assumptions which are exposed by the comparison, with the aim of both gaining insights into the situation and defining possible changes. Ideally this comparison stage should be carried out by the 'problem owners' themselves; where they are not disposed to such conceptual thinking, the analyst might orchestrate and guide this debate.

Arising from this debate stage 6 consists of defining 'feasible and desirable' changes, changes which the problem owners agree are desirable in that they alleviate some problem or move the situation towards some new and more preferable state and which are also politically, economically and organisationally possible.

Finally, in stage 7, the desirable and feasible changes are brought about. The methodology may itself be used again to bring about these changes, the new 'problem situation' being how to make the changes or, now with well defined objectives, more conventional design approaches may be used.

## 8.7 USING SSM IN INFORMATION-SYSTEMS WORK

With its emphasis upon investigating different views of the organisation, of what the organisation might aim to achieve and how it might seek to achieve those aims, SSM has proved appropriate to the real-life concerns of managers and achieved much success as a means of re-engineering organisational activities. It is not surprising, then, that recent years have seen much interest, from both academics and practitioners, in using SSM in information-systems work.

The most obvious way of doing so is to use SSM as a 'front-end' to the activities demanded by conventional life-cycle models of development. Examples of attempts to use SSM in this way include the work of Wilson (1990), the Multiview methodology of Avison & Wood-Harper (1990) and in proposals to use SSM in the feasibility study stage of SSADM (CCTA, 1993). These all use the SSM analysis, albeit in different ways, as a precursor to more traditional development techniques. The task assigned to SSM is, to use the popular phrase, to ensure that they are 'Doing the right thing' (deciding which information-system to build) before turning to traditional ways of 'Doing the thing right' (building the information-system as well as possible).

Miles (1988) characterises this kind of use of SSM as being a 'grafting' approach, for the soft systems thinking is grafted onto conventional IS thinking and no challenge is made to the philosophy or assumptions of the conventional development approach. Miles does suggest an alternative use for soft systems thinking, one in which traditional techniques are 'embedded' in an overall SSM-driven analysis. In such an approach Miles foresees that:

> "Whilst information processing changes are addressed using conventional 'hard' methods, the 'soft' investigation proceeds at the meta-level, generating requirements which might, in turn, constitute a re-design of computer based procedures that may be either still under development or already implemented." p.57

No examples of such an embedding approach have yet been reported however, and it is not hard to understand why this should be so.

From our discussion of systems thinking in general and soft systems thinking in particular we can see that any such meta-level use of SSM would require significant changes to the views taken of the nature of organisations, of information-systems and of the relationship between the two. It would, for example, require that organisations be treated not as goal-seeking mechanisms but as ever-changing social constructs, with the recognition that the introduction of a new information-system, or even the prospect of such, generates changes to work practices, to power relationships and to the total experience of those who work in the organisation.

Further, it would require that information be understood as data that has been given meaning by a particular set of individual or organisational appreciations, in the way described in Chapter 5 and used in Chapter 8. Information is thus seen as an abstract concept and the product of individual or group perceptions, and we move closer to that which Harrington (1991) describes as a 'perception-driven paradigm of information', and away from the more conventional 'resource-driven' view where information is treated as a commodity of the organisation that uses it. With this comes the need for greater consideration to be given to understanding the different images that may be held of the organisation and its needs.

Finally, one would have to take seriously the idea that information-systems have no value in their own right, but are only created to support (in any of the forms described in Chapter 6) other human activity. The starting point for thinking about information-systems must therefore be thinking about the organisational activities that the information system is to serve. And, since the concept of adaptation tells us that the business activities will be continually changing, there will be an emphasis upon managing the relationship between information-systems and business activities over time, to continuously match the information provided by the *serving* information-system to the information needs of the *served* organisation and its members.

Many of the ideas currently used in the field of IS are, however, not sympathetic to such a view of organisations or information-systems. We have already seen, for example, how the life-cycle models of development emphasise the development of separate applications through one-off projects and that techniques such as data flow diagramming or of data analysis assume a single, neutral reality. This means that much work remains to be done both in re-thinking development techniques and in overcoming the practical difficulties of organising IS activity around these new ideas. The change to any 'embedded' approach, however attractive in principle, will inevitably be slow.

Soft systems thinking can, though, already be used to advantage on the smaller scale, in the development of individual information-systems. In past attempts to do this, the SSM analysis and the task of creating an information-system have remained essentially separate, with only the results of the former being carried across to the latter. In the next chapters we turn to seeing how this separation might be avoided. We begin by looking at how soft systems ideas enable an interpretative form of data analysis, and how this can provide the means for a more seamless progression from SSM analysis to the creation of an information-system.

# 9 Interpretative data analysis

## 9.1 INTRODUCTION

The soft systems methodology described in Chapter 8 does not directly address any of the data issues of problem situations, even though the value and importance of investigating these is well established. Unfortunately, as we saw in chapter 7, the best known approaches to data analysis have at their heart objectivist assumptions: they are based on the premise that data structures exist, independently of the observer, in the real-world, and that the result of data analysis will be a description of those real-world structures in the form of a data model. Entity-relationship modelling, normalisation or object-orientation each provide a different language and grammar for such descriptions whilst sharing those same underlying assumptions. This prevents a direct use of those approaches in conjunction with SSM, for to accept those assumptions is incompatible with the phenomenological stance of SSM.

Questions concerning the structure and use of data do though still need to be addressed in SSM-based studies, so an alternative form of data analysis, based upon different presuppositions, is needed. Such alternative forms of data analysis have so far been given little consideration and are certainly not to be found in any current information-system development methodology. This does not mean, though, that data analysis must necessarily be carried out within an objectivist paradigm.

In this chapter we introduce one alternative and interpretative form of data analysis. This is based upon the idea, introduced previously, that values, beliefs and expectations act as a form of 'appreciative filter', and that all data models therefore reflect only one possible and particular view of the situation. We suggest that, rather than focusing upon some ultimately unknowable external reality, data models (of a rather different kind than before) might be derived from the conceptualised systems used in SSM.

Each such notional system, as defined by a System Definition, is meaningful only with respect to a particular set of *cognitive categories* and *associations* between those categories. Recording details of both, in a new form of data model, not only provides further insight into the nature of the system being considered, but also the starting point for later thinking about the design of data storage mechanisms such as databases.

## 9.2   THE NATURE OF INTERPRETATIVE DATA ANALYSIS

The basic premise of any interpretative analysis must be that the only knowledge that one can have of the social world is that which is acquired through distorting sets of values, beliefs and expectations. An interpretative form of data analysis must therefore be accompanied by significant changes to what we understand is happening during data analysis and to our expectations of its possible outcomes.

The essence of the objectivist view of data analysis is that it is possible for an independently existing universe composed of an infinite number of things and types of thing (books, doctors, cassowaries, patients, hospitals, sealing wax, cabbages and kings) to be investigated through a neutral, value-free process of data analysis. The resulting data model reflects and maps that reality, though showing only those things that are selected as 'relevant' and 'important' (perhaps books when looking at libraries or doctors, patients and hospitals when we are concerned with health care).

Thus we arrive at the view of software development in which the developer:

*"... is often encouraged to start from the 'real world', conceived in terms of the entities and actions constitutive of the information flow in the existing organization. These are supposed to be 'given', while the software developer's task is to analyze, to abstract and elaborate a correct model that can be manipulated by the computer. While this may be difficult to do, the task itself - discovering the correct description - is supposed to be clearly defined and independent of the software developer as an individual. Also, his or her responsibility in carrying out this task is restricted to matching the real world in the model with the greatest care"* Floyd (1992), p. 16.

Suppose, though, we take seriously the idea that the world, and particularly those parts of the world that involve human action, may be perceived differently by individuals. Now the primary source of knowledge about the things that are 'relevant' to a problem domain cannot be an external, objective reality and data analysis can only ever investigate a problem situation *as it is understood by those who perceive it as problematical.*

The image of organisations and social life that is now applicable is one of social systems whose members continually construct, share, dispute and confirm meanings, and thereby 'construct' reality. An ultimately unknowable reality can now only ever be appreciated and understood through mental frameworks. These are shaped by the values, interests, expectations and beliefs of societies, human organisations and individuals, which creates the possibility of there always being 'multiple realities' or different interpretations of any situation. The differences between these may be resolved through social conditioning, through discussion and debate or through the exercise of power, to produce socially constructed and agreed interpretations of the world or a particular situation. It is these that might be recorded in an interpretative data model.

The data analyst must now abandon any ambition to create data models that are representations of inherently 'real' objects or 'real' situations. Instead, data analysis becomes a reality-creating process, with the data analyst and those in the situation together defining their domain of discourse. All that can now be aspired to is the creation of data models that are coherent, internally consistent and have meaning, in the context of particular beliefs, values and expectations, to those in the situation.

This is not to say that the physical realities of the organisation, the buildings, manufacturing facilities, number of widgets produced per hour and so forth, can be ignored. These remain as important as ever. Knowledge of such things does though in the context of an interpretative data analysis provide only an incomplete description of the organisation. To truly comprehend the situation one needs to investigate not only the observable structures, processes and actions taken by the organisation but also the meanings that are attributed to such things. Those meanings will determine what is regarded as 'data', 'information' or ephemera, will have shaped the information-systems already in use and will influence what information-systems might be perceived as desirable and useful in the future. In return, the shape and nature of those information-systems will influence and affect the way in which the world is understood by the organisation and its members This is recognised in Pfeffer's (1981) comment that:

> *"Organizations develop and implement information systems, reporting forms, and accounting conventions that determine what is measured and how the world is analyzed and viewed. These information systems and structures determine to some degree how causality is perceived and what elements of the environment are noticed" p. 16*

## 9.3 A BASIS FOR DATA ANALYSIS IN SSM

Abandoning belief in an objective external reality (or, at least, confidence in it as the basis for action) presents the would-be interpretative data analyst with a practical problem: if there is no single 'real' problem situation out there, but only multiple, possibly conflicting, views of what the problem situation might be, then how may these be handled and progress made towards enabling change? There may be many answers to this, and many routes to an interpretative data analysis. One way is to employ soft systems thinking.

One of the basic premises of the soft systems methodology is that no part of the real-world can be neutrally experienced or understood, but that by developing models of notional systems, comparing those models with the real-world and debating their implications one may learn a way towards some form of desirable action. Checkland & Scholes (1990) tell us that for this learning to happen there must be two interacting streams of enquiry: one, the logic-driven stream, is primarily concerned with the organised use of systems concepts whilst the other, the cultural stream, focuses upon the human, social and political context of the intervention. An interpretative form of data analysis would serve the former whilst being informed by the latter.

It is SSM's use of explicitly described conceptualised systems that gives the opportunity for an interpretative form of data analysis. Comparison with the present situation and debate amongst interested parties are only possible because the chosen relevant systems are explicitly and precisely described through Root Definitions, Activity Models and CATWOE declarations. Without such explicit definitions of systems we would never be able to engage in useful discussions, for we could never be sure that, say, 'a system to provide medical care' meant quite the same thing to you as it did to me.

Of course, there remains scope for ambiguity and misunderstanding even with the system definitions of SSM, so that over the years new elements have been introduced to increase their precision. From the idea of making explicit statements of certain assumptions and 'taken-as-given's (Checkland & Smyth, 1976), to that of drawing a picture of the system (Checkland & Scholes, 1990), there have been a number of suggestions about how the SSM user might clarify to themselves, and better communicate to others, the nature of a conceptualised system.

SSM System Definitions are now rather sophisticated devices for capturing the essence of a conceptualised system, containing explicit statements of the weltanschauungen and other assumptions within whose context the conceptualised system must be understood. But they may still be misinterpreted. For, at the most basic level, a System Definition can only be meaningfully understood by a reader if that reader is able to assign meaning to the terms used within it. For example, if the defined system is concerned with recording the costs of medical treatments provided to patients, then without some understanding of what is meant by 'patient' or 'medical treatment', one cannot possibly understand the idea of that system. To understand it (or even misunderstand it), the reader of a System Definition must be able to associate meaningful mental constructs to the written or spoken language used to describe the system.

This obvious fact provides the basis for an interpretative form of data analysis within SSM. If we can identify the *cognitive categories* that must exist in order for comprehension of a given system then these may act as the basic components of an interpretative data model for that system. Now, instead of trying to identify a neutral, objective data structure for a problem situation, we aim instead to create a data model that is relevant to a particular conceptualised and explicitly described system. The resulting model will show the cognitive categories required to understand the nature of the system, together with any implied associations between those categories.

Such a model would be clearly different in kind to the models produced by conventional data analysis, and will only ever be meaningful in respect to the definition of a particular conceptualised system. To remind ourselves of both of these points the model produced shall be described henceforth as a 'System Data Model'.

## 9.4 COGNITIVE CATEGORIES

The concept of a 'cognitive category' introduced above is not dissimilar to the idea of 'classes' used in cognitive science. The network theory of cognition suggests that human beings routinely create and modify mental maps to turn sensory perceptions into a workable understanding of the reality that surrounds them. Law & Lodge (1984) provide a very accessible explanation of these ideas, arguing that classification is something for which human beings have a natural psychological capacity and inclination.

By choosing to see similarities between things the human being is able to group them together, regard them as different examples of the same general thing or class, and so impose structure upon what would otherwise be a chaotic series of perceptual experiences. A perceptual event may then be regarded, not as totally novel and unique, but as *like* some previously encountered experience. Once we have adopted the mental class of 'bird' and begun to use it to group together things that fly and have feathers we are able to comprehend our perceptions of an albatross, even though we have never before seen such a creature and it is in some ways unlike the pigeons with which we are already familiar.

The adoption of particular classes may be done unconsciously, in response to stimuli received from the outside world, but is often learned, for the individual within a culture or social group will be provided with certain classes for knowing about the world by that society or group. Our earlier example of the cassowary, that is perceived differently by the Westerner and Karam native, illustrates well that the classificatory systems that human beings use have their source not in any absolute reality but in cultural history and utility.

Classification has utility, for it allows us to make predictions. Understanding an albatross as *like* a pigeon may suggest that albatrosses lays eggs and that those eggs may be good to eat. Those predictions are not always borne out in practice; albatross eggs may taste awful. Nevertheless, we have a way of understanding and responding to the perceived world. We are confounded only when we meet something totally beyond our previous or learned about experience. The Southern American Indians that first saw mounted conquistadors had never seen anything like these armoured knights on horseback before, and reputedly misinterpreted man and horse as being together a fabulous new creature.

Exactly how we should understand human perception and cognition is, of course, the subject of much debate within psychology. Earlier ideas that classification is done by matching according to set criteria ('all birds have feathers', 'all tables have four legs 'and similar) are now less favoured than the idea of probabilistic allocation to classes (this thing I perceive is more like a pigeon than an elephant so it is probably some sort of bird). However classification is achieved, the result is:

" ... *impossibly complex, impossible to map for any individual. It may in principle be pictured as a network where there are indefinitely many connections between the nodes that make up the classes. As individuals ... move through each day they make use of this network, the similarity relations and the links of association, to make sense of the perceptually lumpy phenomena that they encounter. That is, they use this network to impose some kind of order on what they see and make predictions on the basis of that order.*" Law & Lodge (1984) p.33

### 9.4.1 Meaning attributed to cognitive categories

The concern of a would-be interpretative data analyst is however not quite the same as that of psychologists interested in human cognition. During an interpretative data analysis exercise one does not seek to identify a set of classes to, or map out the mental networks that individuals use to, understand an independently existing real-world. In interpretative data analysis one seeks to identify the classes of thing to be used in thinking and talking about a notional or imagined world, the world of a conceptualised system.

This means that whilst the participants in a problem situation may use thousands of classes to make sense of the world in their everyday life, an interpretative data analysis definitely does not concern itself with all of these. It has the more modest aim of creating data models that show only those *cognitive categories* that are required in order for a particular notion of a system to be understood. Just as SSM's Activity Models show only the minimum set of necessary activities, so an interpretative data analysis will seek to identify the minimum set of cognitive categories necessary to make sense of a given System Definition. Those categories have no independent existence, they are not 'out there' waiting to be discovered. Those involved must invent and re-invent them. They must argue about and eventually agree the meaning of each of those cognitive categories. Only then can one define, as precisely and unambiguously as possible, the meaning of each category in respect to that system and ensure that there is consistency between those definitions.

So, cognitive categories have meaning only in respect to a particular definition of a system, and that meaning is socially decided. This means that they are fully definitive and cannot be in any sense tested or refuted by real-world experience. Imagine, for example, that we conceptualise a system within which doctors provide medical treatments to patients. It might be *unhelpful* to define the term 'doctor' so broadly that it encompasses not only qualified medical personnel but also PhDs in astronomy and native medicine men, but there is no way that this decision would be *wrong*. There would though be 'wrongness' in being inconsistent in our definitions, subsequently defining other categories in ways that are only sensible and meaningful when 'doctor' means a qualified medical practitioner.

This emphasis upon defining the meaning of a category in respect to a particular System Definition means that if several similar systems are conceptualised, the categories of each may differ. Even where the names of the categories identified for each are the same, the meaning of those categories may be different in each case. For example, as part of an analysis of a medical practice one might conceptualise both 'a system to improve the health of a local community' and 'a system to provide income to doctors'. The cognitive categories identified for both these systems might include PATIENT, but there is no reason why the same meaning should be given to this category in both systems. In the first system a 'patient' might be taken to be any person residing within a defined geographical area whose health might be improved or maintained; for the second system only those who pay a registration fee to the practice might be considered to be valid examples of a 'patient'.

## 9.5   THE NATURE OF SYSTEM DATA MODELS

It cannot be repeated too often that a System Data Model is *not* a representation of any real-world situation, nor a model of any individual's view of a situation, nor a design for data storage mechanisms. It reflects a particular idea, that of some notional system that is deemed to be relevant to a problem situation. That system may have similarities with the way in which the real-world situation is appreciated; it may be radically different and have little in common with any person's appreciation of the real-world situation. The System Data Model will reflect these possibilities, perhaps including categories that coincide well with the things about which data is stored in real-world databases, or showing categories for which there are no representatives in presently existing data storage mechanisms. The single, essential requirement imposed by interpretative data analysis is that there should be consistency between the System Data Model and the System Definition to which it relates.

### 9.5.1   Interaction of the two forms of modelling in SSM

Although the definition, as precise and unambiguous as possible, of a notional but purposeful system provides the starting point for interpretative data analysis this does not mean that modelling of the system is finished once data modelling begins. The System Definition and the System Data Model are both reflections of the same idea of a system, both provide a means of communicating that idea, and each must respond to changes in that idea. During an SSM study the originally chosen relevant systems may be challenged, amended or modelled to higher resolution levels; each or any of these may result in changes to how those systems are understood, and to the meaning attributed to particular categories. Conversely, identifying and agreeing the meaning of cognitive categories may itself lead to a sharper idea of what, exactly, the system under consideration consists of. The processes of defining the system and of creating the System Data Model are thus inextricably linked and proceed hand-in-hand (Figure 9.1).

### 9.5.2   A single System Data Model for each system

We saw in the previous chapter that it is common for systems to be explored in greater detail by, in the terminology of SSM, modelling the system at a higher-level of resolution. If the Activity Model of a system shows that a number of activities must logically be carried out by the system, then the SSM-user may conceptualise systems to carry out each of those activities so as to gain an increasingly detailed understanding of the original system.

It should be noted though that whilst taking Activity Models to higher levels of resolution leads to a larger set of Activity Models, there will not be a corresponding multiplication of data models. So far as modelling to higher resolution levels leads to a better understanding of the original system concept, so it may allow us to make definitions of the cognitive categories more precise, to add new definitions and to modify the System Data Model.

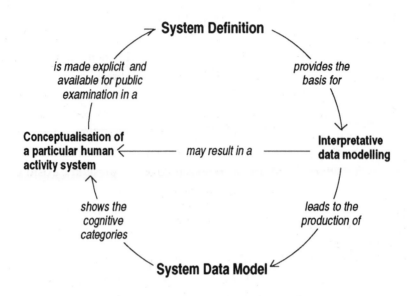

**Figure 9.1** *The interaction of the processes of system modelling and interpretative data modelling*

There will remain though only a single System Data Model for the system, and a single definition of each cognitive category that will be applicable to the sub-systems at all resolution levels. However closely we may examine our idea of 'a system to provide medical care to patients' we must be consistent, at all levels of modelling, about what is meant when we talk of a 'patient'.

## 9.6 IDENTIFYING THE COGNITIVE CATEGORIES OF A SYSTEM

To illustrate how to identify cognitive categories let us use just one of the System Definitions created for use in the Millside Medical Practice study described later in Chapter 10. The system that we shall look at is one concerned with recording the costs of medical treatments provided by doctors to patients, and is described by the System Definition of Figures 9.2 and 9.3.

This System Definition only has meaning with respect to some understanding of what is meant by the terms used within it. That is to say, without some understanding of what is here meant by 'patient' or 'treatment', one cannot possibly understand the idea that lies behind the System Definition. More formally one might say that conceptualisation of the system S(1.7), and understanding the System Definition of that system, depend upon PATIENT and TREATMENT being included in the set of cognitive categories relevant to the system S(1.7).

| SYSTEM DEFINITION OF : | Page ___1___ of __2__ |
|---|---|
| S(1.7), a cost of treatment recording system | Version _____ |

**ROOT DEFINITION**

A medical-practice owned and operated system which enables the cost of treatments to be known by calculating and recording both the cost of the resources used in a treatment and the cost of services provided during the treatment of a patient.

**CUSTOMERS OF THE SYSTEM**

| Advantaged | Disadvantaged | Other Stakeholders |
|---|---|---|
| The medical practice, which is able to recover the costs of treatments | | Patients, who have an interest in that the system should be accurate. |

**ACTORS**

Doctors of medical practice or other members of medical practice

**TRANSFORMATION**

Unrecorded costs of treatments $\Rightarrow$ (T) $\Rightarrow$ Accurately recorded costs of treatments

**WELTANSCHAUUNG**

That patients of the medical practice should pay for treatments and that payments made by patients should cover fully the costs of the treatments that they receive.

**OWNERSHIP**

Medical practice as in system S(1)

**ENVIRONMENTAL CONSTRAINTS**

| Constraints imposed by environment | Constraints accepted in modelling |
|---|---|
| That all treatments require use of resources and provision of services. That when costs of treatment are recorded they must be recorded accurately. That all patients must be charged for treatment in the same way and on the same basis. | All resources to be classed as either equipment or drug. Medical services to be treated in the same way as other services. The cost of a treatment is equivalent to the cost of the services and resources involved. It is possible to identify or define a cost for each resource or service. |

**Figure 9.2**  *Root Definition and CATWOE declarations for a system to record the costs of medical treatments provided to patients of a medical practice*

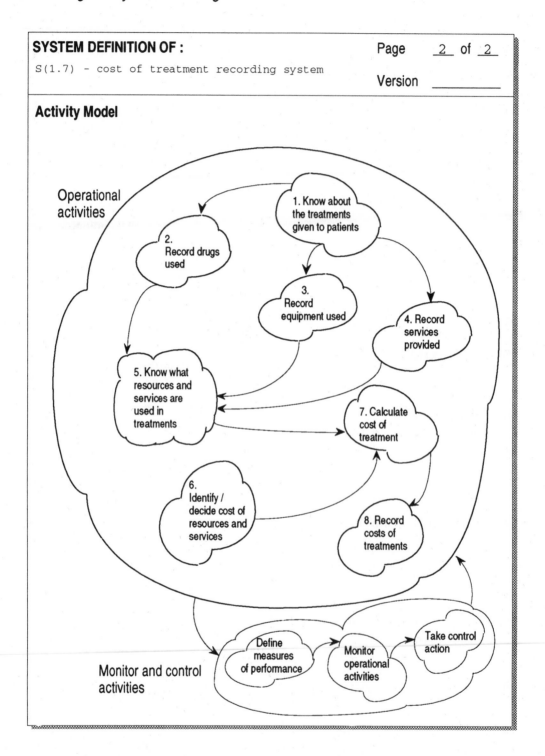

**SYSTEM DEFINITION OF :**

S(1.7) - cost of treatment recording system

Page    2 of 2

Version         

**Activity Model**

Operational activities

1. Know about the treatments given to patients

2. Record drugs used

3. Record equipment used

4. Record services provided

5. Know what resources and services are used in treatments

6. Identify / decide cost of resources and services

7. Calculate cost of treatment

8. Record costs of treatments

Monitor and control activities

Define measures of performance

Monitor operational activities

Take control action

**Figure 9.3**      *Activity Model of S(1.7), a system to record the costs of medical treatments provided to patients of a medical practice*

If the System Definition is well formed and precise then most of the categories relevant to the system should be identifiable from it. A simple but crudely effective way to identify the categories is to:

- Create an initial list of cognitive categories from the nouns, noun phrases and adjectival noun phrases used in the Root Definition, the operational activities of the Activity Model and the CATWOE declarations. This first step is relatively straightforward and mechanical, in as much as it requires the modellers only to identify the labels or names of categories, not to consider the meaning of those categories.

- 'Rationalise' the list by removing duplicates, synonyms and references to the human activity system under study. This second step requires the modellers to address the question of what meaning is to be ascribed to each category.

## 9.7 CREATING AN INITIAL LIST OF CATEGORIES

To illustrate the first of these steps let us begin by looking at just the Root Definition of the system S(1.7). Figure 9.4 shows how each individual noun-phrase of the Root Definition may be decomposed to suggest several cognitive categories.

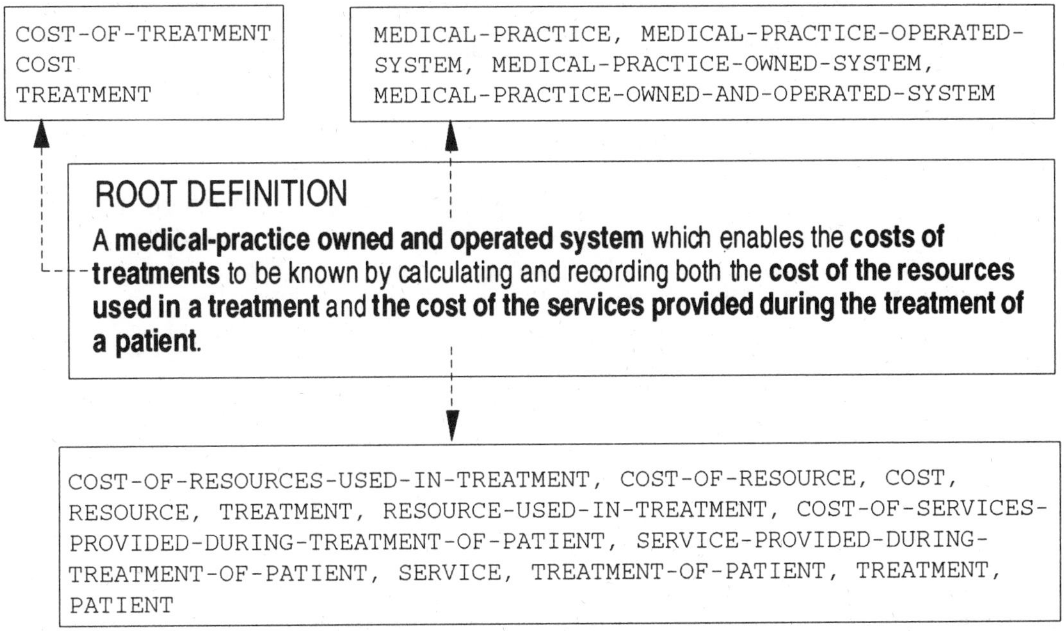

```
COST-OF-TREATMENT
COST
TREATMENT
```

```
MEDICAL-PRACTICE, MEDICAL-PRACTICE-OPERATED-
SYSTEM, MEDICAL-PRACTICE-OWNED-SYSTEM,
MEDICAL-PRACTICE-OWNED-AND-OPERATED-SYSTEM
```

## ROOT DEFINITION

A **medical-practice owned and operated system** which enables the **costs of treatments** to be known by calculating and recording both the **cost of the resources used in a treatment** and **the cost of the services provided during the treatment of a patient**.

```
COST-OF-RESOURCES-USED-IN-TREATMENT, COST-OF-RESOURCE, COST,
RESOURCE, TREATMENT, RESOURCE-USED-IN-TREATMENT, COST-OF-SERVICES-
PROVIDED-DURING-TREATMENT-OF-PATIENT, SERVICE-PROVIDED-DURING-
TREATMENT-OF-PATIENT, SERVICE, TREATMENT-OF-PATIENT, TREATMENT,
PATIENT
```

**Figure 9.4** *Identifying cognitive categories from a Root Definition*

Examining each part of the System Definition of Figures 9.2 and 9.3 in this way yields the initial list of categories shown in Figure 9.5.

| System : S(1.7), cost of treatment recording system | Page 1 of 1 |
|---|---|
| **Category List** | **Version** 1 <br> **Last modified** ____ |

From the Root Definition:

COST, COST-OF-TREATMENT, COST-OF-RESOURCE, COST-OF-RESOURCES-USED-
IN-TREATMENT, COST-OF-SERVICES-PROVIDED-DURING-TREATMENT-OF-
PATIENT, MEDICAL-PRACTICE, MEDICAL-PRACTICE-OPERATED-SYSTEM,
MEDICAL-PRACTICE-OWNED-SYSTEM, MEDICAL-PRACTICE-OWNED-AND-
OPERATED-SYSTEM, PATIENT, RESOURCE, RESOURCE-USED-IN-TREATMENT,
SERVICE, SERVICE-PROVIDED-DURING-TREATMENT-OF-PATIENT,
TREATMENT, TREATMENT-OF-PATIENT

From the operational activities of activity model:

COST, COST-OF-RESOURCE, COST-OF-SERVICE, COST-OF-TREATMENT,
DRUG, EQUIPMENT, PATIENT, RESOURCE, RESOURCE-USED-IN-TREATMENT,
SERVICE, SERVICE-USED-IN-TREATMENT, TREATMENT

From the CATWOE declarations

COST, COST-FOR-RESOURCE, COST-FOR-SERVICE, COST-OF-RESOURCE, COST-
OF-SERVICE, COST-OF-RESOURCES-USED-IN-TREATMENT, COST-OF-SERVICES-
PROVIDED-IN-TREATMENT, COST-OF-TREATMENT, DOCTOR, DOCTOR-OF-
MEDICAL-PRACTICE, DRUG, EQUIPMENT, MEDICAL-PRACTICE, MEDICAL-
SERVICE, MEMBER-OF-MEDICAL-PRACTICE, OTHER-MEMBER-OF-MEDICAL-
PRACTICE, PATIENT, PATIENT-OF-MEDICAL-PRACTICE, PAYMENT, PAYMENT-
MADE-BY-PATIENT, RESOURCE, RESOURCE-USED-IN-TREATMENT,
SERVICE, SERVICE-PROVIDED-IN-TREATMENT, TREATMENT

**Figure 9.5**     *Initial list of cognitive categories for the system S(1.7)*

## 9.8 REFINING THE INITIAL LIST

The richness of the English language means that the initial list of categories produced is likely to be fairly large. Some refinement of the list is now required not only because subsequent work will be easier if we are not dealing with an unnecessarily large number of categories, but also because we have so far only identified the labels of categories. We now need to tackle the more difficult task of agreeing a meaning for each category. For this, debate and discussion amongst all those who are building the system models and the data models is essential.

In practice some discussion about the meaning of categories will have occurred as a natural consequence of creating the System Definition and identifying the cognitive categories. We are now though at the stage where the group must formally address the problem of defining exactly what each term means, and what the system being examined therefore consists of.

The meaning of some cognitive categories will be easier to agree than others. For example, there is likely to be little debate over what is meant by a cognitive category such as PAYMENT-BY-PATIENT, given that we already understand the categories PAYMENT and PATIENT. But what exactly do we mean by PATIENT? A 'patient' might be understood to be *any* person who has been treated by one of the medical practice's doctors, or its meaning may be restricted to people who are formally registered with the practice, regardless of whether they have been treated. If the latter meaning is agreed then this may be seen as the same meaning as for REGISTERED-PATIENT.

Whatever meaning is agreed, it is important that we are consistent and subsequently use the same meaning throughout the modelling. Therefore, after there has been discussion and debate are over what exactly the group will consider 'a patient' to be, the agreed meaning needs to be recorded in some form of data dictionary.

During their discussions the group should not feel constrained by any meanings currently used in the real-world problem situation; cognitive categories can mean whatever you want them to mean for the purposes of modelling the given system. Defining a meaning for a cognitive category that is similar to everyday usage can be helpful, for example, if the data model might be compared, at a later stage, with existing data storage mechanisms. A fresh reinterpretation, though, might lead to new insights.

One could, of course, simply take each of the categories in the initial list and try to agree a meaning for each in turn. It may be more effective, though, to approach the problem indirectly, allowing the discussion of meaning to arise naturally as a result of 'refining' the initial list of categories.

### 9.8.1 Four steps to refining the initial list

An initial list of categories can be refined by the following four actions:

(i)     First, some categories will be referred to in many places within the System Definition. In Figure 9.5 for example, the category TREATMENT is identified from the Root Definition, from parts of the Activity Model and from the CATWOE declarations. The first, trivial, task in refining the initial list is to remove such duplicates.

(ii) Secondly, the initial list may contain a number of synonyms. If two categories have precisely the same meaning then they are synonyms and one can be eliminated. Such synonyms should be removed from the list of cognitive categories, though their existence should be noted in some form of data dictionary. In our example the categories TREATMENT and TREATMENT-OF-PATIENT appear to mean exactly the same thing, so we may decide to use only the latter as the name of a category and record that the former is a synonym or alias for this category.

Some care needs to be taken when dealing with synonyms in this way, for it may sometimes be better to simply change the System Definitions so that the need for the synonym is eliminated. For example, in the context of the System Definition for S(1.7), PATIENT-OF-MEDICAL-PRACTICE and PATIENT mean exactly the same thing; everywhere that the word 'patient' appears unqualified the phrase 'patient of the medical practice' could be substituted without altering the meaning of the sentence. If all those involved in the modelling agree that this is so, then we might act in either of two ways.

One of the synonyms might be used as the name of the category, with all others recorded as alternative labels or aliases for that category. In our example, we have chosen to do this and have retained PATIENT as the name of the category, recording PATIENT-OF-MEDICAL-PRACTICE as an alias. Should we, at some later time, want a category that means a patient of some other sort then we shall have to give it a new name.

Alternatively, if we know or suspect that subtle differences in meaning exist, then it may be better to retain the distinction between the two categories. To do this we could keep each as a separate category, changing the System Definition so that each term is used as most appropriate. In our example we might choose to take this option with respect to the categories DOCTOR and DOCTOR-OF-MEDICAL-PRACTICE, reformulating the System Definition and replacing any unqualified uses of the word 'doctor'. This eliminates the need to record any alias and leaves the possibility of using DOCTOR as the name of another, rather different category elsewhere.

(iii) Thirdly, remove from the initial list any categories that are the names of attributes of another category. An example of such a category is COST-OF-RESOURCE. This is not really a cognitive category of the same kind as, say, PATIENT since it is descriptive of the category RESOURCE. Such categories can be removed from the initial list, but in the data dictionary we shall record that one descriptive attribute of RESOURCE is 'cost-of-resource', i.e. whenever we categorise something as a resource we expect to be able to meaningfully think of that thing having a particular cost.

Deciding whether a category of the initial list is really only an attribute is sometimes difficult and two practical guidelines may be useful. The first of these may be expressed by the phrase "If in doubt, don't take it out". Leaving a doubtful category within the list will have no serious consequences at this stage, and its nature will become apparent later in modelling when we consider the different forms of association that may exist between categories. If necessary it can be eliminated then.

A second useful guideline is to think of an example or instance of the category. If the instance is described in terms of some unit of measurement or the name of a position on a given scale of measurement then it is likely that what we are considering is an attribute of another category. For example, an instance of COST-OF-TREATMENT would be £138.11; since this is a numerical measurement in British currency it is likely that this is an attribute value rather than a category instance. If we find that an instance of a category SEX-OF-PATIENT is 'male' then this is a measurement according to a pre-defined scale of 'male' or 'female' and it is again likely that what we are looking at is an attribute of another category (PATIENT) rather than a genuine cognitive category.

(iv)  Finally, and perhaps least obviously, we disqualify as valid cognitive categories of the system any categories that are descriptive of the system itself or another, higher level system that it serves; in the example MEDICAL-PRACTICE-OWNED-AND-OPERATED-SYSTEM, MEDICAL-PRACTICE-OWNED-SYSTEM, MEDICAL-PRACTICE-OPERATED-SYSTEM and MEDICAL-PRACTICE are all disqualified on this basis. To not do this would lead to the possibility of logical recursion; we would be arguing that to attribute meaning to the system we need to attribute meaning to cognitive categories, one of which is the system itself; thus we would enter an infinite loop whereby to understand the meaning of the system, we need to understand the meaning of the system, *ad infinitum*.

Were the modellers of S(1.7) to carry out these refinements to the original list of categories then a smaller list of categories, such as shown in Figure 9.6, would result.

Note how, because in this case 'treatment of patient' has been chosen as the category name with 'treatment' being a synonym, all references to 'treatment' within other category names have been changed; thus the category SERVICE-PROVIDED-IN-TREATMENT has become SERVICE-PROVIDED-IN-TREATMENT-OF-PATIENT.

## 9.9  RECORDING THE AGREED MEANING

It has already been suggested that some form of data dictionary should be used to record the agreed meaning for cognitive categories, and any aliases or attributes associated with each category. The value of creating such formal data dictionary entries lies in ensuring that having once agreed the meaning of a category we do not inadvertently associate a different meaning with that category later. It is these data dictionary entries, together with any diagrammatic representations of them, that form the final System Data Model.

| System : S(1.7), cost of treatment recording system | Page 1 of 1 |
|---|---|
| **Category List** | Version  4 |

| ID | NAME |
|---|---|
| C02 | DOCTOR-OF-MEDICAL-PRACTICE |
| C16 | DRUG |
| C17 | EQUIPMENT |
| C18 | MEDICAL-SERVICE |
| C19 | MEMBER-OF-MEDICAL-PRACTICE |
| C08 | OTHER-MEMBER-OF-MEDICAL-PRACTICE |
| C09 | PATIENT |
| C11 | PAYMENT |
| C12 | PAYMENT-MADE-BY-PATIENT |
| C20 | RESOURCE |
| C21 | RESOURCE-USED-IN-TREATMENT-OF-PATIENT |
| C22 | SERVICE |
| C23 | SERVICE-PROVIDED-IN-TREATMENT-OF-PATIENT |
| C15 | TREATMENT-OF-PATIENT |

**Figure 9.6**    *Refined list of cognitive categories for S(1.7)*

Either a simple manual data dictionary or an automated software package might be used, the latter providing some advantages in ease of cross-referencing and validation. The data dictionary entries need not be very detailed at first, when their main purpose is to ensure consistency as we move to later stages of modelling; later though we might need to add further information to the dictionary entries. Figure 9.7 shows one possible format for entries in a simple, manual data dictionary.

No 'hard and fast' rules for using the data dictionary need be given. The data dictionary should be used in whatever way suits the group doing the modelling and to record whatever it seems to them it is useful to record. For example, one of the explicit statements of the CATWOE declarations of the system S(1.7) is that the cost of the treatment of a patient is equivalent to the sum of the costs of all resources and services used in that treatment; indeed, the set of activities shown in the Activity Model is only the minimum necessary set of activities if that is the case. This might be recorded through a separate data dictionary entry for the attribute 'cost-of-treatment'.

## 9.10 ASSOCIATIONS BETWEEN CATEGORIES

The discussion that results from identifying and agreeing the meaning of the different

| **Definition:** | C15 | TREATMENT-OF-PATIENT | Page  1  of  2 <br><br> Version ___ 1 |
|---|---|---|---|

| **Type of entry :**      Cognitive category. |
|---|

**Aliases :**
TREATMENT / MEDICAL-TREATMENT / APPROPRIATE-MEDICAL-TREATMENT /
PREARRANGED-AND-SCHEDULED-TREATMENT / PURCHASED-TREATMENT /
TREATMENT-APPROPRIATE-TO-MEDICAL-CONDITION / TREATMENT-GIVEN-TO-
PATIENT / TREATMENT-PROVIDED-TO-PATIENT

**Agreed meaning**

A single episode of patient care whereby a specific
medical intervention is given on a particular occasion
to a single PATIENT.

**Associations in which this category participates**

Not yet identified

**Attributes of the category currently known**

COST-OF-TREATMENT

**Comments**

A patient might be provided with several treatments, of the
same or different type.
A treatment can only be provided to a patient if that treatment
has been authorised by a doctor who is a member of the medical
practice.
Consultation or advice-seeking by a patient is classed as being
a treatment.

**Figure 9.7**      *Example of a simple, manual data dictionary entry*

categories will be a valuable exercise in itself. It may reveal ambiguities and subtle
differences of meaning that would otherwise have remained hidden, and it may result in
a changed understanding of the system being modelled. However, those discussions will
not be complete unless they include some consideration of the way in which the
definitions are inter-related. This is because, for example, our understanding of what
constitutes a PATIENT will probably affect and be affected by our understanding of

DOCTOR-OF-MEDICAL-PRACTICE. The next stage of interpretative data analysis is therefore to define the meaning of categories even more precisely, by investigating the associations that may exist between them. Such associations may exist in several different forms, and we shall now examine each of these in turn.

### 9.10.1 Association through roles

The first type of association that we might identify is that through role. To start thinking about role associations let us introduce into our list of categories for S(1.7) a new category, that of PERSON. It is now quite clear that there is some sort of association between this new category and some of those previously identified. Since we understand that both the members of the medical practice and the patients of the medical practice are human beings we can say that MEMBER-OF-MEDICAL-PRACTICE and PATIENT are *roles* which PERSON may play. We shall want to record this additional piece of information about these categories in the data dictionary, but we may also show it separately in a diagram. Figures 9.8 through 9.10 show how a suitable diagramming notation can be used to differentiate between a number of different possibilities.

Figure 9.8 records that in the context of understanding a particular definition of a system:

- MEMBER-OF-MEDICAL-PRACTICE and PATIENT are both roles that may be played by a PERSON
- Both roles may be played at the same time. That is to say, we can envisage that an individual could be simultaneously a member of the staff of the medical practice and also be a patient of the practice
- These are the only two roles that may be played by PERSON. That is, to make sense of the System Definition we need only be concerned with those individuals that are members or patients of the medical practice. There is no need to be concerned with persons who are neither.

Contrast this with Figures 9.9 and 9.10. Figure 9.9 differs in that it records that our understanding of the categories is such that the two roles of MEMBER-OF-MEDICAL-PRACTICE and PATIENT cannot be played simultaneously. Figure 9.10 differs in that it allows that PERSON may be important in its own right, and that we need to consider the case of persons who are neither members of the medical practice nor patients. Later modelling might remove the need for this: we may find, for example, that we need to consider persons who apply to become patients as 'applicants', and that the addition of this new category allows us to move to a fully defined role association for PERSON.

In modelling the associations between categories of human activity systems it is inevitable that most role associations will concern categories related to human beings. Indeed, the introduction of the category PERSON is almost always required. However, the notion of a role is not restricted to these, since roles may be ascribed to non-human categories. Consider, for example, the case where the meanings given to categories allow for a manufactured item to be sold or be used as a component in some other sold product.

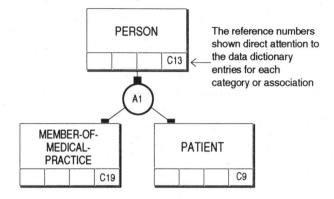

**Figure 9.8**     *Representation of non-exclusive, complete role association*

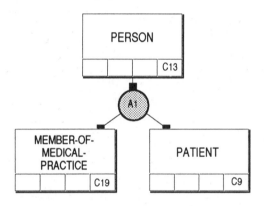

**Figure 9.9**     *Representation of exclusive, complete role association*

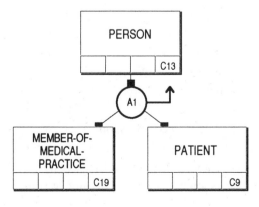

**Figure 9.10**     Representation of non-exclusive, incomplete role association

This situation could be partially represented by regarding 'manufactured component' and 'saleable item' as two roles that a manufactured item might play, as in Figure 9.11.

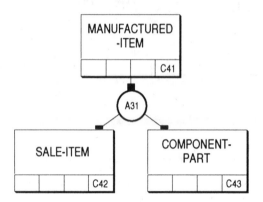

**Figure 9.11** *Example of role associations between non-human categories*

### 9.10.2 Association through specialisation

A second form of association is where one category is defined as a specialised sub-category of another. This kind of association is common in everyday life, where we make sense of the world by defining the world that we experience into sets of related categories. We may employ noun qualifiers to distinguish between, say, the categories of 'tree' and 'oak tree', whilst still recognising that the two types of thing are related in their essential nature. Note though that we sometimes recognise the association between two cognitive categories even though the names used do not make it obvious; an example is that everything that we call 'a sparrow' may also be described as 'a bird'.

This type of association is important because of the idea of inheritance. For example, a young child may first learn to recognise parts of the world that it perceives as being examples of BIRD. Later, the child may learn that the small red-breasted object fluttering on the bird-table is not only a 'bird' but also a 'robin'. Later still their understanding of the world may increase to understanding that all the things that are 'birds' also have their own specific species name or sub-category.

Interestingly, as the child's understanding of the categorisations grows the understanding of what is, or is not, 'a bird' changes. The two year old's understanding of a bird as being something that has wings and can fly gradually becomes expanded, so that by adulthood the category of BIRD can encompass things such as emus.

The important difference between this form of association between categories and role associations is that here the association is fully definitive. Everything that can be regarded as a bird **must** be also regarded as a robin, a thrush, an eagle or some other species. This is obviously different from the situation with role associations where a person may be a member of the medical practice or patient, but may be neither of these.

In the example, there are a number of such specialisation associations. The System Definition of S(1.7) for example specifically states that all resources will be classified as either drugs or equipment. This will be recorded in the data dictionary but Figure 9.12 shows how it might also be represented pictorially. The shading used indicates that there is nothing that is a resource that is not either a DRUG or EQUIPMENT. This is to say that what we mean by a 'resource' is completely defined by the meaning we attribute to 'drug' and 'equipment'.

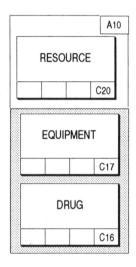

**Figure 9.12**    *Specialisation association for RESOURCE, DRUG and EQUIPMENT*

The case is slightly different regarding the category of SERVICE. It seems that MEDICAL-SERVICE is a sub-category of SERVICE, but this cannot be the only specialised form of service (otherwise the two categories would be equivalent). We could deal with this in two ways. We might choose to record MEDICAL-SERVICE as a sub-category, but indicate that other sub-categories exist, and that we have not completely defined SERVICE. Or we might add to the list of categories the inverse category of NON-MEDICAL-SERVICE. The specialisation possibilities of SERVICE are then completely defined. Figure 9.13 shows how both these possibilities could be represented.

### Inheritance of meaning
An important feature of both role and specialisation forms of associations is that the meaning of the higher-level category is wholly inherited by the lower-level category.

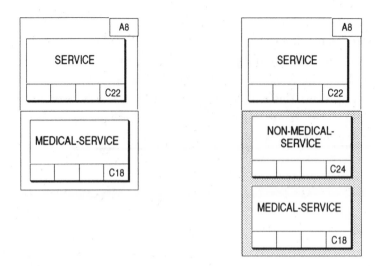

**Figure 9.13** *Alternative representations of the specialisations of SERVICE*

For example, suppose that we understand that a PERSON may be male or female, and that MEMBER-OF-MEDICAL-PRACTICE is a role that may be played by a PERSON. Then, because it is a role of PERSON, our understanding of the category MEMBER-OF-MEDICAL-PRACTICE must include the possibility of being male or female. Because the category DOCTOR-OF-MEDICAL-PRACTICE is a sub-category of MEMBER-OF-MEDICAL-PRACTICE, it too will inherit this possibility, and along with MEMBER-OF-MEDICAL-PRACTICE will also necessarily be involved in any other associations that PERSON may be involved in.

Inheritance is though uni-directional. No part of the defined meaning for PERSON will be inherited from the defined meaning for MEMBER-OF-MEDICAL-PRACTICE, and our understanding of the category of MEMBER-OF-MEDICAL-PRACTICE will be such that it includes properties or actions that are unique to itself and which the category PERSON does not have. Similarly, in the specialisation association between MEMBER-OF-MEDICAL-PRACTICE and DOCTOR-OF-MEDICAL-PRACTICE our understanding of DOCTOR-OF-MEDICAL-PRACTICE will be such that it has properties or may take actions that MEMBER-OF-MEDICAL-PRACTICE does not.

This accords with the way in which we use ideas of inherited properties in everyday life. If one of the criteria for something to be thought of as 'a bird' is that it has wings, and we recognise sparrows as a type of bird then we assume that a sparrow has wings. The characteristics of the cognitive category of BIRD are inherited by all those cognitive categories that are sub-categories of BIRD, including SPARROW. But we do not assume that the inheritance works both ways and we do not assume that the characteristics of a sparrow are inherited by all examples of a bird. Sparrows have, along with the characteristics shared by all birds, some characteristics that are uniquely their own.

In interpretative data modelling we employ the idea of inheritance in precisely the same way. Where a cognitive category is a sub-category of another cognitive category or a role that another may play then certain characteristics will be inherited from the super-category and some will belong only to the sub-category. For the moment we shall consider the term 'characteristics' to cover the meaning ascribed to the category and participation in associations. Thus we can formulate the two rules:

- Where a cognitive category A is a sub-category of another cognitive category B or a role which may be played by B, then the meaning ascribed to A will be to some extent dependent upon the meaning ascribed to B.
- Where a cognitive category A is a sub-category of another cognitive category B, or a role that may be played by B, then if B has an association with a third cognitive category C, then A will also have an association with C.

In the System Definition of the system S(1.7) the categories of DRUG and EQUIPMENT are sub-categories of the category RESOURCE. This means that not only will some part of the meaning ascribed to RESOURCE be inherited by DRUG and EQUIPMENT, but also that these will each participate in any associations in which RESOURCE participates. For example, if we recognise any association between the categories RESOURCE and TREATMENT-OF-PATIENT, then we simultaneously recognise the same association between DRUG and TREATMENT-OF-PATIENT.

### 9.10.3 Association through composition

Another way in which categories may be associated is through composition, where one category is understood to be composed of one or more other categories.

For example, let us imagine that we have identified a category called COURSE-OF-MEDICAL-CARE, and we understand a course of medical care to consist of a number of individual treatments given to a patient over a time. We might record this as in Figure 9.14.

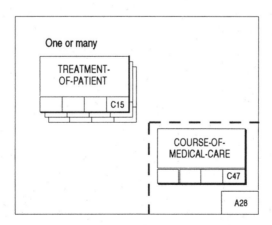

**Figure 9.14** *Representation of a composition association*

Figures 9.15 and 9.16 show how the same conventions may be used to represent more complex compositional associations. Figure 9.15 shows the composition of a System Definition of SSM, whilst 9.16 shows a fuller representation of the manufacturing situation described earlier where a manufactured item can be sold or used as a component in a sold item.

Use of the component association symbol should not be read as implying any form of inheritance of properties or associations. If it happens that a component category can participate in the same associations as the aggregate category then both associations will need to be separately recorded.

### 9.10.4  Association through the potential for action

A fourth way in which two categories may be related is through the potential for one category to perform some action upon the other. Our understanding of a category contains within it assumptions concerning what actions that category may perform with respect to other categories.

For example, our understanding of the category of DOCTOR-OF-MEDICAL-PRACTICE may allow that instances of such a category may *provide* a MEDICAL-SERVICE. Also, a definition of PATIENT as being a person registered by a doctor of the medical practice tells us that DOCTOR-OF-MEDICAL-PRACTICE may *register* PATIENT. Finally, we know from the System Definition that DOCTOR-OF-MEDICAL-PRACTICE may *authorise* TREATMENT-OF-PATIENT.

These possible actions need to be explicitly recorded in the data dictionary, showing each pair of categories linked by any actions that one may perform upon the other, as in Figure 9.17.

Note the distinction made in Figure 9.17 between the actions performable by DOCTOR-OF-MEDICAL-PRACTICE and by OTHER-MEMBER-OF-MEDICAL-PRACTICE. Both are sub-categories of MEMBER-OF-MEDICAL-PRACTICE and therefore inherit from that super-category the potential action of providing a NON-MEDICAL-SERVICE. The potential action of providing a MEDICAL-SERVICE is though restricted to the category DOCTOR-OF-MEDICAL-PRACTICE. Should the thinking behind this diagram ever be encapsulated in a real-life data storage mechanism then there would be data records of the occasions when medical services were provided. One design consideration would be to ensure that no record of such an occasion could be created unless there already existed a data record for the doctor who provided that medical service.

### 9.10.5  Associations arising from dependency of meaning

A final form of association between cognitive categories arises when the meaning of a category is dependent upon the meaning of two or more other categories.

In our example, the meaning of RESOURCE-USED-IN-TREATMENT-OF-PATIENT is obviously dependent upon the meanings attributed to the categories of RESOURCE and

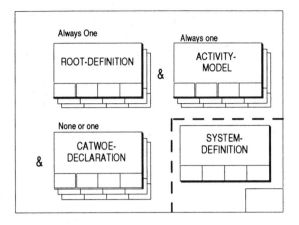

**Figure 9.15**   *Representation of the composition of a System Definition*

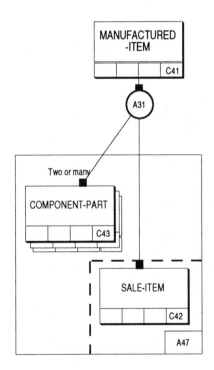

**Figure 9.16**   *Fuller presentation of the manufacturing situation*

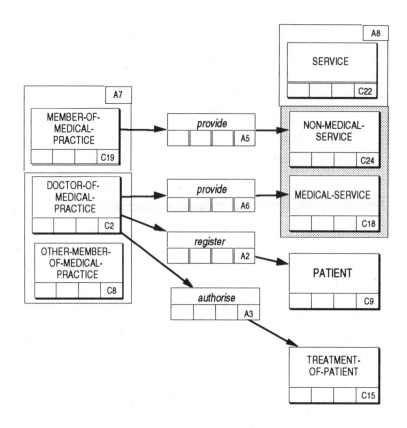

**Figure 9.17** *Representation of some valid actions understood to be possibly performed by the category DOCTOR-OF-MEDICAL-PRACTICE*

TREATMENT-OF-PATIENT. If our understanding of what constitutes a resource or a treatment changes, so too will our understanding of what constitutes a resource used in a treatment; for example, should drugs no longer be classified as a resource then such things as penicillin will no longer be thought of as one of the resources used in the treatment of a particular patient.

Moreover, should we ever abandon use of the category of RESOURCE, then we should be obliged to simultaneously abandon use of the category RESOURCE-USED-IN-TREATMENT-OF-PATIENT. Because the existence and use of this category depends upon the existence and meaning attributed to other categories we may consider it to be *weakly-defined*. Where dependence of meaning occurs and where a category is weakly-defined then this should be recorded in the data dictionary and shown as in Figure 9.18.

Identifying such weakly-defined categories becomes important if we ever wish to use the System Data Model to guide later database design. We may then wish to impose constraints on the database design, such as that it shall be impossible to record anything as a resource used during a patient's treatment unless that thing is already recorded as a

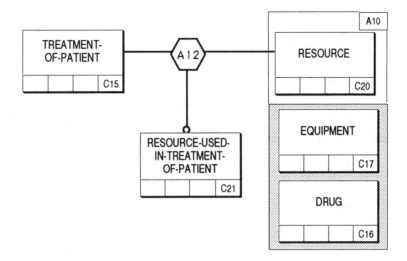

**Figure 9.18**    *Representing dependency of meaning for the category RESOURCE-USED-IN-TREATMENT-OF-PATIENT*

resource, and that details of resources (drugs or equipment) cannot be deleted unless we are certain that all records of their use in treatments can be deleted simultaneously.

## 9.11 CATEGORY-ASSOCIATION TABLES

A possible, though rather time-consuming approach to identifying associations is to consider *all* possible pairs of cognitive categories and then ask whether, in the context of the given system, any valid associations exist between each pair.

By thinking about every possible pairing we may identify associations that we should otherwise have missed. If this happens then it means that some ambiguity or lack of precision exists in the System Definition. It will be necessary to go back to the System Definition or data dictionary entries and make such amendments as are necessary.

If this approach is used then what is created is a category-association table. Such tables may be created and maintained manually, but this is time-consuming and it is better to use a simple database package. The general form of such a table is shown in Figure 9.19.

Note that if an association exists then it will give rise to two entries in the CAT, each describing the association from the viewpoint of one of the participating categories.

An apparent oddity is that the CAT invites the analyst to consider whether a cognitive category may be associated with itself. This is to allow for the possibility of there existing a special form of association, known as reflexive association. Genuine cases of such associations are rare, most apparent cases arising from ambiguities in the System Definition and not identifying all required categories, but one of the virtues of the CAT is that it forces the possibility of such associations to be considered. A further advantage of the CAT is that it fully documents the analysis; the table entries record not only details of

Every possible pairing of categories considered in body of table ↓

Details of any association between the pair of categories ↓

| CATEGORIES | | | | ASSOCIATION | | | | | |
|---|---|---|---|---|---|---|---|---|---|
| ID | Name | ID | Name | ID | Type | Name | | | |
| C2 | DOCTOR-OF-MEDICAL-PRACTICE | C2 | DOCTOR-OF-MEDICAL-PRACTICE | | | | | | |
| C2 | DOCTOR-OF-MEDICAL-PRACTICE | C9 | MEDICAL-SERVICE | A6 | Acts on | provide | | | |
| C2 | DOCTOR-OF-MEDICAL-PRACTICE | C19 | MEMBER-OF-MEDICAL-PRACTICE | A7 | sub-type of | | | | |
| C2 | DOCTOR-OF-MEDICAL-PRACTICE | C9 | PATIENT | A2 | Acts on | register | | | |

**Figure 9.19**    *Basic structure of a category-association table (CAT).*

the associations that have been identified but also explicitly record that certain pairs of cognitive categories *have* been considered and found to have *no* association.

A disadvantage of creating a CAT is that time will be spent considering associations that are either irrelevant in the context of the System Definition, or will be eliminated during later refinement. However, this will be time well spent if it makes the exclusion of such associations a more conscious and considered decision.

## 9.12 RECORDING ADDITIONAL DETAIL

We have now seen how to identify the cognitive categories required to make a particular System Definition meaningful, how those categories, and associations between categories may be defined in a data dictionary or a diagram. All the modelling done so far has been at a purely conceptual level. It has been based upon a System Definition that describes a *notional system*, not any part of the real-world, or any view of what the real-world *is*.

It is possible though that the circumstances of the intervention may lead us to make the notional systems that we model quite similar to the latter. It might be, for example, that those involved in modelling the medical practice are unable to conceive of doctors registering patients in any way other than the way it is done at present. In that case the System Definitions that they create, their understanding of categories such as PATIENT, and their understanding of associations such as 'may register', will all be constrained by their present experiences. In such cases recording additional detail in, and thereby 'constraining', the definitions of categories would be worthwhile.

One might for example wish to include details of the maximum number of instances of the category that could occur. In the example of the medical practice there might exist real-world legislative limits on the number of patients that can be registered with any single real-world medical practice. Perhaps these state that no doctor may serve more than 8,000 patients simultaneously. Choosing to accept this constraint when conceptualising relevant systems means we must record it in the appropriate CATWOE declarations, the definitions of categories and perhaps in the System Data Model.

Another thing that we might decide to record is whether we are assuming that every instance of a category must be involved in a certain association. For example, we might have already shown that for DOCTOR is to register PATIENT is an action that is recognised as possible, but is this compulsory? Does our understanding of the cognitive category of DOCTOR allow for someone who does not treat patients to be considered as an instance of DOCTOR?

We are probably restricting 'doctor' to cover only medically qualified individuals; we would not, in this context, consider someone with a Ph.D. in astronomy to be an instance of DOCTOR. But we might, or might not, further restrict our definition of 'doctor' to someone who treats patients. We could define DOCTOR as someone qualified and capable of treating patients; in that case a qualified medical practitioner would be an instance of DOCTOR even though they are permanently engaged in laboratory research and never treat patients. We would also regard as an instance of DOCTOR someone who has only recently qualified and not yet treated any patients.

We might instead choose to recognise someone as an instance of DOCTOR only if they are qualified and have treated at least one patient. The rationale for doing this could be that it is a patient-treatment system that is being modelled, and *within that context* the existence of doctors is only recognised in so much as they treat patients.

Neither of these possibilities are right or wrong; but it is important that the System Definition and System Data Model reflect the same assumptions about what is meant by DOCTOR. To do this we might show a maximum and minimum number for the association. This allows us to distinguish between the case where DOCTOR may but also may not have registered patients (Figure 9.20) and where the agreed definition of DOCTOR means that at least one registration has been enacted (Figure 9.21).

Adding such additional details to the System Data Model will therefore require considerably closer examination of the assumptions made in the System Definition and cause the analysts to identify many more of the assumptions made during modelling. In some cases there may be considerable debate amongst the group as to what assumptions do or do not apply. Where consensus can be reached then the assumptions should be explicitly stated in the System Definition. If no consensus can be reached then additional details should be omitted.

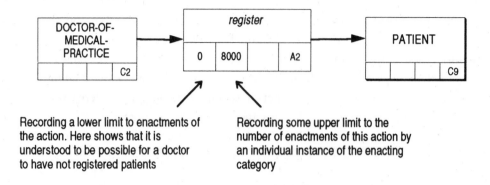

**Figure 9.20** *Showing detail of maximum and minimum enactments of an action association, non-enactment possible*

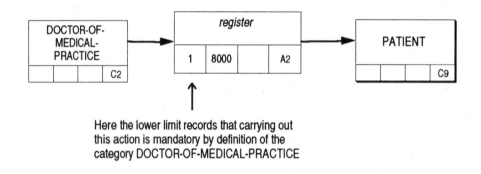

**Figure 9.21** *Showing detail of maximum and minimum enactments of an action association, enactment compulsory*

## 9.13 VALUE OF THE SYSTEM DATA MODEL

Developing System Data Models during an SSM analysis obviously requires additional time and effort, especially if System Data Models are created for every relevant system. It does, in return, offer many benefits.

Some of these are benefits for the process of the SSM analysis. These include that the System Data Model:

- Establishes a vocabulary for discussion and debate in SSM, and ensures that such discussion and debate are organised around a shared understanding of the identified relevant systems. By ensuring that there are no differences in the meaning attributed to the terms of the System Definition we add rigour to the modelling and avoid the dangers of misdirected debate. If two participants attach different meaning to the terms of a System Definition then they cannot be understanding that System Definition in the same way, and if that is the case then they are unlikely to have a very useful discussion through it vis-a-vis the real situation.

There may be two reasons why SSM does not already address this problem directly. First, there may be an unconscious reliance that shared social conditioning (the participants in modelling generally coming from similar professional and cultural backgrounds), together with the interaction through discussion and debate, will always lead to cognitive categorisations within an acceptable range of variation. Formal examination of the categories would in such cases be a relatively non-contentious process, but would give some defence against those assumptions being unfounded. A second possible reason is that ambiguity can sometimes be desirable, allowing for the temporary avoidance of confrontations that might threaten the continuance of the SSM analysis. In such situations then the flexibility of SSM allows that the detailed definition of categories may be postponed until later when more politically feasible.

● Provides further insight into the nature of the system being considered. A central premise of SSM is that the discussion and debate that flows from modelling relevant human activity systems and comparing these with the real-world situation may lead to learning and thence to the identification of desirable and feasible change. That discussion and debate would be enriched if the human activity system models under debate were accompanied by corresponding System Data Models. Considerations of feasibility might then include whether particular options for change are feasible in terms of their data implications. Such insights become more vital as strategic planning of the business activities becomes both more closely linked with, and constrained by, the planning of technical support for the business activities.

● Complements the Activity Model of the System Definition. The Activity Model provides a dynamic, activity-focused view of a system, showing the activities that any real-world expression of the system would logically be required to perform in order to *be* an expression of that system. The System Data Model provides a rather more structural view of the system. It shows those things that a data storage mechanism serving some real-world expression of the system would logically have to be capable of storing data about.

It is, however, where data and information requirements are an important part of the problem situation that there are very direct advantages to developing System Data Models, for they may act as the starting point for thinking about possible data storage mechanisms. In this they provide a route from the phenomenology of SSM to the harder techniques used in computer systems analysis and design.

If one of SSM's systems became realised in the real-world, then whatever precise form the real-world implementation took, there would be a need to do, in some way, the activities shown in the Activity Model for that system. The SSM analysis does not though, unless accompanied by premature design decisions, tell us exactly how those activities will be done. Rather than guess what the real-world implementation might look like and therefore what *information* its enactors may require, we may instead think about how to create *data* storage mechanisms that could be used by any real-world variant of the SSM system. Any such variant will need to, somehow, store and use data about the cognitive categories shown in the System Data Model. The System Data Model can therefore, whilst it is not itself any kind of blueprint for data storage, provide the basis for more conventional entity-relationship, object-oriented or other types of design model.

The dilemma faced by conventional data modelling is, as we saw in chapter 7, never being able to really justify what entities or objects are included in or excluded from the data model: this is now resolved. The decision to include some entity or object is guided by the existence of a particular cognitive category or association in a specific System Data Model, and this in turn is a consequence of some particular conceptualisation of a relevant system. If challenged, then the data analyst can trace the cause of any disagreement right back to the fundamental view taken of the problem situation and to the changes that participants have agreed to be desirable and feasible.

# Q & A: CHAPTER 9

Q.   In conventional forms of data analysis, entity-relationship data models or object-oriented models are created by information-systems specialists after discussions with the potential users. Does the same way of working apply here? Who is it that should create the System Data Models?

A.   It is true that the focus upon technological issues and on providing technical solutions means that data analysis and modelling is usually done by those individuals that have the specialised knowledge required for later database design. The problem-owners (the potential users of an information-system, the managers and staff of the organisation) are generally involved only in so much as they answer questions and are eventually required to confirm that the data model will satisfy their requirements.

In interpretative data analysis things are rather different. We have already seen that a System Data Model is created alongside the System Definitions; changes in one will always be reflected in the other and the same definitions of the cognitive categories must be used in both. This means that it is probably best if a System Data Model is created by the same group who formulated the System Definitions from which it is derived. This does not, of course, exclude the possibility of there being some facilitation provided by someone more experienced in this type of data analysis or able to look ahead to the design consequences of any decision made.

**Q.** **Are the data models talked about in this chapter really any different to those produced by conventional data modelling, in particular when creating 'logical' and 'semantic' data models?**

**A.** Although some of the data models produced by conventional data analysis are described as 'logical' models we must be suspicious about the use of that term. It certainly does not imply that the data structures shown are inevitable and that no other structure is logically possible.

Yourdon (1989) describes the entity relationship diagram as:

*.... a network model that describes the stored data layout of a system at a high level of abstraction. It is quite different from the dataflow diagram, which models the functions performed by a system; and it is different from the state-transition diagram, which models the time-dependent behaviour of a system" p.233*

Yourdon here uses the word 'system' in the hard systems thinking way, that is as a label for natural and man-made systems in the real-world (see Yourdon, 1989 pp. 9-39), so that when he talks of 'the stored data layout of a system at a high level of abstraction', what is referred to is the layout of some real-world data storage mechanism.

In this context a conventional data model may be 'logical' insofar as it is 'non-physical', and does not define precisely how and by what medium data will be stored and transmitted. It may also be an abstracted model, in that it focuses upon certain features but ignores the detail of others. But the model remains firmly rooted in reality.

The systems modelled in SSM, and therefore the System Data Models of interpretative data analysis, are of a different kind; neither represents, even in a highly abstracted form, either 'what-is' or 'what-shall-be'. There is then a major difference in the essential nature of the System Data Model and 'logical' data models of conventional data analysis.

Much the same argument applies to 'semantic' data models, although semantic data modelling is somewhat closer to interpretative data analysis, for some descriptions of it emphasise that its aim is to represent more closely a particular view of the world. In semantic data modelling the aim is to constrain the meaning of data items, especially through integrity and structural clauses in the database definitions. Rather than merely show a relationship between the entities CUSTOMER and ORDER we might, for example, show that such a relationship can exist *only* if the customer is not in debt, that there are *two* types of ORDER that may be placed or that the invoicing address for the ORDER *must* always be the address recorded for CUSTOMER.

This is done to determine how a particular data storage mechanism such as a database will operate; it will, for example, be physically impossible to create a new order if the customer for that order is currently in debt. It does, though, also have the effect of defining more exactly what one should understand such things as 'orders' to be. This is evident in Baskerville's (1993) suggestion for 'semantic database prototyping' in which end-users and designers gain a *shared understanding* by focusing on a prototype and engaging in a social process in which:

> *"... users and designers mutually must adjust their semantics, the rules of their language, their thinking, and ultimately their artefacts." p. 124*

Here there is some recognition that a data model is always to some extent an epistemological device, a coherent means of understanding a problem domain, rather than a description of the real-world. It also provides a formal vehicle and a focus for those negotiations, about how a data model will be understood, that commonly occur in practice but are rarely acknowledged in the literature of data analysis.

Semantic database prototyping is though proposed as a method *"... for permitting end-user validation of a semantic data model" (p. 124)* and it is emphasised that *"... the users must understand that they are validating the structure of the data stores. Otherwise, their comments will address myriad procedural aspects that are not reflected by the semantic data model." (p. 129)*. It is initiated *"... when analysts first meet with the users and conduct a brief study of the problem domain. They produce an entity-relationship diagram." (p. 125)*.

This suggests that it is most appropriate to conventional single application development and does not directly address the difficulties of producing data models in ill-defined problem situations involving a variety of potential users. It is in just those situations that we propose the use of interpretative data modelling.

Q.   **I can see that using SSM and doing this interpretative data analysis would lead to more questioning of the situation and people's assumptions. Suppose though that a conventional data analyst's view of the problem situation just happened to agree with the definition of some notional system. Would the System Data Model for that system, and the data analyst's data model, be much different?**

A.   If there are genuinely shared beliefs about the organisation, its aims and how they should be achieved, then the data models resulting from both types of data analysis might be similar. It is where there are issues and contention in the situation that an interpretative form of data analysis would be of greatest value, more rigorous and most defensible. Instead of hiding differences of opinion under the cloak of false consensus, or merely accepting power as the arbitrator between different views, an interpretative data analysis would recognise, and lay open for inspection, debate and possible modification, the distorting influences of the values and interests of the modellers.

It is though unlikely the results of the two types of data analysis would ever be quite the same, even in seemingly straightforward situations. This is because of the many unquestioned assumptions that a conventional data analyst's model will contain. These arise from using the real-world as the basis for data modelling.

Take, for example, the question of an order. In conventional data analysis this invariably leads to a data structure such as shown in Figure 9.22 where an entity such as ORDER has several related ORDER-LINES.

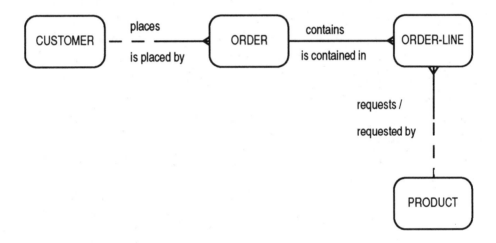

**Figure 9.22** *'Order' and 'Order-line' construct of conventional Entity-Relationship data model*

We do not need to worry about the diagramming conventions used, to think about what is implied by Figure 9.22. It reflects the current procedures: the request to buy several different products is normally placed on a single sheet of paper, an order form, for administrative convenience and to save stationery and postage costs. If the request to purchase a product was sent electronically though there would be no reason to group separate requests together. Each could be sent separately, being stamped with the details of the customer, time and date requested and any other data normally provided by the order-header of the order form.

So if the grouping of requested purchases is not a logical requirement, then why does conventional data analysis always lead to it being shown in the data model? The answer is that conventional data analysis begins by searching for things to include in the data model from the real-world situation. This inevitably leads to the idea of an order being confused with the physical artefact of the order form, and thence to: first, in normalisation, an ORDER-LINE relation being created because of the necessity to remove repeating groups during normalisation: secondly, in Entity-Relationship modelling, ORDER-LINE being created as a 'link-entity' in order to avoid an undesired many-to-many relationship between ORDER and PRODUCT. A convenience of pre-automated data transfer thus becomes institutionalised as part of the data model.

In interpretative data analysis this does not happen, for present processing procedures, including such things as order forms, are not used as the basis for deciding what should be included in the data model. Instead, as in Figure 9.23, customers and products are linked directly by a single association. The idea of grouping together purchase requests will only appear in the data model if a System Definition includes this as a specific requirement for the system, and before this is done the case for doing so will have to be argued. Otherwise the System Data Model, as in Figure 9.23, will only record that one of the valid actions that a customer may perform is to order products: there is no assumption about how this will be done. The data model produced is therefore genuinely at the conceptual level, and previous practice does not taint future thinking.

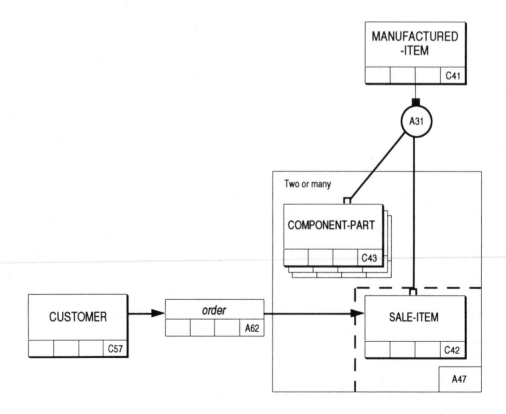

**Figure 9.23**    *Example of an ordering action in interpretative data modelling*

**Q.** **Doesn't the identification and definition of categories and associations take too long to do?**

**A.** It should not do. Once you have the definition of a system to start with then you can identify possible cognitive categories pretty easily. Of course, if there is little agreement about the meaning of the categories, or the discussion about them uncovers some ambiguities in the System Definition, then you might have to go back and change the definition of the system. Any iteration of that kind will take a little more time. Even then, though, it will be saving time in the long run. It is clearly better to sort out any disagreements at the very start of thinking about what might be done and before deciding what changes might eventually take place in the real-world situation. If those disagreements only become evident later then far more revision work will be necessary.

**Q.** **How can we ever know if we have identified the right categories?**

**A.** There cannot in principle be any single 'right' set of categories. If everyone involved in the modelling agrees that the given System Definition makes sense in terms of the categories identified, then they are 'right' for that group.

One thing that the group can choose to do, though, is to check that their understanding of the system remains unchanged if the System Definition is re-written, with replacement of any synonyms. Though the phrasing may now become a little clumsy, what is important is whether the group understand exactly the same thing by the two versions. If any subtleties of meaning have been lost then maybe they have classed as synonyms two separate ideas with slightly different meanings. In that case two separate categories may need to be defined, and the exercise repeated.

**Q.** **If two different groups start looking at the same definition of a system, should they identify the same set of categories?**

**A.** Probably not exactly the same, but then you would not expect that they would. They should come up with two broadly similar sets since they are working from the same System Definition, but the meanings that they ascribe to categories may not be precisely the same. Also, they may have chosen to use different names for the same categories.

It is hard to imagine a case where two sets of participants in the same problem situation might arrive at completely different sets of categories, but if that was possible then it must be preferable for it to be made obvious, and for the two groups to discuss why it has happened, rather than try to discuss the implications of a system that each is understanding in a different way.

**Q.** Is it the diagrams drawn with the conventions shown that constitute the System Data Model?

**A.** No. The real System Data Model is the understanding which participants share about the categories and their meaning. This does though need to be reflected and recorded in some physical equivalent. It is therefore the data dictionary entries, which may include explanatory diagrams, or the data dictionary entries plus such diagrams, that we have often referred to as the System Data Model.

**Q.** The way in which the possible cognitive categories have been identified from the words and phrases of the System Definition seems to place an awful lot of importance upon the way in which the system is described therein. Is not variation in wording and phrasing a potential problem?

**A.** Some practitioners of SSM do choose to employ loosely worded descriptions of relevant systems. It can be difficult to move from these to a System Data Model, but, we would argue, there can also be difficulties in using these as the basis for useful discussions.

Using the language of the System Definition as a starting point for identifying categories is surely justifiable since which words are used *does* matter. It is the choice of words that imparts what the conceptualised system is, or is not. Changing the wording could lead to a different data model, but this should be, for the changed language may now communicate a changed conceptualisation of the system. If it does not, then the changes to the System Data Model will be trivial.

Moreover, some of the differences arising from the use of language will be resolved later. For example, in modelling the associations between DOCTOR and PATIENT the details of the System Data Model will be, to some extent, determined by the fact that in the System Definition of S(1.7) the noun 'treatment' is used. The Root Definition, for example, uses phrases such as "... the cost of services provided during the *treatment* of a patient". One could though have only ever used the verb 'treat', saying for example "... the cost of services provided on the occasions when a doctor *treats* a patient". Now some of the categories would change (TREATMENT-OF-A-PATIENT would disappear as a category) and some associations would be different (we would now show 'treat' as a valid action of DOCTOR-OF-MEDICAL-PRACTICE).

The language with which we would discuss the system S(1.7) would therefore be rather different. For giving guidance towards possible data storage needs, though, such differences in the System Data Model would not be significant, As one expects data to be stored about not only categories but also the enactment of actions, both cases will suggest that data needs to be held about doctors and the occasions when patients are provided with treatments.

Q.    **Are the two processes of identifying the categories and investigating the associations between them really two different views of the same process?**

A.    Yes, and it is really somewhat incorrect to regard the identification of cognitive categories and the identification of associations between those categories as being two separate stages of the analysis. They cannot in principle be divorced from each other; our decisions as to what is, or is not, a valid action for a category forms part of our definition of the meaning ascribed to that category. However, for practical purposes it is more convenient to think of the two processes as being separate though closely connected.

Finally we include one question that the reader may like to consider for themselves:

Q.    **A well-known example of a Zen Buddhist koan is the question:** *Where does my fist go when I open my hand?*

**In interpretative data analysis how should one deal with those nouns of the language (such as *fist*) which describe neither a physical entity nor an event? Do they equate to categories, associations or neither?**

# 10 The Millside Medical Practice: an illustrative use of systems thinking

## 10.1 INTRODUCTION

One of the great strengths of soft systems thinking is that it can be tailored to the particular needs of each situation in which it is used. This means that no description of its use can ever be completely typical or act as a template to guide new applications. This must be remembered when, in this final chapter, we show how soft systems thinking might be used in a particular problem situation, that surrounding the Millside Medical Practice.

The Millside Medical Practice is a partnership of six general practitioner doctors. The practice currently suffers from a number of administrative difficulties concerning the storage and retrieval of patient records and the scheduling of appointments. The two senior partners, Drs Davis and MacKenzie, have already had discussions with a computer consultancy company, Immediate Technology Solutions. Their report suggested that the problems that the practice is experiencing might be solved by the purchase of new computer-based information-systems. They have proposed the use of a relational database together with several pieces of proprietary software and provided a detailed specification of the computer system that they would recommend and offer to supply.

The doctors are concerned that this advice might be coloured by the consultancy company's desire to sell to them an 'off-the-shelf' software solution and that what is proposed may be, to borrow a simile from their own field, a prescription for the symptoms rather than the disease. A second opinion has therefore been requested from an independent consultant, Mr Baker.

This is a problem situation in which 'the problem' seems to be the design of new computer-based procedures for office management and the issues, at first sight, appear to be technical ones. If this is were to be accepted then any of the available information-systems development approaches, which focus on such technical concerns, could be applied here. Instead, we shall see how using soft systems thinking and an interpretative data analysis reveals that there is rather more involved, leads to a more insightful analysis and increases the chance that the medical practice will obtain an information-system that better meets present and future needs.

## 10.2 ENTRY INTO THE PROBLEM SITUATION

Baker knows that the course of any intervention will always differ from that anticipated at its start, changes arising from a growing understanding of what is required or is possible and in response to changes in the situation. Nevertheless, there needs to be some initial agreement over a remit for the study and the first piece of analysis that Baker needs to do is not concerned with the problems of the Millside Practice. It relates instead to the expectations of the doctors regarding the study, what it is that the study will aim to achieve and how he will interact with the problem situation. The first step is therefore to negotiate entry into the problem situation and, in the language of SSM, to consider the *problem-solving* system rather than the *problem content.*

The most obvious products of this analysis will be the formal contracts or informal agreements, setting out the terms of the study, the expected timings and costs. Equally important, though, will be the less tangible outcomes: from thinking about the problem-solving process Baker will form expectations about the scale and scope of the study, have preliminary ideas about how he might investigate the situation, understand the co-operation and facilities that may be available and, in general, know better what he will be doing. For their part, the members of the medical practice will have clearer expectations of the study and the benefits that will accrue from it.

In the case of the Millside situation the first contacts with the senior partners are followed by an after-surgery meeting at which all the partners are present. Several remarks made here alert Baker to the fact that there are some basic issues upon which the partners disagree, and some differences of opinion concerning the future of the practice. It begins to look as if this study may need to concern itself with more than purely technical and design matters, and that there may be underlying issues that need to be brought to the surface.

Baker can see that some of the disagreements are of long standing, and that it would be unfruitful to go into them at this meeting. In his talks with the partners he therefore emphasises the importance of ensuring that any new computer systems should fit the practice, rather than vice-versa, and the need for the design of new computer systems to be preceded by a proper understanding of how the Millside Practice works. Baker then outlines some of the different problem-solving approaches that might be used, recommending that some form of 'soft' analysis might be valuable in the situation.

The outcome of this meeting is that it is agreed that there will be a preliminary ten days work, during which time Baker will investigate the workings of the practice and recommend whether to proceed with the computer-based information-system proposed by Immediate Technology. The results of this preliminary study will be reported to a meeting of all the partners. The work proper, the analysis of the problem content, can now begin.

### 10.2.1 Commentary on this first part of the study

During the first contacts with the senior partners and in the meeting with all the staff Baker has begun the cultural stream of enquiry of SSM. In his personal notes of the first meetings he has recorded a number of comments that suggest that there is, at least, a variety of opinion in Millside. He has also noted how, on non-medical matters, not all partners' views seem to be seen as of equal weight.

Baker's decision to not pursue the nature of the disagreements in the medical practice during the first meetings may seem merely common-sense, but his emphasis upon the need to understand the medical practice's 'business' was not. From previous chapters we may realise why this is certainly required, but by giving it so much emphasis here Baker has carried out a politically adept manoeuvre. Baker has already learned that the Immediate Technology consultant spent little time at Millside and whilst there spoke only to the two senior partners. Baker rightly judges that offering to listen to a wider group's views will be an attractive proposal from the perspective of the other members of the practice, who will now have the opportunity to state their opinions. Furthermore, presenting wider participation and an in-depth look at the business of the practice as being the cautious and wise option means that the senior partners need fear no loss of face from this second consultancy episode.

In terms of an analysis of the problem-solving system it is not yet clear who is to be assigned to the role of client. Is it to be one or both of the senior partners or is it to be all the doctors? The agreement to present his findings to all the partners suggests the latter but this is something which Baker will need to re-consider as the preliminary study unfolds.

## 10.3 APPRECIATING THE PROBLEM SITUATION

To gain as full as possible an understanding of the Millside Practice, Baker arranges a series of interviews with the doctors, receptionists and administrative staff. From these interviews come a number of facts concerning the practice, and perhaps just as valuable, a number of anecdotes and opinions about the way the practice works.

Baker finds that the Millside Medical Practice consists of six doctors, two nursing staff, two reception staff and three medical secretaries (one part-time). The practice is located in an urban area which, although once prosperous, has undergone a gradual decline in the last fifty years. The doctors agree that until recently the practice's list of registered patients probably displayed a higher than the national average level of senior citizen patients, members of minority ethnic groups, single parent families and family units with a lower than average income. The practice has built up a good local reputation for meeting the special needs of these groups, and two doctors, Drs Patel and Edwards, particularly stress that commitment to serving these groups remains strong.

Changes have occurred, though, in the last few years. Re-development of the canal and riverside areas has led to the area becoming a desirable and fashionable area to live and the high reputation of the Millside Practice has led to the majority of the new residents registering with this rather than other local medical practices. The result has been a change in the type of patients registered with the practice, with an influx of younger and wealthier residents with different expectations and requirements. One indication of this is that it has been suggested that a new 'Well Woman' evening clinic should be initiated, with a focus upon maintaining good health rather than the treatment of illness. Dr Singleton is currently organising this, but whether the Millside Practice can or should change in response to all such new requirements is an issue about which the partners cannot agree.

Another area of disagreement concerns how the practice should react to government initiatives and changes in legislation regarding the organisation of medical care. There has been discussion amongst the partners as to whether the practice should remain wholly within the national health care arrangements, take advantage of new legislation by opting to manage its own budget or even whether it should operate as a purely private practice for fee-paying patients only.

All the partners do agree, though, that the increase in registered patients has exposed a number of problems with the way that the practice is presently organised. These include; an excess of paperwork; difficulties in the storage of patient record cards and other material; increased workload; difficulties in scheduling appointments and a lack of waiting-room and surgery space. These problems are not merely inconvenient to the practice's staff but also affect the quality of service provided to patients and Baker decides that it would be worth doing some simple measurements to gauge the disservice caused. At his request the receptionists agree to do an additional task for a couple of days. Alongside each entry in the appointments book they note the time at which each patient actually enters the doctors consulting room. By this simple device some quantitative data is gathered about one aspect of the service given to patients. It is found that:

- 71% of patients began their consultation with the doctor more than 10 minutes after the time for which their appointment was arranged. The receptionists confirm that complaints by patients most often arise from their being kept waiting for long periods after their arranged appointment time.

- The average time between patients entering the doctors' rooms is 12 minutes and 34 seconds. This includes the 'non-patient' time required for the doctor to wash up and prepare for a new patient and for the reception staff to call the next patient. This seems to be the reason for the delays caused to patients, and suggests that perhaps slightly more time should be allowed for each appointment than the 10 minutes currently allowed. Clearly, it would be impractical to expect patients to attend for appointments at more precise times; inevitably the patient for a 10.47 appointment will arrive late or early. Perhaps, instead, it might be possible to build in some slack time into the scheduling so that the average patient's actual waiting time is reduced.

Whatever course the study finally takes, the difficulties posed by the existing patient records will have to be addressed. Normally Baker would want to do some investigation of the actual stored data but one difficulty faced by Baker in this particular study is that the need to respect doctor-patient confidentiality means he cannot have free access to the 'live' patient records. Baker does though obtain blank copies of the forms and documents used, to see the type of data that is presently recorded on these. Discussions with the medical secretaries also reveal that:

- There are currently 35,321 patients registered with the practice's six doctors and the number has been increasing over the last five years (Figure 10.1). Any new information-system must have sufficient capacity for several years' continuation of such growth.

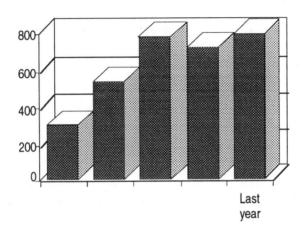

**Figure 10.1**    *Increase in Millside registrations over the preceding five years*

- There is a great variation in the size of the records kept for patients. Some patients have had as many as two hundred treatments in the last five years; others have had none. If, as Immediate Technology has suggested, a database is to be used in the new information-system then it will be necessary to ensure that sufficient space is available for many such large groupings of data relating to a single patient.
- There is, in data processing terms, a large variability in the activity on the existing records. The records of some patients are frequently retrieved and updated. Some other patients make little use of the doctors' services and their records may not have been looked at or changed in several years. This may be important later, during the design of any new computer-based information-system, when access to the most used records might be optimised.

This sort of fact finding allows Baker to build up a rich picture of the problem situation, which he records and, for his own purposes, shows in the Rich Picture Diagram shown in Figure 10.2.

It is now clear that the study might proceed in many different ways. At one extreme Baker might accept as given that 'the problem' concerns the Millside Practice's present administrative difficulties of a large amount of paperwork, the increasing patient list and problems of scheduling appointments and doctors' time. At the other extreme the whole focus of the study might change towards helping the partners reassess the missions and

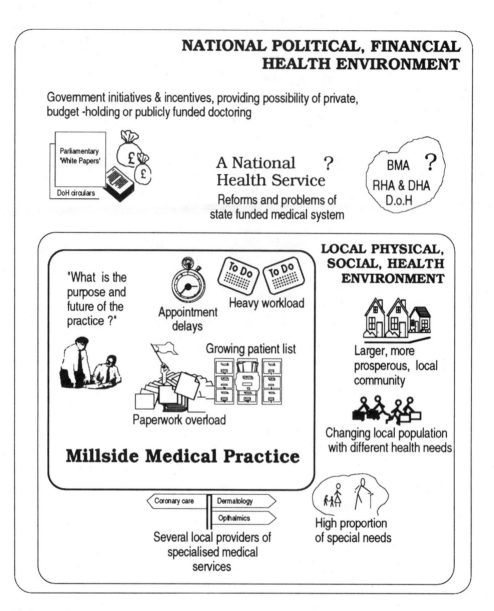

**Figure 10.2**    *Rich picture diagram for the Millside study*

future of the practice. Before continuing any further it is time for the remit of the study to be re-considered, if necessary re-written, and for both Baker and the doctors to be clear what the outcomes of the study will be. Discussions with the senior partners reveal that the former is not a realistic option, but they accept that some of the wider concerns need to be taken account of. Baker then prepares carefully for his second group meeting with the doctors.

## 10.3.1  A second group meeting

In that meeting Baker reports the findings of the preliminary study. As much as possible the language used is neutral and the intention is to give a disinterested outsider's view of the practice and its present situation in purely factual terms. Graphs and pie-charts are used to communicate some of the facts concerning changes in the local area, numbers of patients and other data.

Baker's conclusions are that the problems of administration cannot be completely divorced from questions of the future shape of the practice, and that there may be problems with the software package proposals made by Immediate Technology. Before accepting those proposals the medical practice needs to specify its own particular requirements. Immediate Technology should be asked to tailor its proposals to meet these, provide some alternative solution or the practice should look to other suppliers.

In the discussions that follow it becomes clear that while there are different views about changes in emphasis regarding the Practice's activities there is no real commitment to making large structural changes at present. As one of the partners says:

*"We are not in a position to totally change what we do, or how we work. There have been so many changes in health care nationally already, and there is no certainty about what might happen tomorrow. But we do know for certain about the problems that we have already."*

Gradually, a consensus emerges and it is agreed that Baker should do some further work to define the practice's requirements. The focus of this work should be upon improving the procedures and information-systems that serve the present practice, but flexible and robust answers will be looked for. Ideally, any new procedures and information-systems should be capable of supporting not just the Millside Practice of today, but any new forms of the Millside Practice that the partners may wish to move towards in the future.

Baker's final task in this meeting is to explain what needs to be done next, and he proposes that the next stage will be to identify some relevant systems, though this is done rather indirectly. Baker suggests that to think through the information requirements of the practice requires some detailed knowledge of what the practice's essential 'mission' or purpose is. A way of doing this that has been found useful elsewhere, Baker says, is to think about the different possible things that such a medical practice might aim to achieve, and to then think about what activities would need to be done as a consequence.

Baker is careful to not give the impression that the relevant systems being identified are proposals for the future of the Millside Practice. He emphasises that these are devices to enable further discussion and that the future of the Millside practice will probably never look like any of these.

At the end of the meeting a number of the partners express their feeling that the meeting has been useful in 'bringing things out into the open'. One of the doctors is though concerned that the views of patients, and the views of the reception staff and assistant medical staff have not, so far, been aired. Baker notes these comments and that the views of other stakeholders may need to be brought into future discussions.

### 10.3.2 Commentary on this part of the study

It might seem that a great deal of time and effort has been spent in getting to this point but the value of the work so far has been immense. Not only does Baker now have a clear idea of what is required and of what outcomes would be acceptable but has also gained a level of commitment and ownership for the study that the previous work by Immediate Technology never had. Whatever final recommendations are made, these will have a far greater chance of being accepted and acted upon.

We should note that Baker appears to have resolved the question of whom he is assigning to the role of 'client' in this study, for it was to the senior partners that he turned to resolve the issue of how the study should proceed. Had he instead assigned all the partners to that role, or if the senior partners had wished for greater discussion of the wider issues, then the next meeting might have been of a different kind. One possibility is that a workshop form of meeting might have been arranged in which all were invited to discuss the various issues and their perceived importance. Baker might here have used a group activity, such as asking each partner to name the strengths, weaknesses, threats and opportunities for the practice (a 'SWOT' analysis), to open up discussion or have led the doctors through the creation of their own Rich Picture Diagram.

We can also see that over time, from the first meeting with the senior partners, both Baker and those in the Millside practice have been acquiring a clearer idea of how they might work together and of what this might entail. The negotiations over the terms of the formal remit, the planning of activities and their timing have all led to expectations of which, of the many possible studies that might happen, will happen. Both sides have acquired a clearer 'image' of the study.

Formal techniques such as PERT/CPM project planning can be useful in this 'imaging' process. While they are primarily used to provide benchmarks for measuring progress and expenditure, drawing up project plans and timetables also helps to eliminate vagueness or ambiguity over the nature of the study. Even if there is uncertainty over precisely what will happen from day to day, even if activities can only be specified at a high-level and timings are more guesses than estimates, it is useful to create a project plan for an SSM study.

While clear, shared expectations of what a study is to 'deliver' and of how it is to be conducted will help the study to go more smoothly, there is though a balance to be made. Neither side, those in the situation or the would-be problem solvers, will wish to make hasty decisions or commit themselves to courses of action that may, in the light of further investigation, prove to be inappropriate. In the Millside study Baker has charted a middle course. The last meeting has given him a good idea of what might be (and what might not be) welcomed as outcomes from the study. The official agreement for the study is now fairly focused and identifies the information support systems as the primary concern for future work. But there is still scope to look beyond that area and consider the possible effects of different futures for the practice.

Finally, we may deduce from Baker's actions that he has also imaged the study in ways that he has not shared with the doctors. The decision to avoid using the technical terms of

SSM, and to talk of possible mission statements rather than Root Definitions of relevant systems, both tell us something of how he expects to interact with the doctors. This is not to be a study during which the partners are expected to learn how to carry out SSM. Rather it is to be a study in which soft systems thinking will be used to help Baker facilitate discussion and learning. This illustrates the way in which, in any intervention situation, thinking always occurs on two levels. The most evident of these is the thinking concerning the problem content of the situation; this is the thinking concerned with helping the client or 'solving the problem'. There is though always, happening simultaneously, thinking about the intervention itself. As we saw back in Chapter 2, this was not always recognised in the past, but to do both types of thinking is a requirement when using SSM.

## 10.4 MODELLING RELEVANT SYSTEMS

The decision has been made that the remainder of the study should look at how the administrative procedures of the Millside practice could be improved so as to better support the work of the practice. The proviso has been made though that the study should also give attention to the changes that would be required if the practice moved to being a fund-holder or private practice.

The most obvious choice for a relevant system here would seem to be one concerned with providing administrative support to the Millside medical practice. The notion of 'support' that was discussed in chapter 6 tells us, however, that one cannot begin by focusing upon a support system, one must always look first at the system to which support is to be given. In the Millside situation we have a concrete example of this, for it is impossible to imagine a system to provide administrative support in the absence of any idea of what the activities to be supported are.

Baker could resolve this in the conventional IS manner, by using the present activities of the practice as his guide. He could map out in detail the data flows and data stores currently used and then design an administration system for these, albeit with perhaps some changes to make things more efficient. To do this would, though, build into any new information-system the assumptions of the past. Furthermore it would give no insight into what changes would be required if the Millside Practice were to become a budget-holder or a private practice.

So, for the moment, Baker chooses to put to one side his knowledge of the present administrative arrangements. He tries to understand, instead, what activities would be logically required if the practice remains as part of the national health service arrangements, if it moves to being a fund-holder or if it becomes a private practice. To do this he conceptualises three systems, namely:

- System S1: A system to provide medical care and services to patients in return for payments.
- System S2: A system to provide medical care and services to patients within the organisational procedures required by a nationally organised health service.

- System S3: A system to provide patients with medical care and services within the constraints imposed by available funds managed by the practice

SSM System Definitions are then created for each of the chosen relevant systems, with Activity Models showing the activities that each system would have to perform, if it was to be that system. When each has been explored in detail then it will be possible to consider what "supporting the operations of the Millside Practice" could mean in each case.

Baker is not surprised that when the essence of these systems is discussed with the partners a number of modifications to the Root Definitions and Activity Models are necessary; those in the situation normally have a far greater understanding of the issues and of the constraints that need to be taken into account. The models are repeatedly amended in the light of this learning and Figures 10.3 and 10.4 show one of the resulting System Definitions.

## 10.4.1 Modelling to higher resolution levels

The models produced so far are not of sufficient detail to allow Baker to arrive at any conclusions about data processing implications. For each of them, modelling will need to be done at the next resolution level. For example, the required activity 7 of Figure 10.4 is 'Know costs of treatments provided to patients'. There are many ways in which this might be achieved, and by conceptualising systems to carry out that activity, one will be better placed to understand what it is that must be done.

Baker therefore creates new System Definitions, describing systems for each of the activities shown in the Activity Model of S(1). Figures 10.5 and 10.6 show the Root Definition, Activity Model and CATWOE declaration for one of these, that for the activity 'Know costs of treatments provided to patients' referred to above. The systems S(2) and S(3) are similarly modelled to the next level of resolution.

## 10.4.2 Creating System Data Models

Whilst creating the System Definitions for the Millside Study, Baker has been building three System Data Models, one for each of the three relevant systems first identified. As modelling has moved to higher levels of resolution, these System Data Models have been amended and added to.

This work has a very practical value, for the cognitive categories and associations identified may, at a later stage, have data storage equivalents. For example, Baker has identified a category of PATIENT and some associations in which it participates. As this category arises for each of the three relevant systems being considered, it seems likely that any variant of the Millside practice would need to know and use data about patients. The data dictionary entries that have been made will provide a useful starting point for deciding what sort of data might need to be held.

By the time that Baker decides that the modelling of systems has been done to sufficient detail, the three relevant systems each have their own System Data Model.

| SYSTEM DEFINITION OF : | Page    1   of   2 |
|---|---|
| S(1), a system that provides medical treatment to registered patients in return for payment | Version   _____ |

**ROOT DEFINITION**

A medical-practice owned and operated system to provide those persons registered as patients of the doctors of the Millside Medical Practice with treatments, appropriate to their medical condition, in return for payment.

**CUSTOMERS OF THE SYSTEM**

| Advantaged | Disadvantaged | Other Stakeholders |
|---|---|---|
| Registered patients | | Doctors and other members of the Millside Medical Practice |

**ACTORS**      Doctors of medical practice or other members of medical practice

**TRANSFORMATION**

Need of registered patients for treatment ⟹ (T) ⟹ That need satisfied by purchased treatment

**WELTANSCHAUUNG**

That registered patients should be able to purchase the medical treatments they require and that payments made by patients should cover fully the costs of the treatments that they receive.

**OWNERSHIP**

Millside Medical Practice

**ENVIRONMENTAL CONSTRAINTS**

| Constraints imposed by environment | Constraints accepted in modelling |
|---|---|
| The treatments given to patients will be appropriate to the medical condition of the patient. | That all treatments will be prearranged and scheduled |

**Figure 10.3**    *Root Definition and CATWOE declaration of the system S(1), a system to provide medical care and services to patients in return for payments.*

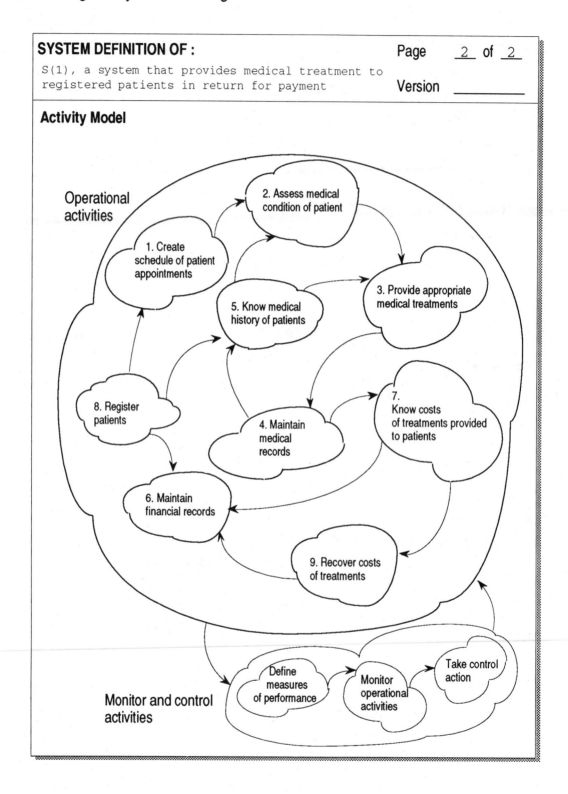

**SYSTEM DEFINITION OF :**   Page   2 of 2

S(1), a system that provides medical treatment to registered patients in return for payment   Version _____

**Activity Model**

Operational activities

2. Assess medical condition of patient

1. Create schedule of patient appointments

3. Provide appropriate medical treatments

5. Know medical history of patients

8. Register patients

4. Maintain medical records

7. Know costs of treatments provided to patients

6. Maintain financial records

9. Recover costs of treatments

Monitor and control activities

Define measures of performance

Monitor operational activities

Take control action

**Figure 10.4**   *Activity model of the system S(1)*

| SYSTEM DEFINITION OF : | Page   1 of 2 |
|---|---|
| S(1.7), a cost of treatment recording system | Version _____ |

## ROOT DEFINITION

A medical-practice owned and operated system which enables the cost of treatments to be known by calculating and recording both the cost of the resources used in a treatment and the cost of services provided during the treatment of a patient.

## CUSTOMERS OF THE SYSTEM

| Advantaged | Disadvantaged | Other Stakeholders |
|---|---|---|
| The medical practice, which is able to recover the costs of treatments | | Patients, who have an interest in that the system should be accurate. |

## ACTORS

Doctors of medical practice or other members of medical practice

## TRANSFORMATION

Unrecorded costs of treatments $\Rightarrow$ (T) $\Rightarrow$ Accurately recorded costs of treatments

## WELTANSCHAUUNG

That patients of the medical practice should pay for treatments and that payments made by patients should cover fully the costs of the treatments that they receive.

## OWNERSHIP

Medical practice as in system S(1)

## ENVIRONMENTAL CONSTRAINTS

| Constraints imposed by environment | Constraints accepted in modelling |
|---|---|
| That all treatments require use of resources and provision of services. That when costs of treatment are recorded they must be recorded accurately. That all patients must be charged for treatment in the same way and on the same basis. | All resources to be classed as either equipment or drug. Medical services to be treated in the same way as other services. The cost of a treatment is equivalent to the cost of the services and resources involved. It is possible to identify or define a cost for each resource or service. |

**Figure 10.5**    *Root Definition and CATWOE declaration of the system S(1.7), a system that enacts the activity 'Know costs of treatments provided to patients'*

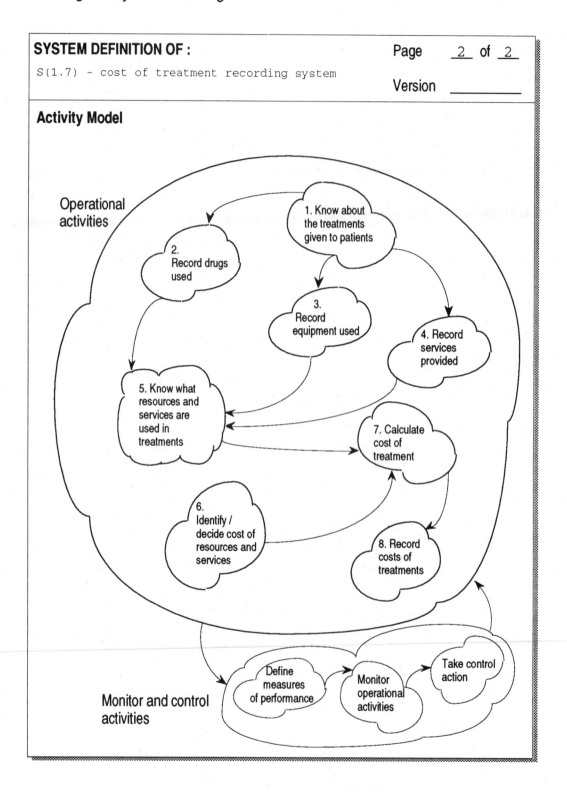

**Figure 10.6** *Activity model of S(1.7), the system to record cost of treatments.*

These show the things about which any real-life implementation of that particular system would have to store data.

### 10.4.3 Commentary on the modelling of systems

Some criticisms could be levelled at how SSM was used in this part of the study. First, although Baker has used the SSM models as the basis for discussion with the doctors, it was Baker who created those models. It would perhaps be better if the modelling had been done more directly by the doctors; they then would be more committed to the results of any analysis using those models.

Baker's choice of what to do was though a response to the particular situation in which he found himself. The continuing stream of cultural enquiry suggested both that the doctors were not interested in learning SSM and that it was unlikely that they could find sufficient spare time for the modelling. Therefore, he created the models, and only afterwards initiated a debate. This is a perfectly valid use of SSM.

We may note that there was some change in the systems modelling when moved to higher levels of resolution. As before, Baker could have modelled and orchestrated discussion over a number of different systems. Baker has instead modelled, for each of the activities at the first level of resolution, only one system at the next resolution level. For example, for the activity 'Know costs of treatments provided to patients' of S(1) he has modelled only the system defined in Figure 10.5 and Figure 10.6: other possible systems to do that activity have not been brought into the analysis. It might be argued that Baker has, in this way, constrained possible debate, but in his defence we must recognise that every application of SSM is bound by the needs of the particular situation. Baker's decision was here determined by the seemingly straightforward nature of the transformation (costs of treatments unrecorded to those costs recorded), the difficulty of involving others in this level of detailed modelling and the constraints of time.

## 10.5 LEARNING AND CHANGE

With the system modelling complete it is time to apply the results to the Millside Medical Practice.

Baker knows that there are a number of ways in which SSM models may be used, the most common being to use the activities of a SSM model as the basis for asking questions of the real-world procedures. For each activity of a model one might ask:
- Is there any way that this activity is done at present?
- If so, how is it done? By whom?
- Is it done well? What shortcomings exist?
- How might it be done differently or better?

This approach would not though be appropriate to the Millside study. First, the agreed remit for the study is not to re-organise the medical practice but to help provide an information-system for the practice. Secondly, he does not expect that the doctors will be able to make sufficient time available for participation in workshops or detailed discussions. Finally, and perhaps most importantly, there is no expectation that many of the activities in the models will be done, in any way, at present. Baker knows, for example, that because the practice presently works within nationally determined health service procedures, activities such as 'Calculate the costs of treatments provided to patients' have no real-world equivalents in the Millside practice.

An alternative use of the systems models might be to follow Wilson (1990) in creating a 'consensus primary task model' from the models that have been created so far. Wilson suggests that from several modelled systems one may identify a set of activities common to all the models. A new Root Definition may then be created (after some experimentation and iteration) so as to define a new system, one whose required activities are, possibly with some activities added, the same as those common to the previously identified systems. Wilson argues that this is reasonable on the assumption that

> *".... no matter what kind of organization is being considered, there will be a description of it that will achieve global consensus, ie a neutral primary task description" p. 94.*

In this way, it is argued, the SSM-user will obtain, even though the originally modelled systems might have been wildly different, a System Definition with which all agree and that represents the 'primary task', the most basic activities required in a problem situation. From this it is hoped that the data required for each activity can be identified, and so the basic data processing needs may be specified.

Baker feels that fully adopting this approach would not be appropriate to the Millside situation as it would concentrate attention on only the non-contentious activities that are common to all the modelled systems. Furthermore, he feels unhappy about working backwards *from* a set of activities *to* the Root Definition of a system.

Some elements of both these uses of the systems models could, though, be used in a data-focused analysis of Immediate Technology's proposals for a new information-system.

### 10.5.1  Using the systems modelling

Baker decides to examine Immediate Technology's proposals from two perspectives, the activities supported and the adequacy of the proposed data storage mechanisms, in the manner shown in Figure 10.7.

#### Support for activities

To decide what activities Immediate Technology's proposed information-system would support, Baker will first look for activities that are common to the three systems that he has modelled. In this way Baker will be able to specify activities that seem to be essential to the operation of any variation of the medical practice. Taken together these are not the activities of any system, they are merely an aggregated set of activities, but one might expect any new information-system for the medical practice to support these.

All the three systems that Baker modelled, for example, require that people be registered as patients, that some such patients be given medical treatments and that some

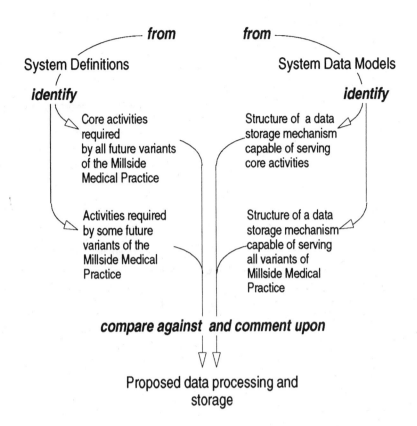

**Figure 10.7**   *Using systems modelling to evaluate the proposed information-system*

knowledge of a patient's medical history be available before treatments are given. Baker can say, then, that any information-system to support the medical practice, whether manual or computer-based, should allow for data about patients, about occasions when doctors registered patients and when treatments were given to patients to be stored, retrieved and updated. He may then ask if Immediate Technology's proposed information-system does so.

Not so essential, but certainly desirable, is that the proposed information-system could accommodate other activities, those that are not common to all the modelled systems. For example, whilst to be able to record details of the treatments given to patients is a core requirement, recording the cost of those treatments is not: this would only be required if the practice in future manages its own finances or goes private. Would the information-system that Immediate Technology is proposing allow the cost of treatments to be recorded and, if not, then how easily could it be modified to do so?

Asking that question for each of the non-common activities provides the second means of analysing activity support, and will allow Baker to assess how stable is the proposed information-system, or how vulnerable it would be to changes in the way that the practice operates in future. For this a comparison table may be constructed. This shows, for each activity of each modelled system, the ease or difficulty of supporting that activity using the proposed information-system (Figure 10.8).

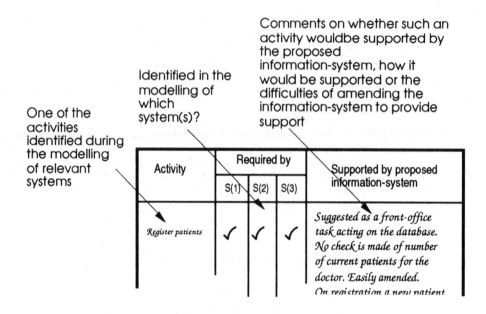

One of the activities identified during the modelling of relevant systems

Identified in the modelling of which system(s)?

Comments on whether such an activity wouldbe supported by the proposed information-system, how it would be supported or the difficulties of amending the information-system to provide support

| Activity | Required by | | | Supported by proposed information-system |
|---|---|---|---|---|
| | S(1) | S(2) | S(3) | |
| *Register patients* | ✓ | ✓ | ✓ | *Suggested as a front-office task acting on the database. No check is made of number of current patients for the doctor. Easily amended. On registration a new patient* |

**Figure 10.8**    *Assessing the support given to the three system's activities by the proposed information-system*

### The adequacy of data storage

Alongside this examination of the activities supported, Baker will evaluate the proposals for data storage. If all the data used by and generated by Millside Medical Practice were stored in a well-designed database then that database should be able to meet both present and future requirements. Such a database would be able to support the data processing required by the practice operating as now, or if in future that was the route chosen, the practice operating as a private or budget-holding practice. If Baker can describe the structure of such a database then this may serve as one way of understanding the extent to which Immediate Technology's proposals will satisfy Millside's needs.

The three System Data Models show the cognitive categories and associations meaningful in respect to the three conceptualised systems. If Baker identifies the categories and associations relevant to the common, core activities then he will have guidance as to the things about which a new information-system must store data.

For example, for the activity 'register patients' the System Data Models of all three modelled systems show an action association of 'register' between the categories of DOCTOR-OF-MEDICAL-PRACTICE and PATIENT. A relational database equivalent of these categories and this association would require two relations storing data about doctors and patients, plus a third relation storing details of the occasions when a patient was registered by a doctor (Figure 10.9). The database structure proposed by Immediate Technology should contain these relations and provide, through foreign keys, the ability to relate the data held within them.

The categories and association

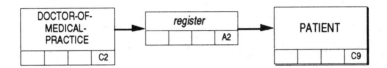

might be implemented in a set of relations as

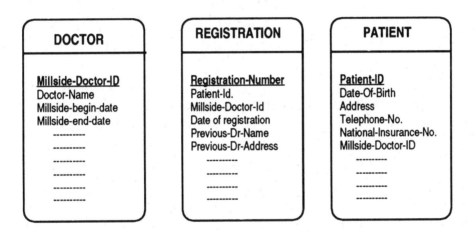

**Figure 10.9**    *Categories and associations relevant to the registering of patients from the three System Data Models, and a relational database equivalent*

In addition, Baker can investigate the flexibility of Immediate Technology's proposals for storing data. Many of the categories and associations in the three System Data Models will have no equivalents in the proposed data structure. For example, while all the System Data Models show a category of DRUG, not all show that drugs are a type of resource or that the resources used in a treatment have a cost. As calculating and recording such costs is not presently required, Baker is not surprised to find that Immediate Technology's proposals do not allow for data about resources or costs to be stored. What, though, if in future such data is needed? Could the proposed data storage design be easily modified?

To investigate such questions Baker combines the three System Data Models. In doing this he creates not a new System Data Model but a 'composite model'. The real-world equivalent of this composite model would be the structure of a database that could equally well accommodate the needs of the Millside Medical Practice operating as at present, as budget-holder or as a private practice. Baker would not suggest that such a database be implemented, for the machine overheads of processing and maintaining its structure would be too great. Understanding what such a totally flexible data structure would look like will, however, be an excellent guide to assessing the flexibility of Immediate Technology's proposed database structure.

So, using the approach shown in Figure 10.7 Baker is able to use the systems modelling of SSM to evaluate both the scope and the flexibility of the information-system that Immediate Technology is proposing.

## 10.6 BRINGING ABOUT CHANGE

A final meeting is now held, in which Baker explains to the assembled group of doctors and administrative staff something of how the work has been done. Looking at the activities required for private practice, budget-holding and remaining in national health service arrangements has, he explains, provided the means for assessing the suitability of the proposed information-system, both for now and for whatever course the Millside Practice chooses to take in the future.

The information-system recommended by Immediate Technology, Baker tells the group, would support most of the core activities, but maybe not in the best possible way. Maintaining the appointments list, for example, is in Immediate Technology's proposals done as a stand-alone task by a proprietary software package. It would be better if this was integrated with the rest of the information-system so that appointments and medical histories of patients could be viewed together. Furthermore, the way in which the proposed information-system would store the practice's data is not entirely satisfactory.

Immediate Technology has recommended the use of a relational database system and provided file definitions of the files to be used. They have also described the operations that will be supported by their proposed information-system. Baker's analysis suggests that if a relational database system is to be used then this needs to include different files and relationships (implemented through foreign keys), and have a different structure, from that which Immediate Technology have proposed. For example:

- Baker's analysis suggests that a separate file should be used to hold details about the doctors working in the practice. In Immediate Technology's recommendations such a file does not exist. The only data items relating to doctors are where the name of a doctor appears in the field 'Registered doctor' within a patient's record or a registration record, the name of the attending doctor is recorded in a treatment record or used in an appointments record. Baker believes that this reduces the flexibility of the information-system and makes it difficult to produce, for example, reports of the drugs used in treatments authorised by a particular doctor.
- Immediate Technology's recommended way of storing details of the treatments given to patients mirrors the notes made by doctors in the existing card records, with an unformatted text description to be added by the doctor. The composite model though suggests that specific fields should be used to note the drugs and other resources used.

- Immediate Technology's recommendations do not include any of the design considerations necessary if the costs of treatments are to be calculated or payments are required of patients. To be able to calculate the costs of treatments would be required if the practice was to manage its own budget or become a private practice; to charge patients is also required if the practice 'goes private'. To accept the Immediate Technology's recommendations would therefore mean that difficult amendments or the replacement of the information-system would be needed if, sometime in the future, the practice took either of these routes.

None of such points of difference indicate that Immediate Technology's proposals should be rejected outright, but they do suggest modifications. A file of data concerning doctors could, for example, be added with little difficulty. For the moment it might contain few fields and be rarely used, but the minimal processing overheads caused by its inclusion would be outweighed by the flexibility that its inclusion would provide.

To provide a computer system that meets the additional requirements might cost slightly more than that proposed by Immediate Technology, additional software would need to be written, for example, to replace the packaged software that was proposed for handling appointments. Baker recommends the modifications despite this, for the additional costs are, he believes, compensated for by the additional flexibility that they provide and may be offset by future savings. Estimated costs are included in the printed report that is made available for all to study and to comment upon. The next stage of the work will be to discuss with Immediate Technology, and other possible suppliers, how the practice's requirements can be met by a computer-based information-system.

It is agreed that Baker will undertake these discussions and act as the practice's agent in the procurement and implementation of a computer-based information-system. This part of the work will not be discussed here, other than to note that Baker's use of soft systems thinking may not be over. Later, perhaps when considering training of staff and how to bring the new information-system into operation, Baker might choose to model systems to implement the new information-system and use these as a guide to what must be done.

## 10.7 FINAL COMMENTS

It is characteristic of work in the information-systems field that, even when the work has been completed, one can never truly know that it was done in the best possible way. This is not a field in which one can devise experiments to 'prove' the superiority of one approach over another, for one can never develop the same information-system twice. Thus, even at the end of the work described, neither Baker nor we can say for certain that the decisions made about how to carry out this study, the choice of systems to model, or how to use those models were correct. The study appears to have been successful and fulfilled the clients' expectations, but perhaps even more successful results might have been achievable.

The Millside study can therefore only be illustrative, and should not be seen as a prescriptive blueprint for how to carry out such studies in future. Within it can be seen some key features of using a systems approach for work in information-systems.

- There has been a focus upon, not the information-system, but upon the essential business and the business activities that the information-system is to serve. Baker's work has throughout been driven by what the medical practice, not the computer system, might do.

- There has been a conscious and consistent use of the basic concepts of systems thinking, especially those concerned with human activity systems.

- Using systems concepts has not precluded use of ideas and techniques borrowed from other disciplines. Baker has not been shy of using interviewing, observation, measuring and charting or document analysis as ways of finding out as much as possible about the operations of the Millside Practice. Nor, in the later stages where he has considered Immediate Technology's proposals, has he ignored the value of the techniques and language of computer systems analysis for discussing technical aspects of the information-system.

- There has been continuous thought about how the study will be done as well as about the content of the study. Baker did not plan out exactly what the study would consist of on day one, and then do that. He instead at every stage reviewed how the study was progressing, how the situation was changing, and tailored his work to the needs of the situation and to the social and political context of the study.

- Perhaps most importantly of all, it has never been forgotten that all information-systems work is work carried out in a social setting. Baker was always conscious that the result of this work would affect the lives of the doctors, the administrative staff of Millside and, indirectly, the lives of the patients that they served. Although he was unable to arrange the full participation that he may have wished for, Baker nevertheless involved those in the Millside Practice as much as was possible in the work. His intention has always been to understand their appreciations of the situation and to facilitate the specification of an information-system appropriate to these.

It is not impossible that the same sort of things might have been done even if systems thinking had not been used; some might be said to be the hallmark of good consultancy practice. Systems thinking, though, besides providing valuable concepts and tools for analysis, demands attention be given to roles in the intervention as well as the problem situation, to how the study will be done and to understanding social and political constraints. As information-systems penetrate further into our lives this alone should commend to us its future use.

# Bibliography

ACKOFF R L & EMERY F E (1972) *On Purposeful Systems.* Tavistock, London.

ACKOFF R L (1957) Towards a behavioural theory of communication. *Management Science* **4** pp. 218-234.

ACKOFF R L (1967) Management Misinformation Systems. *Management Science* **14** (4) pp. B-147 to B-156.

ACKOFF R L (1974) *Redesigning the Future.*Wiley, New York.

AHITUV N & NEUMANN S (1990) *Principles of Information Systems for Management, 3rd edition.* WCB, Dubuque IA.

AKTAS A Z (1987) *Structured Analysis and Design of Information Systems.* Prentice Hall, Englewood Cliffs NJ.

ANGYAL A (1941) A Logic of Systems. Reproduced in F. E. Emery (ed.) (1969), q.v., pp. 36-37.

ANTHONY R N & DEARDEN J (1980) *Management Control Systems, 4th edition.* Irwin, Homewood Ill.

ANTHONY R N (1965) *Planning and Control Systems; A framework for analysis.* Harvard University Press, Cambridge Ma.

ASHBY W R (1956) *An Introduction to Cybernetics.* Chapman & Hall, London.

ASHWORTH C & GOODLAND M (1990) *SSADM: A Practical Approach.* McGraw-Hill, Maidenhead.

AVISON D E & WOOD-HARPER A T (1990) *Multiview: An exploration in Informatin Systems Development.* Alfred Waller, Henley-on-Thames.

BASKERVILLE R (1993) Semantic database prototypes. *Journal of Information Systems* **3** (2) pp. 119-144.

BATINI C, CERI S & NAVATHE S B (1992) *Conceptual Database Design: An Entity-Relationship Approach.* Benjamin/Cummings, Redwood Ca.

BEDEIAN A G (1993) *Management, 3rd edition.* Dryden, Fort Worth, Texas.

BEER S (1966) *Decision and Control.* Wiley, Chichester.

BEER S (1967) *Cybernetics and Management, 2nd edition.* English U.P., Oxford

BEER S (1972) *Brain of the Firm. The Managerial Cybernetics of Organization.* Allen Lane, London.

BEER S (1979) *The Heart of Enterprise*. Wiley, Chichester.

BEMELMANS T M A (ed.) (1984) *Beyond Productivity: Information Systems Development for Organizational Effectiveness*. North-Holland, Amsterdam.

BENYON D (1990) *Information and Data Modelling*. Blackwell Scientific, Oxford.

BERLINSKI, D (1976) *On Systems Analysis: An Essay Concerning the Limitations of Some Mathematical Methods in the Social, Political, and Biological Sciences*. MIT Press, Cambridge Mass.

BERTALANFFY L von (1950) The Theory of Open Systems in Physics and Biology. *Science*, Vol 111, pp.23-29.

BERTALANFFY L von (1951) General Systems Theory: a new approach to unity of science. *Human Biology* **23** pp. 303-361

BERTALANFFY L von (1968) *General Systems Theory*. Braziller, New York.

BLACK G (1968) *The Application of Systems Analysis to Government Operations*. Praeger, New York.

BLACKLER F & BROWN C (1986) Alternative models to guide the design and introduction of the new information technologies into work organisations. *Journal of Occupational Psychology* **59** pp. 287-313.

BLUNDEN M (1985) Vickers' Contribution to Management Thinking. *Journal of Applied Systems Analysis* **12** pp. 107-112.

BOEHM B W (1976) Software Engineering. *IEEE Transactions on Computers* Vol C-25, No 12. pp. 1226-1241.

BOGUSLAW R (1973) Systems Concepts in Social Systems. In: Miles R F Jr. (ed.) (1973b) q.v., pp. 177-190.

BOULDING K (1956) General Systems Theory - The skeleton of Science. *Management Science* **2** (3), pp. 197-208

BOULDING K (1985) *The World as a Total System*. Sage. Beverley Hills, California.

BRANDON D H (1963) *Management Standards for Data Processing*. Van Nostrand, New York.

BRITTAN J N G (1980) Design for a Changing Environment. *The Computer Journal* **23** (1) pp. 13-19.

BRONOWSKI J (1973) *The Ascent of Man*. Little, Brown and Co., London.

BROOKES C H P, GROUSE P J, JEFFERY D R & LAWRENCE M J (1982) *Information Systems Design*. Prentice-Hall, Sydney.

BROOKS F P (1987) No silver bullet: essence and accidents of software engineering. *IEEE Computer* **20** (4) pp. 10-19.

BULMER R (1967) Why the Cassowary is not a Bird. *Man* (new series) **2** (1) pp. 5-25.

BURRELL G & MORGAN G (1979) *Sociological Paradigms and Organisational Analysis.*
Heinemann, London

CANNING R G (1956) *Electronic Data Processing for Business and Industry.* Wiley, New York.

CANNING R G (1957) *Installing Electronic Data Processing Systems.* Wiley, New York.

CANNING R G (1972) That Maintenance Iceberg. *EDP Analyzer* **10** (10) pp. 1-14.

CANNING R G (1973) A Structure for EDP Projects. *EDP Analyzer* **5**, (11) pp. 1-13.

CCTA (1993) *Applying Soft Systems Methodology to an SSADM Feasibility Study.* HMSO, London.

CHECKLAND P B & CASAR A (1986) Vickers' Concept of an Appreciative System: a systemic
account. *Journal of Applied Systems Analysis* **13** pp. 3-17

CHECKLAND P B & SCHOLES J (1990) *Soft Systems Methodology in Action.* Wiley, Chichester.

CHECKLAND P B (1971) A systems map of the universe. *Journal of Systems Engineering* **2** (2) pp.
107-114.

CHECKLAND P B (1972) Towards a systems-based methodology for real-world problem
solving. *Journal of Systems Engineering* **3** (2) pp. 87-116.

CHECKLAND P B (1975) The development of systems thinking by systems practice - a
methodology from an action research program. In: Trappl R & Hanika F de P (eds.) (1975)
q.v., pp. 278-283.

CHECKLAND P B (1978) The origins and nature of 'hard' systems thinking. *Journal of Applied
Systems Analysis* **5** (2) pp. 99-110.

CHECKLAND P B (1981) *Systems Thinking, Systems Practice.* Wiley, Chichester.

CHECKLAND P B (1983) O.R. and the Systems Movement: Mappings and Conflicts. *Journal of
the Operational Research Society* **34** (8) pp. 661-675.

CHECKLAND P B (1985) From optimising to learning: a development of systems thinking for
the 1990s. *Journal of the Operational Research Society* **36** (9) pp. 757-767.

CHECKLAND P B (1989) Soft Systems Methodology. In: Rosenhead J (ed.) (1989) q.v., pp. 71-
100.

CHECKLAND P B (1990) Private correspondence with the author concerning an ISCOL
consultancy project.

CHECKLAND P B, FORBES P & MARTIN S (1990) Techniques in Soft Systems Practice 3:
monitoring and control in conceptual models and in evaluation studies. *Journal of Applied
Systems Analysis* **17** pp. 29-37.

CHEN P P-S (1976) The entity-relationship model: toward a unified view of data, *ACM
Transactions on Database Systems* **1** (1) pp. 9-36.

CHERRY C (1957) *On Human Communication: a review, a survey and a criticism.* Wiley, New York.

CHURCHMAN C W & VERHULST M (eds.) (1960) *Management Science, Models and Techniques, vol. 2.* Pergamon, New York

CHURCHMAN C W, ACKOFF, R.L. & ARNOFF E L (1957) *Introduction to Operations Research.* Wiley, New York.

CIBORRA C U (1984) Management Information Systems: a Contractual View. In: BemelmansT M A, (ed.) (1984) q.v., pp.135-145.

COAD P & YOURDON E (1990) *Object-Oriented Analysis.* Prentice-Hall, Englewood Cliffs N.J.

CODD E F (1970) A relational model of data for large shared data banks. *Communications of the ACM* **13** (6) pp. 377-387.

CODD E F (1979) Extending the Database Relational Model to Capture More Meaning. *ACM Transactions on Database Systems* **4** (4) pp. 397-434.

COUGER J D & KNAPP R W (eds.) (1974) *Systems Analysis Techniques.* Wiley, New York.

CRELLIN B (1988) An Organizational Review of Objective Setting and Appraisal within the Context of Culture at the International Stock Exchange. M.Sc. Dissertation, Lancaster University, Bailrigg, Lancaster.

CULNAN M J & SWANSON E B (1986) Research in Management Information Systems, 1980-1984: Points of Work and Reference. *MIS Quarterly* **10** (3) pp. 289-301.

CURTIS G (1989) *Business Information Systems: analysis, design and practice.* Addison-Wesley, Wokingham.

CUTTS G (1987) *SSADM: Structured Systems Analysis and Design Methodology.* Paradigm, London.

CYERT R M & MARCH J G (1963) *A Behavioural Theory of the Firm.* Prentice-Hall, Englewood Cliffs N.J.

CYERT R M & WELSCH L A (1970) (Eds. ) *Management Decision Making,: Selected Readings.* Penguin, Harmondsworth.

DATE C J (1990) *An Introduction to Database Systems, Vol. 1, 5th edition.* Addison-Wesley, Reading Mass.

DAVIS W S (1983) *Systems Analysis and Design: A Structured Approach.* Addison-Wesley, Reading Mass.

De CHAMPEAUX D & FAURE P (1992) A comparative study of object-oriented analysis methods, *Journal of Object-Oriented Programming,* **5** (1) pp. 21-33.

De MARCO T (1978) *Structured Analysis and System Specification.* Yourdon, New York.

De NEUFVILLE R & STAFFORD J H (1971) *Systems Analysis for Engineers and Managers.* McGraw Hill, London.

DEWEY J (1910) *How We Think.* D.C. Heath, New York.

DOWNS E, CLARE P, & COE I (1992) *Structured Systems Analysis and Design Method: Application and Context. 2nd edition.* Prentice Hall, Hemel Hempstead.

DRETSKE F L (1981) *Knowledge and the Flow of Information.* Blackwell, Oxford.

DROR Y (1971) *Design for Policy Sciences.* American Elsevier, New York.

EDEN C (1989) Using cognitive mapping for strategic options development and analysis (SODA). In: Rosenhead J (ed.) (1989) q.v., pp. 21-42.

ELLIS, W D (1938) *A Source Book of Gestalt Psychology.* Routledge & Kegan Paul, London.

EMERY F E & TRIST E L (1960) Socio-technical systems. In: Churchman C W & Verhulst (eds.) (1960) q.v., pp. 83-97.

EMERY F E & TRIST E L (1965) The Causal Texture of Organizational Environments. *Human Relations* **18** pp. 21-32.

EMERY F E (ed.) (1969) *Systems Thinking: Selected Readings.* Penguin, Harmondsworth.

EVA M (1992) *SSADM Version 4: A User's Guide.* McGraw-Hill, Maidenhead.

FEIGENBAUM D S (1968) The Engineering and Management of an Effective System. *Management Science* **14** (12) pp. B721-B730.

FINDEISEN W & QUADE E S (1985) The Methodology of Systems Analysis: An introduction and Overview. In: Miser and Quade (1985) q.v., pp. 117-149

FINKELSTEIN C (1989) *An Introduction to Information Engineering: From Strategic Planning to Information Systems.* Addison Wesley, Sydney.

FISHER D L (1969) Management Controlled Information Systems. *Datamation* June, pp. 53-57.

FLOYD C (1992) Human Questions in Computer Science. In: Floyd C, ZullIghoven H, Budde R, Keil-Slawik R (eds.) (1992) q.v.

FLOYD C, ZULLIGHOVEN H, BUDDE R, KEIL-SLAWIK R (eds.) (1992) *Software Development and Reality Construction.* Springer-Verlag, Berlin.

FORRESTER J W (1961) *Industrial Dynamics.* MIT Press, Cambridge Mass.

FORRESTER J W (1969) *Principles of Systems.* Wright Allen Press, Cambridge Mass.

FORRESTER J W (1984) Bounded Rationality and the Politics of Muddling Through. *Public Administration Review* Jan/Feb 1984, pp. 23-31.

FREDERICKSON N (1990) Introduction to soft systems methodology and its application in work in schools. In: *Soft Systems Methodology: Practical Application in Work in Schools.* Frederickson N (ed.) (1990) University College London, London. pp. 1-10.

FRIEDMAN A L & CORNFORD D S (1989) *Computer Systems Development: History, Organization and Implementation.* Wiley, Chichester.

GALBRAITH J (1973) *Designing Complex Organizations.* Addison-Wesley, Reading Mass.

GALBRAITH J(1974) Organizational Design: An Information Processing View. *Interfaces* **4** (3) pp. 28-36.

GALLIERS R D (1991) Strategic Information Systems Planning: myths, reality and guidelines for successful implementation. *European Journal of Information Systems* **1** (1) pp. 55-64.

GANE C & SARSON T (1977)*Structured Systems Analysis: tools and techniques*. IST, New York.

GIBSON C F & NOLAN R L (1974) Managing the four stages of EDP growth. *Harvard Business Review*, Jan-Feb 1974, pp. 76-88.

GLADDEN G R (1982) Stop the Life-Cycle, I Want to Get Off. *ACM SIGSOFT Software Engineering Notes* **7** (2) pp. 35-38.

GORRY G A & SCOTT MORTON M S (1971) A Framework for Management Information Systems. *Sloan Management Review* **13** (1) pp. 55-70.

GORRY G A & SCOTT MORTON M. S. (1989) Retrospective commentary on A Framework for Management Information Systems. *Sloan Management Review,* **30** (3) pp. 49-61.

GOULDNER A W (1959) Organisational Analysis. In: Merton R K, Broom L & Cottrell L S Jr. (eds.) (1959) q.v., pp. 400-428.

GRAHAM J (1972) *Systems Analysis in Business*. Allen and Unwin, London.

GREGORY R H & VAN HORN R L (1963) *Business Data Processing & Programming*. Chatto and Windus, London.

HALL A D (1962) *A Methodology for Systems Engineering*. Van Nostrand, Princeton N.J.

HALL P A V (1982) In Defence of Life Cycles. *ACM Sigsoft Software Engineering Notes* **7** (3) p 23.

HARRINGTON J (1991) *Organizational Structure and Information Technology*. Prentice Hall, Hemel Hempstead.

HARRISON W L (1985) *Computers and Information Processing*. West Publishing, St. Paul Mn.

HARTMAN W, MATTHES H & PROEME A (1968) *Information Systems Handbook.*. Philips-Electrologica, Apeldooorn, Netherlands.

HICKS J O Jr (1984) *Management Information Systems: a user perspective.*West Publishing, St.Paul Mn.

HIRSCHHEIM R & BOLAND R (1989) Series Foreword. In: Friedman A L & Cornford D S (1989) q.v., pp. xiii-xiv.

HIRSCHHEIM R & KLEIN H K (1989) Four paradigms of information systems development. *Communications of the ACM* **32** (10) pp. 1199-1216.

HITCH C (1953) Sub-optimization in Operations Problems *Journal of Operations Research Society of America* **1,** pp. 87-99

HOOS I (1972) *Systems Analysis in Public Policy: A Critique*. University of California Press, Berkeley, Ca.

HOOS I (1976) Engineers as Analysts of Social Systems: A Critical Enquiry. *Journal of Systems Engineering* **4** (2) pp. 81-88.

HORNBY P, CLEGG C W, ROBSON J I, MACLAREN C R R, RICHARDSON S C S & O'BRIEN P (1992) Human and organizational issues in information systems development. *Behaviour & Information Technology* **11** (3) pp. 160-174.

HUGHES J G (1991) *Object-Oriented Databases*. Prentice Hall, Hemel Hempstead.

IBM (1974) Study Organization Plan Documentation Techniques. In: Couger J D & Knapp R W (eds.) (1974) q.v., pp. 94-127.

IIVARI J (1991) A paradigmatic analysis of contemporary schools of IS development. *European Journal of Information Systems* **1** (4) pp. 249-272.

IVES B & LEARMONTH G P (1983) The Information System as a Competitive Weapon. *Communications of the ACM* **27** (12) pp. 1193-1201.

JENKINS G M & YOULE P V (1971) *Systems Engineering*. Watts, London.

JENKINS G M (1969) The Systems Approach. *Journal of Systems Engineering* **1** (1) pp. 3-50.

JENKINS G M (1983) Reflections on Management Science *Journal of Applied Systems Analysis* **10** (1) pp. 15-40.

JORDAN N (1968) *Themes in Speculative Psychology*. Tavistock, London.

KATZ D & KAHN R L (1966) *The Social Psychology of Organizations*. Wiley, New York

KENT W (1978) *Data and Reality*. Elsevier, Amsterdam.

KIM W & LOCHOVSKY F H (eds.) (1989) *Object-Oriented Concepts, Databases, and Applications*. ACM Press, New York.

KIM W (1990) *Introduction to Object-Oriented Databases*. MIT Press, Cambridge Mass.

KLEIN H K & HIRSCHHEIM R (1987) A comparative framework of data modelling paradigms and approaches. *Computer Journal* **30** (1) pp. 8-15.

KLINE M B & LIFSON M W (1971) Systems Engineering and its Application to the Design of an Engineering Curriculum. *Journal of Systems Engineering* **2** (1) pp. 3-22.

KLIR J & VALACH M (1967)*Cybernetic Modelling*. Illife, London.

KROENKE D M (1992) *Database Processing: Fundamentals, Design, Implementation. 4th edition*. Macmillan, New York.

KUHN T S (1962) *The Structure of Scientific Revolutions*. University of Chicago Press. Chicago.

LAW J & LODGE P (1984) *Science for Social Scientists*. Macmillan, London.

LEWIS P J (1989) Prototyping Information Systems: Lessons from Practice. In: Whiddett D (ed.) (1989) q.v. pp. 143-161.

LEWIS P J (1991) The decision making basis for information systems: the contribution of Vickers' concept of appreciation to a soft systems perspective. *European Journal of Information Systems* **1** (1) pp. 33-43.

LEWIS P J (1992) Rich picture building in the soft systems methodology. *European Journal of Information Systems* **1** (5) pp. 351-360.

LIEBENAU J & BACKHOUSE J (1990) *Understanding Information: An Introduction.* Macmillan, Basingstoke.

LINDBLOM C E (1959) The Science of Muddling Through. *Public Administration Review* **19**, pp.79-88. Reprinted in Pugh D S (ed.) (1990) q.v. pp. 278-294.

LONGWORTH G (1992) *A User's Guide to SSADM version 4.* NCC Blackwell, Oxford.

LOOMIS M E S (1987) *The Database Book.* Macmillan, New York.

LUCAS H C Jr, LAND F F, LINCOLN T J & SUPPER K (eds.) (1980) *The Information Systems Environment.* North-Holland, Amsterdam.

LUCAS H C Jr. (1986) *Introduction to Computers and Information Systems.* Macmillan, New York.

LYNCH H J (1969) ADS: A Technique in Systems Documentation. *Database* **1** (1) pp. 6-18.

MACHOL R E (1965) (Ed.) *System Engineering Handbook.* McGraw-Hill. New York.

MACIASZEK L A (1990) *Database Design and Implementation.* Prentice Hall, Sydney.

MACRO A (1990) *Software Engineering: Concepts and Management.* Prentice Hall, Hemel Hempstead.

MARCH J G & SIMON H A (1958) *Organizations.* Wiley, New York

MARCH J G (1982) Theories of Choice and Making Decisions. *Society,* Nov-Dec, pp. 29-39.

MARCH J G (1988) *Decisions and Organizations.* Blackwell, New York.

MARKUS M L & ROBEY D (1983) The Organizational Validity of Management Information Systems. *Human Relations* **36** pp. 203-225.

MARTIN C & POWELL P (1992) *Information Systems: A Management Perspective.* McGraw-Hill, Maidenhead.

MARTIN J (1975) *Computer Data-Base Organization.* Prentice-Hall, Englewood Cliffs N.J.

MARTIN M P (1991) *Analysis and Design of Business Information Systems.* Macmillan, New York.

MAURER J G (ed.) (1971) *Readings in Organization Theory: Open-Systems Approaches.* Random House New York.

McCRACKEN D D (1982) Life Cycle Concept Considered Harmful. *ACM SIGSOFT Software Engineering Notes* **7** (2) pp. 29-32.

McFADDEN F R & HOFFER J A (1991) *Database Management, 3rd edition.* Benjamin/Cummings, Redwood, CA.

McGINNES S (1992) How objective is object-oriented analysis?. Paper presented at the *CAiSE '92 4th Conference on Advanced Information Systems,* Manchester, UK, May 1992.

McLEOD R Jr. (1990) *Management Information Systems: a study of computer-based information systems, 4th edition.* Macmillan, New York.

McNURLIN B C & SPRAGUE R H, Jr. (1989) *Information Systems Management in Practice, 2nd edition.* Prentice-Hall, London.

MERTON R K, BROOM L & COTTRELL L S Jr. (eds.) (1959) *Sociology Today.* Basic Books, New York.

METHLIE L B (1980) Systems Requirements Analysis - Methods and Models. In: Lucas H C Jr, Land F F, Lincoln T J & Supper K (eds.) (1980) q.v., pp. 173-185.

MEYER B (1988) *Object-Oriented Software Construction.* Prentice Hall, Hemel Hempstead.

MILES R F Jr. (1973a) Introduction. In : In: Miles R F Jr. (ed.) (1973b) q.v., pp. 1-11.

MILES R F Jr. (ed.) (1973b) *Systems Concepts: lectures on contemporary approaches to systems.* Wiley, New York.

MILES R K (1985) Computer Systems Analysis: the constraint of the hard systems paradigm. *Journal of Applied Systems Analysis* **12** pp. 55-65.

MILES R K (1988) Combining 'Soft' and 'Hard' Systems Practice: Grafting or Embedding? *Journal of Applied Systems Analysis* **15**, pp. 55-60.

MISER H J & QUADE E S (1985) *Handbook of Systems Analysis.* Wiley, Chichester.

MOWSHOWITZ A (1976) *The Conquest of Will: Information Processing in Human Affairs.* Addison-Wesley, Reading Mass.

MUMFORD E & HENSHALL D (1979) *A Participative Approach to Computer Systems Design.* Associated Business Press, London.

MUMFORD E & WEIR M (1979) *Computer Systems in Work Design, the ETHICS method.* Associated Press, London.

MUMFORD E, LAND F F & HAWGOOD J (1978) A participative approach to the design of computer systems. *Impact of Science on Society* **28**, (3) pp. 235-253.

NOLAN R L (1973) Managing the Computer Resource: a stage hypothesis. *Communications of the ACM* **16** (7) pp. 399-405.

O'BRIEN J A (1991) *Introduction to Information Systems in Business Management, 6th edition.* Irwin, Homewood, Ill.

ODELL J J (1992) Dynamic and multiple classification. *Journal of Object Oriented Programming* **4** (8) pp. 45-48.

OLLE T W, HAGELSTEIN J, McDONALD I G, ROLLAND C, SOL H H G, VAN ASSCHE F J M & VERRIJN-STUART A A (1991) *Information Systems Methodologies: a framework for understanding, 2nd edition*. Addison-Wesley, Wokingham.

OPTNER S L (1960) *Systems Analysis for Business Management*. Prentice-Hall, Englewood Cliffs N.J.

PATCHING D (1990) *Practical Soft Systems Analysis*. Pitman, London.

PETTIGREW A M (1979) On Studying Organizational Cultures. *Administrative Science Quarterly* **24**, pp. 570-581.

PFEFFER J (1981) Management as symbolic action: the creation and maintenance of organizational paradigms. *Research in Organizational Behaviour* Volume 3, pp. 1-52.

PLISKIN N, ROMM T, LEE A S & WEBER Y. (1993) Presumed versus Actual Organizational Culture: Managerial Implications for Implementation of Information Systems. *The Computer Journal* **36** (2) pp. 143-152.

POPPER K R (1959) *The Logic of Scientific Discovery*. Hutchinson, London.

POPPER K R (1963) *Conjectures and Refutations: the growth of scientific knowledge., 5th edition 1974*. Routledge and Kegan Paul, London.

POPPER K R (1972) *Objective Knowledge: an evolutionary approach*. Clarendon Press, Oxford.

PORTER M E & MILLAR V E (1985) How information gives you competitive advantage. *Harvard Business Review* **63** (4) pp. 149-160.

PRINCE T R (1970) *Information Systems for Management Planning and Control*. Irwin, Homewood Illinois.

PUGH D S (ed.) (1990) *Organization Theory : selected readings, 3rd ed.ition*. Penguin, Harmondsworth.

QUADE E S & BOUCHER W I (eds.) (1968) *Systems Analysis and Policy Planning*. American Elsevier, New York.

QUADE E S (1971) The systems approach and public policy. *Journal of Systems Engineering* **(2)** 1 pp 23-34.

REYNOLDS G W (1992) *Information Systems for Managers, 2nd edition*. West Publishing, St Paul Mn.

RISHE N (1988) *Database Design Fundamentals*. Prentice-Hall, Englewood Cliffs, N.J.

ROSENHEAD J (ed.) (1989) *Rational Analysis for a Problematic World*. Wiley, Chichester.

ROYCE W W (1970) Managing the Development of Large Software Systems: concepts and techniques. Proceedings of IEEE WESCON.

RUMBAUGH J, BLAHA M, PREMERLANI W, EDDY F & LORENSEN W (1991) *Object-Oriented Modeling and Design*. Prentice-Hall, Englewood Cliffs, N.J.

SACKMAN H (1967) *Computers, System Science and Evolving Society: The Challenge of Man-Machine Digital Systems*. Wiley, New York.

SCHACH S R (1993) *Software Engineering, 2nd edition*. Irwin, Homewood, Il.

SCHLAER S & MELLOR S J (1988) *Object-Oriented Systems Analysis: Modeling the World in Data*. Yourdon, Englewood Cliffs N.J.

SCOTT W R (1987) *Organizations: Rational, Natural and Open Systems, 2nd edition*. Prentice Hall, Englewood Cliffs, N.J.

SILVER G A & SILVER M L (1989) *Systems Analysis and Design*. Addison-Wesley, Reading Mass.

SIMON H A (1957) *Models of Man, Social and Rational : Mathematical Essays on Rational Human Behaviour in a Social Setting*. Wiley, New York.

SIMON H A (1960) *The New Science of Management Decision*. Harper and Brothers, New York.

SIMON H A (1965a) Administrative Decision Making. *Public Administration Review* **25** pp. 31-37.

SIMON H A (1965b) *The Shape of Automation for Men and Management*. Harper and Row, New York.

SIMON H A (1969) *The Sciences of the Artificial*. MIT Press, Cambridge Mass.

SIMON H A (1976) *Administrative Behaviour, 3rd edition*. The Free Press, New York.

SMYTH D S & CHECKLAND P B (1976) Using a systems approach: the structure of root definitions. *Journal of Applied Systems Analysis* **5** (1) pp. 75-83.

SOMMERVILLE I (1982) *Software Engineering*. Addison-Wesley, London.

SOMOGYI E K & GALLIERS R D (1987) From Data Processing to Strategic Information Systems - A Historical Perspective. In: Somogyi E K & Galliers R D (eds.) (1987) q.v., pp. 5-25.

SOMOGYI E K & GALLIERS R D (eds.) (1987) *Towards Strategic Information Systems*. Abacus, Tunbridge Wells.

TRAPPL R & HANIKA F de P (eds.) (1975) *Progress in Cybernetics and Systems Research, Vol. 2*. Hemisphere, New York.

VICKERS G (1965) *The Art of Judgement*. Harper and Row, London.

VICKERS G (1968) *Value Systems and Social Process*. Tavistock, London.

VICKERS G (1970) *Freedom in a Rocking Boat*. Allen Lane, London.

VICKERS G (1983) *Human Systems are Different*. Harper and Row, London.

VICKERS G (1984) *The Vickers Papers, edited by Open Systems Group*. Harper and Row, London.

VROOM V H (1974) A New Look at Managerial Decision Making. *Organizational Dynamics,* **5**, pp. 66-80. Reprinted as 'A Normative Model of Managerial Decision-making' in Pugh D S (ed.) (1990) q.v. pp. 309-328.

WADDINGTON C H (1973) *O.R. in World War 2: Operational Research against the U-boat*. Elek, London.

WAGNER H M (1969) *Principles of Operations Research*. Prentice-Hall, Englewood Cliffs N.J.

WAND Y (1989) A Proposal for a Formal Model of Objects. In: Kim W & Lochovsky F H (eds.)(1989) q.v., pp. 537-559.

WARD J, GRIFFITHS P & WHITMORE P (1990) *Strategic Planning for Information Systems*. Wiley, Chichester.

WARING A (1989) *Systems Methods for Managers*. Blackwell Scientific, Oxford.

WATERS S J (1974) *Introduction to Computer Systems Design*. NCC, Manchester.

WEAVER P L (1993) *Practical SSADM Version 4: A Complete Tutorial Guide*. Pitman, London.

WHIDDETT D (ed.) (1989) *Implementation of Small Computer Systems: Case Studies of Applications*. Ellis Horwood, Sussex.

WILSON B (1984) *Systems: Concepts, Methodologies and Applications*. Wiley, Chichester.

WILSON B (1990) *Systems: Concepts, Methodologies and Applications, 2nd edition*. Wiley, Chichester.

WISEMAN C & MACMILLAN I C (1984) Creating Competitive Weapons from Information Systems. *Journal of Business Strategy* **5** (2) pp. 42-49.

WOOD-HARPER A T & FITZGERALD G (1982) A Taxonomy of Current Approaches to Systems Analysis. *The Computer Journal* **25** (1) pp. 12-16.

WOOD-HARPER A T, ANTILL L & AVISON D E (1985) *Information Systems Definition: The Multiview Approach*. Blackwell Scientific, Oxford.

WYMORE A W (1976) *Systems Engineering Methodology for Interdisciplinary Teams*. Wiley, New York.

YOURDON E. (1989) *Modern Structured Analysis*. Prentice-Hall, Englewood Cliffs N.J.

YOUSSEF L A (1975) *Systems Analysis and Design*. Reston Publishing, Reston Va.

ZWASS V (1992) *Mangement Information Systems*. WCB, Dubuque IA.

# Index